About the Author

Professor L.P. Singh spent about two decades as a mendicant in search of truth and salvation. He was awarded D. Litt. Degree from Ranchi University, Ranchi in 1972. He retired as a professor of Philosophy from Magadh University, Bodh Gaya in January 1996 and in February of the same year he became Senior Fellow of the Indian Council of Philosophical Research, Govt. of India for three years. In 2000 A.D. Professor Singh was awarded Fellowship of Indian Institute of Advanced Studies, Shimla for three years from 2000 to 2003. He became a visiting Research Professor in 2004 at the Catholic University of America, Washington D.C. He was also awarded Indo-French Cultural Fellowship in 1994. During his sojourn at Paris, he delivered lectures at the Department of Philosophy, Sorbonne University IV, Paris. He also addressed the students and staff members of Nihon and Toyo University, Tokyo in 2006. He delivered a special lecture at the Faculty of Humanities and Social Sciences, Khon Kaen University, Thailand in 2013. He presented several papers at the National and International Conferences and Seminars such World Philosophical Congress 1975, International Congress of Orientalists, Mexico City 1976, First Sanskrit Symposia, Mexico City 1982, World Sanskrit Congress, Lieden, Holland, International Conferences at East China Normal University, Shanghai, Xiaotong University, Xi'an in December 2013. He also presented papers at the School of the Social sciences and the Humanities, East China Normal University and at the School of Social Sciences, Shanghai University, Shanghai, China in 2014, Presented a Paper on Advaita Vedanta at International Conference of Philosophy held in January, 2018 at Doha (Qatar) , Presented paper on Integral Humanism at Beijing World Philosophy Congress held on August 2018. Prof. Singh has been elected General President of Indian Philosophical Congress in 2020 founded by Rabindra Nath Tagore and S. Radha Krishnan. He chaired many International sessions. About 21 Research Scholars worked under his supervision and were awarded Ph.D. degrees. He has written many books of high academic value, published several papers at the National and International proceedings and Journals of high academic repute. Prof. Singh is a distinguished professor of philosophy and a social activist.

Tantra, Veda and Mysticism

L.P. Singh

CONCEPT PUBLISHING COMPANY PVT. LTD.
NEW DELHI-110059

ISBN-13: 978-93-5439-005-0

First Published 2022

Published and Printed by

Concept Since 1974

Concept Publishing Company Pvt. Ltd.
A/15-16, Commercial Block, Mohan Garden,
New Delhi-110059 (INDIA)
T : 91 11 41101460, 91 11 25351460, 91 11 25351794
E : publishing@conceptpub.com; *W* : www.conceptpub.com

Cataloging in Publication Data--Courtesy: D.K. Agencies (P) Ltd. <docinfo@dkagencies.com>

Singh, Lalan Prasad, 1936- **author.**
Tantra, Veda and mysticism / L.P. Singh.
pages cm
Includes bibliographical references and index.
ISBN 9789354390050

1. Mysticism—India. 2. Hindu philosophy. 3. Philosophy, Indic. I. Title.
LCC BL2015.M9S56 2022 | DDC 294.5422 23

To

The Sweet memory of my most loving

friend Kamal Morarka

The Man of Renaissance and Resurgence

and

Dedicated To

Mrs. Bharati Morarka

The Woman of

Great Culture, Compassion, Courage,

Awakening and Social Activist

Preface

This analects is a collection of some of the papers that were presented at various international and national conferences and seminars and published as part of their proceedings. They broadly highlight my foray into the world of Indian mysticism, metaphysics, Tantra and Veda that form the essence of our cultural and philosophical thinking. The theme that runs in these papers essentially tries to explain that life is a narrative of cosmic drama of which God (Brahman) is the choreographer and witnessing entity. He is the substance and substratum of cosmic drama and the "end of all knowledge" as Raman Maharsi says and the only Truth and Reality. All science and philosophy are geared to understand and unravel His ontological mysticism. This is a task that seekers have been trying to explore and experience through ages. In my own humble way, I have also made some efforts to comprehend the truth and reality of His being. It is a hazardous journey that I embarked upon, traversing wheels of fire in search of truth and salvation.

This analect is my humble presentation to the world of academia and the common masses. I do not claim any originality. It only reflects my stray thoughts. Despite being a village boy, I have had the fortune of meeting and interacting with some of the greatest minds of India like Swami Muktananad, Anand Mayi Ma, Gopinath Kaviraj, Dr. Karan Singh, Hon'ble Rajnath Singh, Venkat Raman, Morarjee Desai, General K.M. Cariappa, Bhairo Singh Sekhawat, S. Nijalingappa, Somnath Chatterjee, Satyen Bose, Radha Binod Pal, Suniti Kumar Chatterjee, Humayun Kabir, Ashok Mehta, Samar Guha, Nath Pai, Madhu Limaye, KM Munshi, JP, Ram Manohar Lohia, Hem Barua, Nanaji Deshmukh, UP Singh, Gulzari Lal Nanda, Ajay Ghosh, D.S. Kothari, S.C. Dubey, L.P. Vidyarthi, R.S. Srivastava, H.S. Gill, G.C. Pandey, Natwar Singh, V. C. Pandey, Lokesh Chandra, Digvijay Singh, Amrita Pritam, Yashwant Singh, Ajay Singh, D .Y. Patil, Muchkund Dubey, Basavaraja Patil, Pranab Mohanthy, Shashi

Ranjan Sahu, M.A. Baby, P.C. Halder, K.N. Rao and K.M. Singh. I was also greatly inspired by Chandrasekhar, the Renaissance Man of Modern Indian History. He was a phenomenal mind. I was highly impressed by his vision of India as a secular, socialist and democratic country and had the fortune of enjoying his immense love, affection and trust. Kamal Morarka who had a great mind and was a visionary and thinker, often shared the vision of his mentor Chandrasekhar. He considered socialism and democracy as the foundation of India. He would say that any deviation from this fundamental principle to alter the political grammar and trajectory of the multi-cultural fabrics and ethos of India would be disastrous for National Unity. In this context, it may not be out of place to quote the economist and diplomat JK Galbraith "The Indian commitment to the semantics of socialism is at least as deep as ours to the semantics of free enterprises". All these intellectuals have enriched my life and thought. I owe a debt of gratitude to all of them. I am equally grateful to Mrs. Bharati Morarka for her help and encouragement in my academic pursuits. She is a woman of culture, courage and compassion, a thinker and a social activist.

However, my father and mother had been my greatest teachers. Whatever little I have achieved in my life, is all due to their blessings. My father, who didn't have any schooling, was a great mind. I have not inherited one percent of his talent and merit. My mother was a very pious woman. She was full of love, compassion and divinity. My wife and my eldest brother also played invaluable role in my making.

I have included some of the important letters and other documents refelecting my association with academicians and social activists.

My sincerest thanks are reserved for my sons Arvind, Amitabh, Ashutosh and Raja and daughters-in-law Kavita, Chiyako, Priya and Naina and my daughters Mili and Varsha. Without their caring love and affection, it would not have been possible for me to channelize my loneliness into philosophical pursuits following untimely demise of my wife, twenty-five years ago.

I cannot forget my friends Shri Suresh Chandel, Dr. Anil Khatri , Shri Srikant Sharma, Shri Ravinder Sharma, Shri Aakash Sharma, Shri H.L. Pandey, Shri Rampal Negi and Shri P.S. Rana for rendering throughout their invaluable help and encouragement. My heartfelt thanks to them.

The real elixir of my academic has, of course, been Ms. Rachana Singh Rathore, Ms. Anju, Ms. Menka Solanki, Ms. Mori Kawa Reiko, Ms. Jennifer, Ms. Seema Singh and Ms. Shina from whom I received immense love and affection. To Kishu, Rishi, Anirvan, Shivam, Misti and Alia, who kept inspiring me to self-reflect and change the semantics of my life so that I can pursue the journey of a meaningful search in finding truth in mysticism and metaphysics, I extend my deepest appreciation.

I profusely thank Ashok Mittal, the owner of the Concept Publishing Company Pvt. Ltd. for undertaking the publication of my fifth book. Last but not the least, I am grateful to Sandeep Jha for his help and cooperation in ensuring that my academic work finds expression in my papers and books on time.

New Delhi
30.08.2021

Prof. L.P. Singh

Contents

1
Tantra and Veda

The evolution of psycho-spiritual philosophy in India is based largely on intuition and mysticism. The irresistible urge for the Beyond is the sheet anchor of the religio-philosophical culture in India. The problems of inner life and the mysteries of the world of becoming and the world of spirit are the *raison d'etre* of philosophical revolution and spiritual renaissance. All Indian philosophical schools are unanimous in their belief that the ultimate Reality is beyond the reach of human words and concepts.[1] The evolution of cult and culture in India is inspired and fed by intuitive vision and subjective ṛealization and not by reason and argument. The orientation to the goal of liberation from the meshes and trammels which connotes total cessation of metempsychosis is both the beginning and the end of the religio-philosophical movement of India.

The original sources of cultural life in India are Tantra and the Veda. When the rest of the world was passing through the dark ages of a barbarian civilization, India was enjoying a most developed and sublime form of cultural life.[2] The cultural heritage of India is to be found primarily in her intuitional science of Tantra and the religio-philosophical schools of the Vedas. Tantra and the Veda are the warp and woof of the cult and culture of India. Tantra is a cult and the Veda a religio-philosophical school. For the development of a robust civilization both spiritual humanism and sublime philosophy are required. There is no doubt that the sources of the philosophical ideas, religious beliefs, social codes lie in the Veda but the spiritual humanism and cult are the discoveries and achievements of pre-Vedic India.

Indian culture has had an extremely long and complex development. It has a longer history of continuous growth than any other living cultural tradition. Historical perspective of cultural tradition is immensely useful in studying and understanding the subterranean cultural spirit of India but it is a very difficult task to present a chronological sequence of the cultural evolution of India. In broad outline, the cultural history of India can be divided into two major periods of development: (i) Tāntric, and (ii) Vedic.

The Tāntric period is dimmed by obscurity but it may be placed approximately between 5000 B.C. and 3000 B.C. This period of Indian culture and civilization is known as pre-historic. The Harappa and Mohenjo-daro civilizations bear the stamp of Tāntric culture. The excavations at Harappa have proved beyond doubt that among the male gods the most remarkable figure is that of the deity Śiva. He has three faces and is seated on a throne with legs crossed in the fashion of a yogi. There are a number of animals such as tiger, buffalo, rhinoceros and deer under the seat.[3] Scholars have regarded him as Lord Śiva for he is described as *Trimukha* (three-faced), Paśupati (Lord of animals) and Mahāyogi (the great ascetic). The idea of three-faced is of great significance. It stands for *Tri-kāladarśī* (knower of past, present and future). The heterogeneous character of the herd of animals signifies the great spiritual power which Śiva possesses and which neutralizes the ferocity of the tiger and renders him harmless even for a deer. He indisputably was a great yogi. Sir John Marshall opines that the huge seal surrounded by four wild animals is proto-Śiva, which has much in common with Śiva of later Hinduism. This rich cultural heritage of India, as described in the words of Prof. Piggot, is 'the unchanging traditions of the temple' and 'not the secular instability of the court'.[4] The prehistoric India had a most developed form of universal religion. The non-Āryans were the first to discover the spiritual cult which makes Tantra the oldest universal religion of the world.

The discovery of the Indus Valley Civilization has revolutionized our concept of Indian history and culture. The excavation report has firmly established that the Indus Valley civilization is the oldest living civilization of the world. The indigenous indabitants of India were highly developed both intellectually and spiritually. And there is no evidence to indicate any affinity between the Indus Valley civilization and the Middle East. A.L. Basham says: "This great civilization owed little to the Middle East, and there is no reason to believe that it was formed by recent immigrants; the cities were built by people who had probably been in the Indus Valley for several centuries. The Harappa people were already Indians when they planned their cities, and they altered hardly at all for a thousand years."[5] The most significant feature of the Harappa culture is its inner conservatism.[6] For the survival of any culture some amount of conservatism is essential. Moreover, the conservatism of any great civilization signifies the cultural fullness and richness of the tradition. Only a weak civilization is easily influenced by an alien culture.

We observe that the Tāntric tradition of ancient India contrary to the general belief has greatiy influenced the Āryan civilization. This influence can be traced in the Vedic culture. Further, it is generally believed that the Indian culture has its roots in the Vedas. This is not correct. The Vedas are later than Tantras. Recent researches and discoveries have proved this and also that it is wrong to think that the primitive non-Āryans were pagan and uncivilized. On the contrary, many of the sublime forms of religious worship and the concept of deities are of Dravidian origin.[7] The myth of Āryan superiority over the non-Āryans has been exploded by the excavations of the Harappa civilization. When the Āryans (Ārya means cultured) came to India through the North-West Frontier of India, they had contemptuously imposed the name Anārya (uncultured) on the indigenous population. Their misplaced sense of superiority had blinded them to the fact that the native people of India were highly advanced in the fields of philosophy, religion, fine arts and social sciences, which later had a great impact on the Vedic culture of the Āryans.

The Vedas

The Āryans were not the indigenous inhabitants of Bhāratavarṣa whose geographical boundary then was very vast. It encompassed the present Iran (*Aranyavraja*), Afghanistan (*Gāndhāra*) and some portion of Asiatic Russia. They came to India from the northern part of Central Asia, their original home. And the Vedas are their greatest contribution. They had, in fact, started the composing of Vedic hymns in their original home. Only the later hymns were composed in India. The *Ṛg-Veda* is supposed to be the most ancient and is considered by European Indologists as a true and only Veda.[8] The hymns of the *Ṛg-Veda* veer round myths and allegories, obscure gropings and immature composings, primitive ceremonials and barbarous propitiatory rites. They are addressed to different manifestations of Nature like Indra, Agni, Varuṇa etc. But it will be unreasonable to say that all the hymns of the *Ṛg-Veda* are bereft of deep philosophical speculations. We find in the later *Ṛg-Vedic* hymns the speculative transition from the early polytheism to philosophical monotheism and monism. The beginning of rationalization was felt in the *Ṛg-Veda* also. The philosophical doubt is expressed thus: 'Of whom they ask, "where is he", of him indeed they also say, "He is not".'[9]

But the deep philosophical ideas and ideology of the Vedic civilization are the gift of the cultural metamorphosis of the Āryans and non-Āryans. When the Āryans came into contact with the Tāntric Sādhanā of the non-Āryans, exoteric utterances of the Vedic hymns were transformed into esoteric experiences inaccessible to senses and mind. That is why we find in the later hymns a harvest of philosophical richness and subtlety. Sri Aurobindo views: 'Only in the later hymns do we perceive the first appearance of deeper psychological and moral ideas borrowed, some think, from the hostile Dravidian, the "robbers" and "Vedas-haters" freely cursed, in the hymns themselves — and, however acquired, the first seed of the later Vedantic speculations.'[10]

The Āryans had a language but not a script of their own. The Dravidians, on the other hand, had their own script. This explains why the Āryans on coming into contact with the Dravidians wrote the Vedas in the Śāradā script for which they were condemned and cursed, because this was undigestible for the orthodox Āryan mind. The Vedic hymns though inspired are not of divine origin. The Vedas are not the Voice of Providence but are the achievements of human mind, which fathomed the deepest layer of consciousness in the course of deep meditation, an art which they learnt from non-Āryan Tantra. The Vedas were handed down from mouth to mouth, from one generation to another, from unknown antiquity not because they were taught by God or were themselves revealed to the sages but because the Āryans were profoundly ignorant about the art of writing. The Vedas were called Śruti because they were passed on by one mind to another and not because they were revealed at some unknown period of history at the beginning of each creation. However, the Vedas are considered to be the earliest literary and philosophical monument of the Indo-Āryan race. It is very difficult to ascertain when they came into existence, Many guesses have been made. Max Müller dates them from 1200 B.C., Hang from 2400 B.C. and Bal Gangadhar Tilak from 4000 B.C.[11] This is speculative and very misleading. For one, all the Four Vedas were not composed at one time or at one place. The *Ṛg-Veda* was composed in Central Asia. It bears me stamp of pure Āryan composition. The *Yajura-Veda* was composed in Aranyavraja (present Iran) and in some part of Asiatic Russia. The influence of Tantra on the Veda starts from the *Yajura-Veda*. The Tantric tradition and culture greatly influenced the exoteric mind of the Āryan. There is a marked transition, from literature to philosophy, in the composition of the Vedic hymns. The *Ṛg-Veda* speaks about the Āryan sentiment and language. It is a monumental work of literature. Its hymns are famous for their literary grace and poetic depth. The description of dawn (*uṣā*) is highly suggestive.

The *Yajura-Veda* represents the age of transition. The matter-of-factness of *Ṛg-Veda* was as transformed into the philosophical monotheism of *Brahma-vāda*. Philosophy took the place of literature. Speculation subordinated poetic wonderings. The *Yajura-Veda* lays stress on the philosophical speculation and exploration of reality by entering the Beyond that is within, by an ascension of intuition.

The *Atharva-Veda* was composed in the present India. But by that time the Āryans had greatly been influenced by non-Āryan Tantra. The racial blending and the culural metamorphosis had started. In course of time this produced a new healthy and robust civilization, and India reaped the harvest of both cultures, and a new civilization was born. Thus in the *Atharva-Veda* the impact of *Tantra Sādhanā* is greater than that of the Vedic ritualism. The Āryans were so influenced by the inuitional science of Tāntra that many of them abandoned their ceremonial sacrifices and got initiated into the Tāntric cult. Those (*Brahmins*) who adopted Tantra were known as Miśras. A large number of them still carry the surname 'Mishra'. This is a clear evidence of the cultural blending of Vedic and Tāntric traditions. P.R. Sarkar says. 'The *Atharva-Veda* was compiled mostly in India and during this period, as a result of their coming in closer contact with the non-Āryans, there emerged a mental or social blending amongst the Āryans who were highly influenced by non-Āryan Tantra. This fact is clearly reflected in the *Atharva-Veda* which cannot be regarded as a picture of Āryan civilization. In the subtle philosophy of the *Atharva-Veda,* particularly in the "Shruti" of Nishingha Tapaniiya, non-Āryan Tantra is more prominent than the Vedic ideal of the Āryan civilization.'[12]

In view of the above we can safely conclude that the philosophical wealth of the Vedas is product of the cultural blending of Indo-Āryan civilization. And as already said it was due to the influence of intuitional science of Tantra that the teachings of the Vedic hymns became the vehicles more of spiritual illumination than of systematic reflection.

The Śivādvaya school of Tantra philosophy is more comprehensive and coherent then and in a way far superior to the Vedantic school of Advaita. Vedantic Māyāvāda is a negative philosophy. It cannot give any logical explanation of the existence and nature of *Māyā* and the world of appearance. It declares the world to be an illusion. This is no explanation. The whole world is reduced to illusion. Who is the perceiver of this illusion? Whose projection is this illusion? Certainly it is neither the projection of *jīva* or Īśvara nor of *Brahman*. But when *Brahman* is the substratum of all, who except *Brahman* can be the cause of this original sin. Dr. Gopinath Kaviraj says: 'According to Śaṅkara, *Brahman* is Truth and *Māyā* is inexplicable (*Anirvacanīya*). Hence, the endeavour to show the superiority of *Advaita* philosophy is turned against its very system. It tarnishes the picture of its philosophical perfection and profundity. He cannot accept Māyā as reality and, therefore, his *Advaita* becomes exclusive and the whole system is based on renunciation and elimination and is not all embracing. *Māyā* is the power of *Brahman*, immanent in *Brahman* but *Brahman* is Truth and from the philosophical point of view *Māyā* is *Ṣāda-Ṣad-Vilakṣaṇī*. And by accepting *Māyā* as *Brahmayī*, *Nityā* and *Satyarūpā*. *Brahman* and *Māyā* (of Tantra) become one and coexistent.'[13] The *Śivādvaya* of Tantra philosophy means the eternal coexistence of the two (Śiva and Śakti).

Tantra and the Veda are the two aspects of Indian culture. But the impact of Tantra on the life and culture in eastern India is more than in western-northern India. The Āryans called the eastern part as Magadha (मगध) which means the land inhabited by '*Maga*'. The word '*Maga*' means non-Āryans or those who do not believe in the Veda. The Himālayan region was, therefore, always the choicest abode of Tāntric *Sādhakas*. That is why the most developed form of the Tāntric school of Kashmira Śaivism originated in Jammu and Kashmir. The impact of the Veda in our socio-religious life is tremendous. There cannot be any ceremony in the Hindu society without the recitation of a Vedic mantra.

Tantra and the Veda are the greatest achievements of Indian culture. They have enriched our socio-spiritual life. The Veda is an idea, Tantra is an ideology. The Veda is a religion, Tantra is a cult. The Veda is a philosophy, Tantra is a science.

Vedic Literature

The word Veda means *jñāna* or spiritual knowledge. The Vedas are called *śruti* not because they are revealed scriptures but because they were handed down from one generation to another by intellectuals who had a photographic memory. It is not *apauruṣeya,* i.e. of divine origin. The great Sāyaṇa has defined it as 'a book which reveals the knowledge of supernatural methods *(alaukika upāya)* for the achievement of the desired object and avoidance of the undesirable'.[14] According to Hindu mythology the real Veda, first revealed by God to the seers, consisted of one hundred thousand verses, and had four divisions. According to the *Viṣṇu Purāṇa,* in the beginning of the Dvāpara Yuga, Kṛṣṇa Dvaipāyana revived the Vedic study and classified the monumental work into four ancient divisions: *Ṛg, Yajura, Sama* and *Atharva*. To resuscitate the Vedic literature and give it a proper form, he imparted the teachings of the Veda to his four principal disciples. He taught the *Ṛg-Veda* to Paila, the *Yajura-Veda* to Vaiśampāyana, the *Sāma-Veda* to Jaimini and the *Atharva-Veda* to Sumanta. And thus Kṛṣṇa Dvaipāyana became known by the name of Veda Vyasa the classifier of the Vedas.

The Vedic literature is divided into four great works, i.e. *Ṛg-Veda, Yajura-Veda, Sama-Vada* and *Atharva-Veda.* Each of these again has four divisions, viz. Sa§hitās, Brāhmaṇas Āraṇyakas and Upaniṣad. The great Vedic commentator Yāska divides the Veda into two, i.e. Saṁhitās and Brāhmaṇas. The Āraṇyaka and the Upaniṣad form part of the latter. According to him the Upaniṣads are part of the Āraṇyakas. There are some Vedic scholars who include Kalpa-sūtras also in the body of the Vedic literature. The Samhitās and the Brahmaṇas are loosely called Karma-Kāṇḍa and the Āraṇyakas Upāsanā-Kāṇḍa and the Upaniṣad Jñāna-Kāṇḍa.

The Ṛg-Veda

The *Ṛg-Veda* comprises one thousand and seventeen hymns. It is divided into ten banks *(maṇḍals),* and represents the earliest phase of the evolution of literary and religious consciousness of the human mind. Naturalism and anthropomorphism constitute the beginning of Vedic culture. In the first phase of the Vedic thought, we find no trace of religio-philosophical consciousness. The Āryans were pagans. They had no religion. They worshipped Nature out of fear, the force dominating their personalities. They thought that through sacrifices they could influence Nature through gods, of their own creation and representing the different elements, like Indira, Marutas, Vāyu, Agni, Sūrya, Uṣā, etc. They conceived that these gods would be pleased by their ceremonial rites and, in return, shower blessings on them. Thus every Āryan chieftain hired the services of priests to please those gods. J.N. Farquhar, commenting on Ṛg-Vedic people, says; 'Men believed that the sacrifices were mighty as influence the gods and bring down gifts from them.

Therefore, every chieftain and noble among the Āryans was eager to secure the help of a skilled priest, and was god to pay him handsomely for services which brought victory and wealth from the gods."[15] Almost all the hymns were composed in the praise of different gods who presided over the different elements of Nature. Unlike the Greek gods or the mythical gods of the Purāṇas, the Ṛg-Vedic gods represent the divine powers of Nature. The Ṛg-Vedic deities are neither personal nor impersonal gods. We think that the Āryans of the Ṛg-Vedic age had no conception of God as such. They were simply wonder struck by the cosmic arrangements. Nonetheless the Ṛg-Vedic age was the age of great cultural turmoil when the nomads were being tamed and domesticated by Nature herself. It has rightly been said that, 'It was the forces of nature and her manifestation on earth here, the atmosphere around and above us, or in the Heaven beyond the vault of the sky that excited the devotion and imagination of the Vedic poets. Thus with the exception of a few abstract gods of whom we shall presently speak and some dual divinities, the gods may be roughly classified as the terrestrial, atmospheric and celestial.'[16] The *Ṛg-Vedic* seers offered prayers to nature gods with awe and reference. The hymns of the *Ṛg-Veda* are primeval worship.

Indra is the most prominent of gods in the *Ṛg-Veda.* He is primarily a deity of the thunderstorm. He is praised for his power and heroism, and as the god of war. The anthropomorphism of the *Ṛg-Vedic* hymns is evident. Indra has been extolled as a heroic person who could cut asunder the earth and sky.[17] He has been identified with Sūrya, the Sun-god. He is a deliverer from the darkness:[18]

Indra has been given the most prominent place in the *Ṛg-Vedic* pantheon as he delivers man from the black hued darkness. The night was the most horrible and was considered to be the nightmare. In that age of twilight of civilization, people were exposed to prey of animals at night. Life was most miserable after sunset.

Uṣās (dawn) is the goddess of the *Ṛg-Veda.* It is evident from the hymns that it is the sense of security and survival which is the motive force behind the native prayers, the ceremonial and the allegorical expressions of Ṛg-Vedic culture. *Uṣās* has been described as the daughter of sky, lady of the light and giver of wealth and joy.[19]

Sūrya (the Sun-god) is another *Ṛg-Vedic* deity. He has been described as the shelter of all creatures.[20] *Sūrya* thwarts the darkness and hence he liberates mankind from the wail of miseries. Agni (the Fire-god) is another deity who occupies a place of distinction in the

Vedic pantheon. Here also we find the same yearning for wealth and joy. The *Ṛg-Veda* says that one can obtain wealth and happiness through the worship of *Agni.*[21]

The Atharva-Veda

The *Atharva-Veda* is a monumental work of Hindu Tantra. Composed in India, it is quite different from the *Ṛg-Veda* both in content and form. The influence of Tantra is felt on every mantra of the *Atharva-Veda.* It gives the whole picture of life. It is not an isolated work of philosophy or religion but deals with the ideal of man's ultimate beatitude, the intuitional science (*Vidyā Tantra*), witchcraft (*Avidyā Tantra*), statesmanship, warfare, etc. But due to the influence of Tantra, the orthodox Āryan does not recognize the *Atharva-Veda* as part of the revealed scripture (*Śruti*). Dayānanda Saraswati, the founder of Ārya Samāj, also condemns it as a heretical literature. The word '*travyi*', which is commonly used to signify the Vedic scriptures, denotes that the orthodox section of the Hindus does not recognize the *Atharva-Veda* as the fourth Veda. Pāṇini, the greatest grammarian of India, also supports the orthodox view and describes the Veda as '*trayi*'.

The *Atharva-Veda* is a landmark in the history of intuitional science. It is a sacred text. Many of its hymns are benevolent and pregnant with deep philosophy. The content of many of its *mantras* is borrowed from the *Ṛg-Veda* and the *Yajura-Veda,* yet itbecame the victim of the strong wave of aversion only because it was of non-Āryan origin. It could not escape the blight of contempt because it was a textbook of Tantrism. An Atharvan has been contemptuously described as 'a lean black man, sharp, irascible, and amorous'.[22]

The *Atharva-Veda* mainly deals with the Tāntric Cult, and covers all the branches of Tantrism. Tantra is a science of psychic power. It lays down certain principles and techniques for exploiting the unfathomable potentialities of human mind. Thus, it is double edged. It can be utilized for the betterment of human society but when it falls in the hands of anti-social elements, it becomes dreadful. The class of esoteric formulas designed to establish harmony in family village life, victory in war, development of intellect, reconciliation of enemies and the royal duty (*Rāja Karma*) are obviously auspicious and sublime in their form and content. Even the class of charms which are meant to cure *takman* (fever)[23] are scientifically dealt within it. On the basis of Atharvanic literature, we have developed mesmerism, hypnotic suggestion, self-hypnotism, mental healing etc., which are employed in curing many diseases.

The *Atharva-Veda* is a compendium of *Vidyā Tantra*, *Upa-Vidyā Tantra* and *Avidya Tantra*. As a work of *Vidyā Tantra*, it propagates the philosophy of *Brahma Vadā*. It is said Vaidarbhi, the son of Bhṛgu approached sage Pippalāda and asked: 'What is *Brahma Vidyā*? What is the relation between *Brahman* and the world? Do kindly enlighten me on this subject.' In reply, the sage said that the nucleus of the cosmological order is *Brahman*.[24] Just as the spokes are attached to the nave of a wheel, similarly every object of this cosmos is *Brahma*-centric. *Ṛk*, *Yaju* and *Sāma* are all dependent on *Brahman*.

Ṛṣi Pippalāda while throwing light on the mysticism of the *Atharva-Veda* tells Sukeśa, the son of Bhāradvāja, that as the nave of a wheel controls the spokes, similarly *Brahman* controls all the sixteen basic factors (*kalās*) of the universe. Ten organs (five sensory and five motor), five vital principles or *prāṇaḥ* (*Prāṇa, Apāna, Samāna, Udāna* and *Vyāna*) and the ego constitute the sixteen *kalās* — the basic factors of the universe — and are completely dependent on Him. They are the causes of life and death. The Supreme One can be known only through intuition or Prajñā. By knowing Him one bypasses death.

The mysticism of the *Atharva-Veda* is like Bergson's 'open religion'. It is a spiritual stream in whose holiness the Āryan and non-Āryan minds used to take a dip to refresh and restore their divine beings. The esoteric experiences are not to be confused with the instinctive experience. It is not a drift into unreason or obscurity. The mysticism of the *Atharva-Veda* lays stress on the intuitive realization of *Brahman*, the supreme unification of Self with *Brahman*, which is the sole objective of *Tantra Sādhanā*.

Schweitzer also says that 'becoming one with the Infinite is a pure act of the spirit which has nothing to do with ethics.'[25] Some of the Atharvans might have been disillusioned by the astounding achievements of a mental voyage. These Atharvans have simply laid down the esoteric process for the unfolding of the hitherto closed mental chamber. But it is up to the *Sādhaka* to utilize these mental propensities which when utilized for some intellectual or material gain without doing any harm to others are known as *Upa-Vidyā* Tantra. Most of the charms and sorceries of the *Atharva-Veda* belong to *Upa-Vidyā*.

The spell blows hot and cold from the same mouth. It is neither moral nor immoral. When it is used against inimical and demoniac forces, it is a moral practice; when the same is employed in inflicting injuries on noble souls, it is condemned. The *Atharva-Veda* takes this view. Hymn II.12.[26] stops the bitterest enemy who tries to thwart the holy sacraments. But at the same time it does not prevent anybody from frustrating the evil designs of an enemy (VII. 70.). Hymn II.7. promises protection against curses and sinister plottings.

Yātu Vidyā (esoteric practices) of the *Atharva-Veda* was very popular among the non-Āryans. Many Āryans also were enamoured of this *Vidyā* and could not resist getting themselves initiated in this cult. But they were cursed and condemned. The orthodox Āryans, in fact, condemned everything non-Āryan. *Yātu Vidyā* was also condemned. The *Ṛg-Veda* (VII, 104,15,16) says: 'May I die today if I am a sorcerer.' Here Tantra is declared as devilish, yet, in response to their conscience, the Āryans, at one time, had to recognize the greatness of *Yātu Vidyā*. In *Śat. Br.* (X, 5, 2, 20) Tantra was accepted in principle as one of the holiest forms of literature. 'Those skilled in sorcery' were given an honourable place. But the hatred of the Āryans was so deep seated that they were not ready to accept even *bheṣajam* (the science of medicine) as it belonged to the altruistic province of the Atharvan. It could not escape the blight of sneer. The *Tait. S.,* VI ,4, 9, 3 (cf. *Maitr. S.,* IV, 5, 2; *Śat. Br.,* IV,15,14) says, "a Brahman shall not practise medicine."[27] The non-Āryans were advanced in the field of physical and intuitional sciences. The Atharvans have always kept contact with the depths. They were never satisfied with the superficial life. They were aware of Tantra *Sādhanā* (*Yātu Vidyā*) and knew that the fountain of life, from which the creative instincts sprang forth, was not psyche but Self. Man is a spiritual being. He becomes truly human only when his intuitive self is awakened. So long as his life is confined to Vedic rites and sacradotal ceremonies, his life is incomplete and insipid. The Vedic rituals might have some social value, but they are the sign of spiritual homelessness. Only ascension to consciousness could bring the realization of total being. According to Tantra there is no salvation by proxy. But Vedic rituals can be performed by hired priests (who gradually became professionals and social parasites). But there was no scope for priesthood in Tāntric culture. The Brahmanical literature naturally, therefore, started a tirade against Tāntric tradition.

Nārāyaṇīya Tantra says that the Vedas have been originated from the Yāmalas, authoritative works of Tāntric literature. According to it the *Sāma-Veda* has been originated from *Brahma Yāmala* and the *Ṛg-Veda* from *Rudra Yāmala.* The *Yajura-Veda* reflects *Viṣṇu Yāmala* and the *Atharva-Veda* from *Śakti Yāmala.* The verses, referred to by the great Siddha Sarvananda in his compendium called *Sarvallāsa Tantra* *are* a clear evidence that Tantra preceded the Vedas.

To our view neither the Vedas have been originated from Tantra nor the latter forms part of Vedic exegesis. Śrī Gauḍapāda has written another Tāntric text named *Śri-Vidyā Ratna Sūtra* to propagate the mysticism of the *Śrī Vidyā* cult.[28] *Prapaṁcasāra* is also ascribed to Śrī Śaṅkarācārya. Rāghava Bhaṭṭa in his commentary on *Śāradā Tilaka* has also supported this view.

Śrī *Vidyārṇav*[29] gives a detailed account of the hierarchy of Guru and disciples of Śrī Śaṅkarācārya. It is a Tāntric literature belonging to the Śāktāgama school. According to this book Śaṅkarācārya was not a grand disciple of Gauḍapāda. In between Gauḍapāda and Śaṅkara, there were five *ācāryas.* The harries of the seven *ācāryas* are given in the following order: Gauḍapāda, Pāvaka, Parācārya, Satyanidhi, Rāmacandra, Govind and Śaṅkarācārya.

On the basis of available research material it can be safely concluded that Śaṅkarācārya was a great admirer and follower of *Tantra Śāstra.* The mystic power that he had cannot be achieved through the Vedantic method. Śaṅkarācārya has displayed occult power to defeat his adversaries on many occasions. This power can be achieved only through *Śakti Sādhanā*. Śaṅkara was a profound devotee of the *Śrī Vidyā* cult, *Śrī-Cakra* is still being worshipped in his Śṛṅgerī Muṭṭa. Dr. Gopinath Kaniraj is of the opinion that Śaṅkarācārya will have to be recognized as one of the greatest exponents of the *Tripurāgama* branch of the *Śākta* school.[30]

The Veda is a religio-philosophical system. Tantra is a science of religion and philosophy of science. Tantra does not believe in the lifeless Vedic rituals. Truth cannot be attained through the exercise of intellect. Tantra is *Sādhanā*. It is reduced so esotericism and *siddhi* or realization attained as an experimentally verified fact. There is a famous story about Maharsi Śāṇḍilya, who studied the whole of Vedic literature but could not attain salvation. After this he went through the literature of the *Pañcarātra* School of *Vaiṣṇava* Tantra and performed *Sādhanā* according to the *Pañcarātra* system and attained enlightenment.

REFERENCES

1. यतो वाचो निर्वतन्ते अप्राप्य मनसा सह। *Taittirīya Upaniṣad,* 11.4.1.
2. *The Wonder That Was India,* pp. 4-9, Sidgwick and Jackson, London, 1956.
3. *Ibid.*, p. 22.
4. *Pre-Historic India*, p. 155. Harmondsworth, 1950.
5. *Ibid.*, p. 15.

6. *Ibid.*
7. *Ancient India*, p. 19.
8. Śrī Aurdbihdo, *On the Veda*, p. 4. International University Centre, Pondicherry, 1956.
9. *Ṛg-Veda*, II. 12, *A Source Book in Indian Philosophy*, p. 4.
10. *On the Veda*, p. 3.
11. *A History of Indian Philosophy*, vol. I, p. 10.
12. *Cosmic Society*—An Anthology, p. 16. Renaissance Universal Publication, New Delhi, 1967.
13. *Bhāratiya Saṁskṛti aur Sādhanā*, vol. I, p. 5.
14. *Black Yajura-Veda.*
15. *Outline of Religious Literature of India* (2nd ed.), p. 7.
16. *A History of Indian Philosophy*, vol. I, p. 17.
17. 'I will extol the most heroic Indra who with his might forced earth and sky asunder.'— R. T. H. Griffith, Hymns ofthe *Ṛg-Veda* (3rd ed.), p. x.89. E.J. Lazarus & Co., 1920-26.
18. 'Sūrya is he : throughout the wide expanses shall Indra turn him, swift as car-wheels, hither, like a stream resting not but ever active : he hath destroyed with light the black-hued darkness.' — *Ibid.*
19. 'Dawn on its with prosperity, O Uṣās, daughter of the sky. Dawn with great glory, goddess, lady of the light, dawn thou with riches, bounteous on'— *Ibid.*, 1.48.
20. 'Aloft as beams now bring the god who knows all creatures that are born, That all may look upon the Sun.'—A.A. Macdonell, *Hymns from the Ṛgveda*, p. 150. Oxford University Press, London, 1922.
21. (i) 'Agni, worthy to be magnified by the ancient ṛṣis and by the present ones, may he conduct the gods hither'.
    (ii) 'May one obtain through Agni wealth and welfare day by day, which may bring glory and high bliss of valiant offspring.'— Hermann Oldenberg, *Sacred Books of the East* XLVI, Vedic Hymns, part II, p. 2. Clarendon Press, Oxford, 1897.
22. Rajendralal Mitra, *Gopatha-Brāhmaṇa*, Introduction, p. 4.
23. *Hymns of the Atharva-Veda*, p. 1.
24. अराइय रथनाभो कला यस्मिन् प्रतिष्ठिति।
    त्वं वैद्यं पुरुषं वेद यथा मा मृत्यु परिव्यथः।। *Atharva-Veda.*
25. S. Radhakrishnan, *Eastern Religion and Western Thought* (2nd ed.), p. 95. Oxford University Press, 1940.
26. Atharva-Veda.
27. ब्राह्मणेन भेषजम न कार्यम्। *Atharva-Veda.*
28. *Tripura Rahasya*, p. xi.
29. The manuscript of this book is lying at the famous temple of Raghunath at Jammu. See Steins catalogue of Raghunath Temple Library.
30. *Bhāratiya Saṁskṛti aur Sādhanā*, vol. 1, pp. 13, 115.

2
Ontological Mysticism
The Future Metaphysics

Metaphysics is a branch of philosophy. It is a quest for reality. The word Metaphysics was coined by Aristotle. The term metaphysics is derived from the Greek *Ta Meta ta Physika* which means after the physics. Its field of study is nature of *being* and *existence.* Aristotle had divided Metaphysics into three main parts, *(i) Ontology, (ii) Natural theology* and *(iii) Universal Science.* With the advancement of knowledge natural theology which deals with the study of God and the universal science which is the study of logic and reasoning have become in independent discipline. Metaphysics is the study of reality, visible and invisible; what constitutes reality, natural and transcendental. Metaphysics is concerned to understand the substance of reality. It reflects on why things exist at all. The whole philosophy in a sense is an enquiry and reflection in some form of metaphysics. Technically speaking metaphysics is the study of all reality. It is the most fundamental subject and it tries to understand what existence and beings mean.

To my mind Metaphysics begins with Parmenides. The critical and the comparative study of Parmenides and Heraclitus is necessary for understanding the origin and development of different Western schools of Metaphysics. As against Heraclitus doctrine of eternal flux Parmenides placed the reality and truth of the world in thought and concept. This became the basis of all subsequent schools of idealism. The whole idealistic philosophy is based on the dictum that truth lies in reason not in the world of senses. Parmenides became the source of both of materialism and idealism. The two contradictory thoughts remain unreconciled in Parmenides contradicting each other. However, Parmenides was not aware of any contradictions while formulating his concept of *Being* as the sole reality. Empedocles and Democritus deduced from the doctrines of Parmenides the materialistic aspects of his thoughts. The basic principle of Parmenides was that being cannot come out from not-being and that being neither originates nor destroys. Empedocles and Democritus caught hold of the concept of matter, i.e. based on the "modern doctrine of indestructibility of matter". Matter has neither a beginning nor an end. The apparent origination and passing away of things is simply the combinations and the dissolution of particles of matter which are indestructible. This is the main view of Democritus. And on the basis of that he recreated the doctrine of Parmenides on the basis of his own philosophy that being cannot come out from not being or passed into not being. On the other hand Plato ceased the idealistic aspects of Parmenides doctrine and developed it into a grand metaphysical system of idealism. Plato identified the concept and the idea with the being of Parmenides. However, it is a debatable point who is the right and truthful interpreter of Parmenides doctrine of *Being*. Plato was a great thinker and a pioneer; he had the honour and the distinction of establishing a school of philosophical thoughts and traditions in the West. But it is also true that the whole philosophy of Plato is based upon the doctrines of Parmenides.

The third and last great thinker of Eleatic school is Zeno. Zeno is acknowledged as the father and the discoverer of dialectic in the West. In support of Parmenides doctrine of Being, Zeno tried to destroy the very basis of the world of *becoming*. The world of *becoming* has two essential features—multiplicity and change. The *Being* of Parmenides is absolutely one and it does not recognise and believe in plurality or multiplicity and change. *Being* is one, individual, eternal and unchangeable. The multiplicity, plurality, change and motions speak of the world of senses which is false and an illusion. To disprove the very basis of multiplicity and motion, Zeno proved through his dialectical reasoning that admission and acceptance of motion and change are illusion and impossibility. He demonstrated through his argument that multiplicity and motions are unreal and contradictory propositions. Two propositions and views which contradict each other cannot both be true on the basis of dialectical arguments. He refuted the very basis of multiplicity and motion. Zeno's dialectic against motion is based upon antinomy of infinite divisibility as for example, the flight of an arrow. Arrow is where it is. It cannot be where it is not, therefore arrow is not moving.

The Western Metaphysical doctrine was culminated in Kant, Hegel and Karl Marx. Kant for the first time makes a distinction between the phenomena and neumena. According to Kant *thing in itself* is unknown and unknowable. Kant rejected the Berkeley's transcendental idealism as form of empirical realism. The Kantian exegesis has been a source of great debate and discussion. The important argument that constitutes the *Critique of Pure Reason* is the refutation of all kinds of rational proof of the existence of God. Kant's contention is that God or the absolute is beyond the reach of reason. There is a great similarity between the teachings of Upanishads and that of Kant.[1]

Hegel is one of the most original and difficult philosopher. He is the last who is considered as philosophical system builder. According to him the reality is the Absolute. The Absolute is spiritual. He does not agree with Spinoza's doctrine that substance has attribute of extension and thought. Apart from this distinction the metaphysical system of Hegel has great similarity with Spinoza. Hegel draws the doctrine of absolute from the concept of reality which does not admit any self-contradictions. He does not accept anything real except the whole. The whole is the absolute of Hegel but he does not accept the views of Parmenides and Spinoza who believed in simple substance. Hegel's whole is like an organism. The post-Kantian thinkers were greatly influenced by Spinoza's monism and Kant's idealism. Hegelian metaphysics is a complex system.

The dialectical materialism of Karl Marx occupies an important position in the history of Metaphysics. According to some his whole doctrine is based on ontological materialism. I think Marx was aware of Aristotelian concept of matter. According to Aristotle matter is not real, it is a possibility. It is called *potentia*. If we accept with this concept of matter then we have to understand dialectical materialism of Karl Marx on a higher state of reality.

In the first part of the Twentieth century there was a reaction against metaphysics. Logical positivism rejection and hostility to metaphysics is based on the employment of the criterion of meaning which is known as the verification principle. But the verification principle is itself not verifiable. However, there has been significant development in the world of metaphysical enquiry. Ludwig Wittgenstein says, "There are, indeed, things that cannot be put into words. They make themselves manifest. They are what is mystical."[2] He further writes, "the correct method in philosophy would really be the following: to say nothing except what can be said, i.e. propositions of natural science, i.e. something that has nothing to do with philosophy—and then, whenever someone else wanted to say something metaphysical, to demonstrate to him that he had failed to give a meaning to certain signs in his propositions. Although it would not be satisfying to the other person—he would not have the feeling that we were teaching him philosophy—this method would be the only strictly correct one. My propositions serve as elucidations in the following way: anyone who understands me eventually recognizes them as non-sensical, when he has used them—as steps—to climb up beyond them. (He must, so to speak, throw away the ladder after he has climbed up it.) He must transcend these propositions, and then he will see the world aright."[3] He concludes, "What we cannot speak about we must pass over in silence."[4]

Einstein's doctrine of Relativity and the Quantum Mechanics are instrumental in the return of metaphysics in the last century. This recent development in science has rejected the classical physics postulated by Newton which was based on ontological materialism. Newton's work entitled *'Philosophiae Naturalis Principia Mathematica'* postulates that the all objects at rest remain in that state unless it is moved by some external force. And he explained the movement of the planets around the sun in the elliptical orbits in terms of force of gravity.

In spite of all the unprecedented and spectacular discoveries and progress in scientific knowledge the problem of the origin of the universe and the real nature of the substance out of which the universe has been created remains a great mystery. The concept of dark energy which is present in enormous amount in the whole universe remains a mystery. According to modern science the biggest problem with the energy of the universe is cosmological constant problem.

This has been established beyond doubt that there are many universes which are governed and contained by different value of dark energy.

Stephen Hawking in the beginning of his book entitled '*The Grand Design*' writes, "How does the universe behave? What is the nature of reality? Where did all this come from? Did the universe need a creator? Most of us do not spend most of our time worrying about these questions, but almost all of us worry about them some of the time. Traditionally these are questions for philosophy, but philosophy is dead. Philosophy has not kept up with the modern development in science, particularly physics."[5]

Philosophy is not dead, rather science has become a philosophy. Problem of 'why' has been the fundamental issue of philosophy since its very inception and the problem of 'how' comes within the domain of scientific investigation and discovery. Now science is trying to understand, reflect and solve the problem of "why". It is a welcome step. This is a metaphysical enquiry in which scientists are taking greater interests.

Scientist propagating their theories on the foundation of ontological materialism coming out of Plato's cave to new awareness of Truth and Reality. Truth and Reality postulated by ontological mysticism (ontological spiritualism). There is a convergence of science and philosophy today. Philosophy is not only alive and vibrant but it has made science a living subject. The problem whether the matter is wave or particle is rooted in misunderstanding and the wrong notion of wave and particle. Matter is neither wave nor particle it is consciousness. Whole cosmos is the modification of cosmic consciousness (*Brahman, Ataman*), Emptiness (*Sunyata* or *Tao*). Whole cosmos is the modification of cosmic consciousness. Consciousness is the *Reality* and the sole *Truth.* Science and metaphysics are the quest for truth and reality. The classical science was concerned with the objective truth. The theory of relativity and quantum mechanics have transcended the boundary of classical science in search of the understanding and knowledge of true nature of reality and entered into the subjective domain of philosophy. If science would not have entered and made inroad into *"subjectivity"* it would have become dead and would have lost charm, beauty and relevance. Unless we understand the true nature and structure of truth we would become the victim of such dilemma. Einstein has revolutionized the science by his famous formulation of $E = mc^2$. He was the first scientist who came face to face with truth. For him matter is not dead but it is energy and alive. By this formulation he rejected the age old scientific dogma of dead matter. The universe is vibrating with life. It is a living reality because it is a modification of consciousness. Consciousness is the quintessential nature and structure of the cosmos. Both science and metaphysics culminate in spirituality. It is the goal and the end of the quest for science and metaphysics. This is ontological mysticism. According to Spinoza, the human body is a modification of infinite substance (God) insofar as it is expressed in the attribute of extension. According to him the material world is a modification of God. Hence, it follows from Spinoza's philosophy that there is consciousness which corresponds to the vital processes of our body. Ervin Schrodinger, one of the founding fathers of quantum mechanics, writes, "And then, on the other hand, we say that consciousness is that by which this world becomes manifest, by which indeed, we can quite calmly say, it first becomes present; that the world consists of the elements of consciousness—this world within which we have just discovered the emergence of the brain as a highly specialized phenomenon, something which has emerged but which might quite well have remained non-existent and which is, in any case, by no means *sui generis*. And now we are asked to believe that this special modification in the evolution of the higher mammals had to happen in order that the world should dawn on itself in the light of consciousness; whereas, if it had not emerged, this world would have remained nothing but a drama played to an empty house, not present to anyone and hence not in a real sense present at all ! If this is really the ultimate wisdom to which we can attain in this question, then to me it seems to be utter bankruptcy of our picture of the world.

And we thought at least to acknowledge it, and not act as though it did not matter to us, or jeer, in our rationalistic wisdom, at those who try to find a way out, however desperate.[6]

The Danish physicist Neil Bohr (1855-1962) came out with a new theory of *complementarity* to explain the dilemma of wave and particle. A single model may not be adequate to explain all observations made of atomic or sub-atomic systems in different experiments. For example, 'electron diffraction is best explained by assuming that electron is a wave, whereas the photoelectric effect is described by assuming that it is a particle. The idea of two different but complementary concepts to treat quantum phenomena was first put forward by him. Wave and particle dilemma is due to incomplete understanding of reality. The reality is beyond wave and particles. The nature is not governed by whims and caprices. There is some system, some rules, some principles, behind the movement of the phenomenal world. The uncertainty principles which explains certain natural functions like Newtonian Classic Physics which also explains gravitational movement of some natural bodies but which does not give scientific explanation of particle and waves but it has limitations.

The principles of uncertainty entail absence of our proper knowledge and understanding of the movement of particles and wave which has given rise to the principles of uncertainty. The movement of particles and waves would be explained by some law. Einstein did not agree with the Copenhagen interpretation of Quantum mechanics. Einstein's rejection of Bohr's doctrine of *complementarity* are based on some scientific thinking and reflection.

It is to be ascertained whether Einstein is right in his assertion that God does not play dice with the world. If we accept the theory of complementarity then the logical doctrine of principles of identity and contradiction will have no place in science.

Washington Post writes, "In science, revolutions take time. So, the day after news broke of a possible revolution in physics 'particles moving faster than light'—a scientist leading the European experiment that made a discovery calmly explained it to the few present at CERN the giant particle acceleration straddling the Swiss-French border. The physicist, Danrio Anterio made no sweeping claims."[7]

In the *Washington Post* of 25th September, 2011 highlighted the new discovery by science which has almost falsified the findings of Einstein that nothing travels faster than light. Some particles according to the report travel faster than the speed of light. It is called the "God Particle". However, I believe that the cosmic consciousness has the speed of infinity. It may be called in mathematical terms that the cosmic consciousness travels with absolute speed and at the same time it has a zero speed. The whole cosmos exists in between zero and infinite speed. The cosmic consciousness which is called in Hinduism as a *Brahman* or *Siva*, Tao in Lao Tzu metaphysics and *Sunyata* (emptiness) in Buddhism is the ultimate reality. It has absolute speed and absolute stillness (pause). From philosophical perspective we can say that consciousness has got infinite speed and from other perspective it may be called that it has a zero speed. Conceptually, there is no dilemma between absolute speed and absolute pause.

The root of knowledge is metaphysics, the trunk is science and the branches are all other schools of social sciences and humanity. Knowledge bereft of ontological mysticism is Pyrrhonism. In mystical experience, knowledge and wisdom become one. Monism is true philosophy and ultimate basis of science. Oneness with reality is the goal of spirituality and the proper understanding of reality is the end of scientific journey. I feel the convergence of science and spirituality will herald a new era of ontological mysticism. Science and spirituality are the integral form and part of human existence. A French mathematician Marquis de Laplace (1749-1827), has made a very logical and rational assertion that all our knowledge is problematical. And in that background we have to examine the different scientific doctrines.

I think that the Einstein's assertions about the speed of the travelling light is the fastest, i.e. it is a relative truth. So there is every possibility of its limitation and falsifications. As I have already asserted that the phenomenal world exists between zero and infinity and hence any scientific formulation which has not reached infinity has every possibility that it would be falsified by other scientific formulation. Scientific formulation being relative in nature, it does not entail that the Einstein assertions were totally wrong. As I have already stated, every scientific postulation is relative and subject to being corrected, improved and modified by another scientific postulation. Marquis de Laplace writes, "Strictly speaking it may be even said that nearly all our knowledge is problematical; and in the small number of things which we are able to know with certainty, even in mathematical sciences themselves, the principle means for asserting truth—induction and analogy, are based on probabilities; so that the entire system of human knowledge is connected with the theory set forth in the essay. Doubtless it will be seen here with interest that in considering, even in the eternal principles of reason, justice and humanity; only the favourable chances which are constantly attached to them, there is a great advantage in following these principles and serious inconvenience departing from them; their chances like those favourable to lotteries, always end by prevailing in the midst of the vacillations of hazard."[8]

There has been a constant debate between the domain of philosophy and science. We have been making arbitrary distinction between philosophy and science, between speculative and logical aspects of science. However, it would be wrong to assume that philosophy must develop into logic of science, which has been asserted by A.J. Ayer. He writes in his concluding celebrated book '*Language, Truth and Logic*' that, a person who is engaged in understanding the logical relationship of the different hypotheses and defining it in form of symbol is a philosopher. According to him, it is one and the same thing to address such people who are engaged in logical relationship of hypothesis as a philosopher or a scientist. He concludes with this sentence that "What we must recognise is that it is necessary for a philosopher to become a scientist, in this sense, if he is to make any substantial contribution towards the growth of human knowledge."[29] A.J. Ayer being a positivist he is biased for science. He could not comprehend the whole gamut of philosophical thinking and speculation. There is no necessity of philosopher becoming a scientist, when scientists are becoming philosophers in pursuit of truth, beauty and reality. Pure physics and pure mathematics are branches of philosophy. The root of knowledge is ontological mysticism, the trunk is philosophy and science and other forms of knowledge are different branches.

However, mediating between two planes of perception and reflection given by science and philosophy would be the greatest intellectual adventure and most rewarding of our times.

I would analyse, examine and evaluate the findings and the postulations of classical physics, theory of relativity and quantum mechanics in the larger background of metaphysical reflection and ontological mysticism.

According to classical physics the universe is governed by the laws that are susceptible to rational understanding. And the chief purpose and objective of classical physics has been the application of those laws for extending our knowledge about the phenomenal world. Newton was a deeply religious man. He considered these laws as the manifestation of God's perfection. However to great extent the classical physics became a tool for understanding the laws that governed the phenomenal world. However, the classical physics failed to explain some problems that govern the events on sub-atomic level. It failed to make enroots into some atomic phenomena with any certainty. Strictly speaking quantum physics does not believe in the world of waves and particles, of position and velocity. We enter into the world of inconsistency and contradictions when we try to explain the quantum world in the language of classical science. Actually the measurement of the object measured and the subject doing the measuring are inexplicably involved.

Metaphysicians and the scientists have been trying since time immemorial to understand and explain the origin and the development of the universe. Stephen Hawking writes "In the beginning the universe was infinitesimally small and infinitely dense, and it burst." This is known as the *"big bang theory"*. The scientists before the postulation of Einstein's theory of relativity and Max Planck's, Heisenberg's, Schrodinger's and Neil Bohr's postulation of quantum mechanics believed that the universe constituted of space-time was smooth and flat. But with the advent of the new discovery and concept of *big bang*, the doctrines who believed the static and the flat universe is broken down. The question which is unanswered till today is why the infinitesimally small and infinitely dense universe did burst. Scientists do not have answer to this "why". If there has been no other force, in that case, the infinitesimally small and infinitely dense would have remained in the state of eternal animated state. Kashmir Saivism, Vedanta, Buddhism have answered this "why" problem. I believe that Kashmir Saivism provides a scientific and metaphysical explanation of this problem. According to Kashmir Saivism, *Parama Siva* is the fundamental reality.

Siva (cosmic consciousness) and *Sakti* coalesce into one undivided unity of transcendentality. The cosmic consciousness is illuminating *(Prakasa)* and knowing entity and *Sakti* (cosmic matrix) is veiling *(Vimarsa)* and activating entity. *Siva* (cosmic consciousness) is consciousness in *stasis*. The creative matrix is consciousness dynamic. It is in the nature of the ultimate reality to create and manifest in the form of universe. So long the cosmic principles (*Sakti*) remain merged in cosmic consciousness, it does not get any scope of activation and manifestation. The theoretical dualism of cosmic consciousness (*Siva*) and cosmic matrix (*Sakti*) is symbolically represented by a grain of gram having two seeds closely joined and covered with the sheath of *Maya*. The evolution starts only when they come apart. When the cosmic matrix which is the cosmic energy starts acting and reacting, the differentiation is started. This differentiation between cosmic consciousness and cosmic principles of energy is the cause of creative ideation and the modification of consciousness in the form of universe. This differentiation in the form of modification of cosmic consciousness is meant objectivisation of the ultimate reality. Evolution is known according to Kashmir Saivism as *Abhasa.* According to *Abhasavada,* world is real, in the sense that it is an aspect of supreme reality. Dr. Gopinath Kaviraj says, "The peculiar metaphysical position of the Tantra consists in the theory of *Abhasa*, which is consistent with this position. It rejects the *Vivartavada* of neo-Vedanta, because the world is not originally a false appearance due to Error. It is real in the same way as an image is real but it has no existence apart from the medium in which it is manifested. To the Vedantist, the world appears as such, to the ignorant, owing to his ignorance, and in the last analysis, it is resolved into *Maya* which is not identical with *Brahman* and is materialistic, but to a *Tantrist* the world is real and is the expression of the *Cit-Sakti* or Free Will of the Lord and is really spiritual in essence like the Lord Himself."[10] *Bindu*, *Nada* and *Kala* are the three stages of evolution. Involution is the process of crudification of cosmic consciousness which undergoes metamorphosis. The cosmic consciousness is transformed and modified into matter. According to the variation in the degree of bondage of creative matrix (*Sakti*) the cosmic consciousness (*Siva*) has taken different modifications. But the fundamental reality is one and the same. Creation is nothing but the thought projection of the *Brahman*. The *creative matrix,* the *magna matter* conceives, bears and nourishes the entire universe. *Siva* is pure consciousness and *Sakti* is the activating principle. This universe is nothing but the creative ideation of the causal matrix. The creative matrix (*Sakti*) is constituted of sentient, mutative and static principles. These three principles after the formations of these three triangular forces which are belligerent in nature burst from the *Bindu* (the point) and in the form of *Nada* (*Sabda*) and *Kala* (curvature). The triangle of forces bursts from one of the vertices. The point from which the triangular forces burst out it is called *Kama Bija* (the seed of the universe). The seed of creation is expressed in a metaphysical word as *Nada* (word). It is dominated by sentient principles.

The universe is a curvature and it has taken different forms and modification of the ultimate fundamental reality, that is cosmic consciousness and it has been originated in the form of different galaxies and other celestial bodies is inherent in the theory of evolution of Kashmir Saivism known as *Abhasavada.* In spite of all the knowledge and the monumental achievements in the field of scientific discovery, the scientists have not been able to explain the origin of the universe out of the ultimate energy which is considered mysterious. Lisa Randall accepts the inability of modern science in explaining the origin, nature and the function of the energy that resulted in the expansion of the universe. She writes, "The shocking observation was that the measurements of the characteristics of the universe required the presence of this new form of energy that's not carried by matter. This energy is not carried by particles or other stuff, and it doesn't clump like conventional matter. It doesn't dilute as the universe expands but maintains a constant density. The expansion of the universe is slowly accelerating as a consequence of the mysterious energy, which resides throughout the universe, even if it were empty of matter."[11]

Lisa Randall does accept the inability and profound ignorance about the cause of the *big bang*. Why the universe which was in the beginning infinitesimally small and infinitely dense banged or erupted. The evolution and the beginning of the universe in spite of the *big bang* theory is a mystery. However, the *big bang* theory does explain to great extent the expansion and evolution of the universe. It was Einstein who first conceived the idea of the expanding universe and formulated his historic scientific theory of general relativity.

Taoism, Buddhism and Hinduism are based on monastic and mystic traditions. In reality, Taoism, Buddhism and Hinduism are not religions, but they are a way of life divine. Erwin Schrodinger writes, "In Christian terminology to say: 'Hence I am God Almighty' sounds both blasphemous and lunatic. But please disregard these connotations for the moment and consider whether the above inference is not the closest a biologist can get to proving God and immortality at one stroke. In itself, the insight is not new. Te earliest records, to my knowledge date back some 2500 years ago or more. From the early great Upanishads the recognition ATMAN=BRAHMAN (the personal self-equals the omnipresent, all comprehending eternal self) was in Indian thought considered, far from being blasphemous, to represent the quintessence of the deepest insight into the happenings of the world. The striving of all the scholars of Vedanta was, after having learnt to pronounce with their lips, really to assimilate in their minds this grandest of all thoughts. Again, the mystics of many centuries, independently, yet in perfect harmony with each other (somewhat like the particles in an ideal gas) have described, each of them, the unique experience of his or her life in terms that can be condensed in the phrase: DEUS FACTUS SUM (I have become GOD)."[12]

The phenomenal world of plurality is only an appearance, it is not real. This has been demonstrated by Buddhist monks before the Chinese Empress that the many faceted crystal remains one object. This has already been quoted before in the context of the Buddhist monk demonstrating it before the Chinese empress. Schrodinger also talks very high of the *mahavakaya* of *Tattavamasi*—Thou art that. This *mahavakaya* symbolizes the basic truth, 'I am this Whole Word' or 'I am the Cosmic Being (*Brahman*)'.[13]

In the history of human civilization twenty first century will herald a dawn of a future metaphysics in form of ontological mysticism. There is a convergence of metaphysics and mysticism. The twenty first century will usher a new era of spiritual renaissance. This renaissance would come in which mankind would discover that the ethical and spiritual truths are the highest truths and highest practicality. It would liberate mankind from the miserable obsession of the reality which is based on ontological materialism. The integration of multi-dimensional kaleidoscope of science with monastic and spiritualistic kaleidoscope is ontological mysticism.

East is monastic and the West is theistic. East is mystical and the West is dualistic. East is spirituality and West is science. Ontological mysticism is the happy and harmonious blending of East and West and science and spirituality. Nature has not set any limit to the realization of human hopes and aspirations. Spirituality is a path of truth, virtue and *nirvana*. Science gives us knowledge, spirituality brings wisdom. In the state of spiritual sublimity we are face to face with truth and reality.

Integrating and mediating between these two planes of ratiocination and reflections given by science and spirituality would be the greatest intellectual and moral adventure and the most rewarding achievement of today. The impact of ontological materialism which has disastrous impact on our civilization is that it is far more developed materially than spiritually. With the scientific and technological advancement the forces of nature at our command, in such an unprecedented way, have polluted the very civilization which was born out of love and compassion. We value material achievements and we do not keep in our mind the importance of ethical and spiritual values. Albert Schweitzer writes, "The essential nature of civilization does not lie in its material achievements but in the fact that individuals keep in mind the ideals of the perfecting of man, and the improvement of the social and political conditions of people, and of mankind as a whole. And that their habit of thoughts is determined in living and constant fashion by such ideals."[14]

Modern science has succeeded in revealing some of the mysteries of nature and in the course of their penetration deeper into the knowledge of natural harmony it has become conscious of the fact that it is harmony and order which rules the universe. And this harmony and order is beyond the realm of scientific ratiocination and experiments. This natural harmony and order is the result of the activation of some hidden reality which I consider as cosmic consciousness. However, scientists do accept the existence of an *ontological order* which is beyond the reach of scientific enquiry. Prince Louis De Broglie considers that the truth is that humanity has been able to adapt itself to live in this world in which there is some isomorphic relation with our mind. If there would not have been so, perhaps humanity would not have been able to survive. He writes, "How remarkable is the harmony between the resources of which our mind disposes and the profound realities which conceal themselves behind natural appearances. To bring this harmony more completely into the light, to glimpse yet more the ontological order of which Duhem spoke—such appears to be the true mission of pure science. Removed from all utilitarian preoccupation, solely devoted to the search for truth, it appears to us as one of the noblest activities of which we are capable. By the wholly ideal nature of the goal it pursues, by the intensity and the disinterested character of the efforts that it demands, it possesses a moral value which cannot be denied."[15] Henri Bergson, the author of *"Creative Evolution"*, has warned against the power of destruction that man has acquired for the first time in the history with the technological advancements and the monumental discoveries of modern physics. He thinks that, we are living in an era of inexpiable strife which has surpassed the limit and the magnitude of horrors of all the wars of the past have witnessed the potential of destruction that could destroy the whole humanity from the surface of the earth.

And he thinks "Let us add that this increased body awaits a supplement of the soul and that mechanism demands mysticism."[16] Humanity does not know that the future depends on itself. It is for it to see if it wishes to continue to live, says Bergson.

Prince Louis De Broglie writes, "Confronted by the dangers with which the advances of science can, if employed for evil, face him, man has need of a "supplement of soul" and he must force himself to acquire it promptly before it is too late. It is the duty of those who have mission of being the spiritual or intellectual guides of humanity to labour to awaken in it this supplement of the soul."[17]

The theory of relativity and quantum mechanics has brought a revolution in human thinking and understanding of both nature and man.

However, Einstein dreamt of postulating a unified theory for the understanding of universe and man. It was a revolution in itself. I consider that the ontological mysticism may be considered as a unified theory because it does explain the mystery of the universe and the mystery of the soul. We cannot have any understanding and knowledge of an object divorced from the subjective involvement. Quantum mechanics believes that the subject and object relation which tinged and modified the object in the process of observation by the observer is neither irrelevant nor completely surveyable. After any number of observations the object is left in a state where which some features (the last observed ones) are known, but others those inferred with by the last observations are not known. This speaks of our limitation and this is why any explanation or, faultless description of physical object is not possible. Schrodinger writes, "I say this interpretation suggests itself: that there is a fully determined physical object in existence, but I can never know all about it.

However, this would be a complete misunderstanding of what Bohr and Heisenberg and those who follow them actually mean. They mean that the object has no existence independent of the observing subject. They mean that recent discoveries in physics have pushed forward to the mysterious boundary between the subject and the object, which thereby has turned out not to be a sharp boundary at all. We are to understand that we never observe an object without its being modified or tinged by our own activity in observing it. We are to understand that under the impact of our refined methods of observation and of thinking about the results of our experiments that mysterious boundary between the subject and the object has broken down.[18] According to classical mechanics once sufficient data is provided it gives yes or no answer for all the further questions. While quantum mechanics simply leaves unanswered some questions in theory to be answered by our experience and further reflections. According to Heisenberg in the drama of existence we are both actor and passive spectator. Further he says that we do not know what is red and what is blue. He also raised the fundamental epistemological problems which is still unanswered. According to quantum mechanics, we are not in position to provide any information about the physical objects or the phenomenal world without having personal experience. This experience or interaction is very important. Even while perceiving an object we modify the object by the light rays with which we hit the object. In the process of perception, the light rays reflect into the retina of the eye and it transmits the inferred object to our mind. So in the process of obtaining knowledge about an object, we tinged and modified the object. This is an eternal problem of philosophy and Kant has rightly argued that the things in itself is unknown and unknowable. Kant, however, does agree that all knowledge begins with experience but it does not mean that it is not always derived from experience. Experience teaches us that certain things have such and such properties but it does not provide complete knowledge that it could not be different. Any emphasis on the theory of complete logical clarification would lead to scientific impossibility. Heisenberg says, "It has been pointed out before that in the Copenhagen interpretation of quantum theory we can indeed proceed without mentioning ourselves as individuals, but we cannot disregard the fact that natural science is formed by men. Natural science does not simply describe and explain nature; it is a part of the interplay between nature and ourselves; it describes nature as exposed to our method of questioning."[19] Quantum mechanics is a paradox. According to quantum mechanics scientists explain its experiments in vocabulary of classical physics.

And at the same time, it asserts that those concepts do not agree accurately with nature. The paradoxical nature of quantum mechanics combines objective and the subjective elements. It is all about possibilities and not certainty. Heisenberg further says, "This looks as if we have introduced an element of subjectivism into the theory, as if we meant to say. What happens depends on our way of observing it or on the fact that we observe it."[20]

While making experiments to understand the atomic structure one starts with the belief that one is making experiments with physical objects and facts which are considered as real. But in the process of experiments, one realizes that the atoms or elementary particles are not real. They belong to the world of possibility rather than as one of the things or facts. The science then becomes an esoteric because scientists cannot define the meaning of concept with absolute certainty. The quantum mechanics postulation that every knowledge depends on both subject and object which are inextricably interwoven is the echo of the Pythagorean and the Democrats formulations who postulated that all our perceptions, experiences and observations have strong personal and subjective tinge.

Rene Descartes, the founder of the modern philosophy postulated that there is no possibility of intimate connection between mind and matter. According to him essence of matter is extension in space and that of mind being thought. And he is considered as the father of the dualism. The world of mind and the world of matter are two completely different worlds independent like two parallel rail lines running together without any meeting point.

However, he postulated that these two independent entities do meet at the mysterious pineal glands. Against the background of the rationalist doctrines of Descartes, Berkeley and the empiricists and the idealist thinkers that did agree as mind and matter fundamentally belong to different world and nature, they could have never interacted. Berkeley argued that matter and mind do interact contagiously and he argued that matter must be of the same nature and substance as mind. And hence the essence of matter must be thought rather than its extension otherwise there is no possibility of their meeting. On the other hand, Locke postulated the *"real essence of substance"* is unknown and unknowable. The theory of empiricism fathered by Locke culminated in *solipsism* of David Hume. The epistemological and philosophical problems raised by Hume are still unanswered. According to Locke, knowledge is the perception of agreement or disagreement of two ideas. This thesis of Locke had logical corollary in Berkeley's formulations *"Essest Percipi"*, which means that the existence of things lies in their being perceived. To be perceived is identical with existence. This line of argument culminated in extreme scepticism which is known as solipsism of Hume. According to Hume, we have experience or perception of only ideas. He refuted any induction or causation. If the extreme form of Hume's scepticism and solipsism is accepted it would annihilate the very basis of empirical science. I feel Hume's assertions have certain limitations but it is not wholly and completely false. Even modern scientists are grappling with the problem of nature and the understanding of complete and irrevocable knowledge. The scientists and mathematicians from the time of Greek and philosophical thinkers of Hinduism and Buddhism have been of the opinion that the knowledge acquired by empirical science is true till we have the experience and total experience of the ultimate reality. The complete knowledge is integral and total and direct which could be obtained only through intuitional science and meditative insight.

Sir James Jeans writes, "Most scientists would agree that they are nothing more than pictures-fictions, if you like, if by fiction you mean that science is not yet in contact with the ultimate reality. Many would hold that, from the broad philosophical standpoint, the outstanding achievement of the twentieth century physics is not the theory of relativity with its welding together of space and time, or the theory of quanta with its present apparent negation of the laws of causation, or the dissection of the atom with the resultant discovery that things are not what they seem; it is the general recognition that we are not yet in contact with the ultimate reality. To speak in terms of Plato's well-known simile, we are still imprisoned in our cave, with our backs to the light and can only watch the shadows of the wall. At present the only task immediately before science is to study those shadows, to classify them and explain them in the simplest possible way."[21]

We do not have knowledge of the thing in itself. This throws a new light on the relation on the integration and the intimate relation between the subject and the object. The barrier between subject and object would not have been broken down which has been accepted by Heisenberg and Schrodinger if both the subject and the object would not have belonged to same reality or substance. This is the fundamental metaphysics of ontological mysticism. The Subjectivisation of the so called external object is knowledge and the Subjectivisation of supreme subjectivity (cosmic consciousness) is wisdom or *nirvana*. This speaks of a hidden reality of which both the subject and object are modification and manifestation. I consider that the cosmic consciousness is the only truth and reality. The dualism of subject and object is real till we have the experience and the realization of ultimate truth and reality (cosmic consciousness). Lisa Randall writes, "Understanding nature, life and the universe poses extraordinarily difficult problems. We all would like to better understand who we are, where we came from and where we are going—and to focus on things larger than ourselves and more permanent than the latest gadget or fashion."[22] This is the basic and fundamental concern for both science and philosophy. Philosophy has been in quest of truth and reality which would bring the realization and experience of cosmic consciousness.

"Know thy self" has been the central objective of the Eastern philosophical and mystical tradition. Schrodinger also comes to the same conclusion while speaking about the importance of the knowledge and the experience of *"who are* we?" He writes, "I do think I am prejudiced against the importance that science has from the purely human point of view. I had expressed by the original title of these lectures, and I have explained in the introductory passages, that I consider science an integrating part of our endeavour to answer the one great philosophical question which embraces all others, the one that Plotinus expressed by his brief: who are we? And more than that, I consider this not only one of the tasks, but the task, of science, the only one that really counts."[23] The laws of causation is the fundamental rule of science. But, it has its own limitations. The principle of uncertainty has not totally rejected the concept of causation but in explaining the functioning of atomic structure it has failed. I personally believe that the principle of uncertainty is incomplete. There cannot be any irrevocable and universal theory or postulation; it is based on potentiality and possibilities. However, the categorical imperative postulated by Kant as a moral concept has great relevance today. Dictate of beauty and adherence to moral norms and values has important place in our life. Though I am aware that the moral values are not universal and absolute in character, it has certain limitations of time, place and cultural milieu which are considered as the greatest value in one tradition that is considered as the greatest sin in other traditions. For example according to the Hindu tradition one who knows the *Brahman* or God (cosmic consciousness or ultimate reality) one becomes *Brahman* or God. But in Islamic tradition, anybody proclaims himself or herself to be God is considered the greatest sin and blasphemy. However, one will have to give place to moral values and character and scientific knowledge to spiritual awareness and sublimity. Planck in reply to the question when he was asked that the progress of science consists in discovery of new mystery the moment one thinks that something fundamental has been solved. In answer to this question he says, "Science cannot solve the ultimate mystery of nature. And that is because, in the last analysis we, ourselves are the part of nature and, therefore, part of the mystery that we are trying to solve."[24]

Erwin Schrodinger while enumerating the problem of reality or individual he comes to the conclusion that the concept of individual or reality is wrapped up in mystery. Take for example the concept of particles. What are these particles if they are not individuals?

When we examine the nature and the form of ultimate particles in our environment which is considered as an attribute of individual sameness becomes enigmatic, as we know that an atom is constituted of a number of particles and a molecule is constituted of several atoms. The molecules are of different size, i.e. small and big but there is no limit, beyond which we call it a big molecule. According to modern science size of the molecule has no upper limit. It may contain hundreds of thousands of atoms. Schrodinger writes, "It may be a virus or gene, visible under the microscope. Finally, we may observe that any pulpable object in our environment is composed of molecules, which are composed of atoms which are composed of ultimate particles and if the latter lack individuality, how does, say my wrist watch come by individuality?"[25] Where is the limit? How does individuality arise at all in objects composed of non-individuals? Schrodinger has raised a very fundamental, scientific and philosophical issue. I personally feel that in absence and without reference to transcendental reality (cosmic consciousness) the objective world loses its identity and meaning. Scientific materialism is not clear and sure about the material reality out of which the phenomenal has been created. Science only deals with the partial aspects of reality which is considered the very nature and form of the objective world. Science does admit that the quasi-metrical aspects of reality do not explain the whole truth. There is hiatus in ratiocination and reasoning but it does not mean that we should all together reject the process of ratiocination and reasoning. It does explain that there is something which transcends the world of reason and scientific materialism.

As I have already mentioned before that the world is real till we realize and experience the ultimate nature and the form of the absolute (cosmic consciousness).

Gaudapada, the founder of Advaita Vedanta, developed the line of argument that the world is real only till we realise and experience the ultimate reality (cosmic consciousness) or *Brahman*. According to him there are four stages of our consciousness, i.e. awake *(jagrata),* dream *(svapana),* dreamless (*susupti)* and enlightenment (*turya*). *Turya* is known as the transcendental state of pure consciousness. It is a state of truth *(sat),* consciousness *(cit)* and wisdom *(bliss).* When one experiences the transcendental reality which is called *samadhi* also the world disappears. Gaudapada argues that the world disappears in the state of *turya* or *samadhi* (state of cosmic consciousness) because the world is not real in the sense of absolute reality. And hence only which is unreal can disappear in the state of salvation or *nirvana*. Sankara's whole philosophical basis is the exposition of Gaudapada's doctrine of *Advaita* which is developed in *Mandukya Kyarika*. Sankara's famous aphorism, states that the *Brahman* is real and the world is unreal and there is complete Identity between *Jiva* and the *Brahman*. There is a qualitative difference between the dreamless sleep, state of pure consciousness, i.e. *turya* and senselessness (*murchha*). When a man goes into deep sleep or that is termed as dreamless sleep, he does not enter into the state of pure consciousness. When he wakes up, he infers that from 10 pm to 4 am his I-ness or the sense of individuality was absent and on that basis he infers that this is the only proof that he was in a state of dreamless sleep. The identity of the individual *Jiva* is established on the basis of the absence of his I-consciousness before and after the dreamless sleep. On the basis of this inference that when his I-ness was absent he was in the state of dreamless sleep. But the dreamless sleep is not the state of pure cosmic consciousness.

Mandukya Karika and *Avadhuta Gita* have enunciated the non-dual school of thought from the transcendental point of view, but when we discuss the nature and reality from empirical point of view, the world is a relative truth. It is a modification of Spinoza's substance, the *Vedantic Brahman*, the Buddhist's *Sunyata* (emptiness) and Taoist's *Tao*. There is a creation. I have already discussed in previous chapters and explained the nature of world as a modification of cosmic consciousness. Buddhism and Vedanta have discussed the truth from transcendental and empirical points of view. The whole philosophical and the scientific formulations are based on ontological mysticism.

From one perspective there is a *Brahman* and from the other there is a world. Both the scientific and the spiritual perspectives are required for understanding truth and nature. The question of, Who am I? is not a heuristic hypothesis. Reality, existence, being, *Brahman* or God are not empty words. These are pregnant with deep metaphysical and scientific import. Schrodinger writes, "Hence this life of yours which you are living is not merely a piece of the entire existence, but is in a certain sense, the whole; only this whole is not so constituted that it can be surveyed in one single glance. This, as we know, is what the Brahmins express in that sacred, mystic formula which is yet really so simple and so clear. *Tat tvam asi,* this is you. Or, again, in such words as 'I am in the east and in the west, I am below and above, I am this Whole world'."[26]

I am in complete agreement with the observation of Schrodinger, "Briefly stated, it is the view that all of us living beings belong together inasmuch as we are all in reality sides or aspects of one single being which may perhaps in Western terminology be called God while in the Upanishads its name is *Brahman*. A comparison used in Hinduism is of the many almost identical images which a many-faceted diamond makes of some *one* object such as the Sun. We have already conceded that we are here dealing not with something logically deducible but with mystical metaphysics—just like the acceptance of a real object-world (usually called an external world, but it includes one's own abode)."[27]

For proper understanding and comprehension of ontological mysticism, one will have to equip oneself with proper frame of mind, cultivated by mystical and moral discipline of non-attachment, discrimination and the longing for the realisation of truth in its wholeness. Without proper understanding the study of philosophy and science in a dilettanet fashion will land him in confusion and contradiction. The path of spirituality and ontological mysticism is like walking on the razor's edge. The Upanishadic seers have rightly stated "Arise, awake, and learn by approaching the excellent ones. The wise ones describe that path to be impassable as a razor's edge, which when sharpened, is difficult to tread on."[28]

From the ontological mystical perspective, ultimate reality is one and homogenous being and existence. It is cosmic consciousness. There is only one consciousness. World and reality are constituted of this cosmic consciousness. It is beyond the reach of both philosophy and science. Neither exact science is really possible nor can any philosophical knowledge comprehend the nature of reality. It is mystical and metaphysical.

Notes

1. *Taittiriya Upanisad*, Verse II. IV.1.
2. *Tractatus Logico-Philosophicus*, 6.522.
3. *Ibid.*, 6.53, 6.54.
4. *Ibid.*, 7.
5. Stephen Hawking & Leonard Mlodinow. *The Grand Design*, Bantam Press, London, 2010.
6. Ervin Schrodinger. *My View of the World*, Ox Bow Press, Woodbridge,

Connecticut. 1983, p. 40.

7. *Washington Post*, 25th September, 2011. *Faster than Light: Revolution or error. Particles burst Einstein's Speed Limit* by Brian Vastag.
8. Marquis De Laplace. *A Philosophical Essay on Probabilities*, Dover Publications, Inc., New York, 1951, pp. 1-2.
9. A.J. Ayer. *Language, Truth and Logic*, London, Victor Gallanez Ltd., 1936, p. 248.
10. *Tripura Rahasyam*, Sarswati Bhavan Granthamala, vol. 15. Varanasi, 1965, pp. 11-12.
11. Lisa Randall. *Knocking on Heavens Door*, Harper Colin Publishers, p. 123.
12. Erwin Schrodinger. *My View of The World*, Ox Bow Press, Woodbridge, Connecticut. 1983, p. 93.
13. *Ibid.*, p. 98.
14. Albert Schweitzer. *Philosophy and Ethics, The Philosophy of Civilization*, A & C Black Ltd., London, W. 1, 1929, pp. 2-3.
15. *Quantum Questions, Mystical Writings of the World's Greatest Physicists*. Ed. by Ken Wilber, Shambhala Publications, Boston, Massachusetts, 2001, p. 123.
16. *Ibid.*, p. 126.
17. *Ibid.*, The Mechanism Demands Mysticism, p. 129.
18. Erwin Schrodinger, *Science and Humanism, Physics in our Times*. Cambridge University Press, 1952, pp. 50-51.
19. Werner Heisenberg, *Physics and Philosophy. The Revolution in Modern Science*, Harper Perrenial, New York, 2007, p. 55.
20. *Ibid.*, p. 24.
21. *Quantum Questions, Mystical Writings of the World's Greatest Physicists*. Ken Wilber, In the *Mind of Some Eternal Spirit*, p. 135.
22. Lisa Randall. *Knocking on Heavens Door*, Harper Colin Publishers, p. 412.
23. Erwin Schrodinger, *Science and Humanism, Physics of Our Time*. 1952, p. 51.
24. *Pure Rationalist Has No Place Here, Quantum Questions*, p. 163.
25. Erwin Schrodinger, *Science and Humanism, Physics of Our Time. Form not substance—The Fundamental Concept*, 1952, p. 18.
26. Erwin Schrodinger, *My View of the World*, pp. 21-22.
27. *Ibid.*, p. 95.
28. *Katha Upanisad* I. iii. 15, Verse 14.

3
Advaita Vedanta and Cosmic Religious Feeling

Advaita Vedanta is the culmination of philosophical and religious quest of man's identity and destiny. In the quest of his own identity and destiny philosophy and religion were discovered. With the growth and evolution of the faculty of thinking man started questioning. This questioning was to understand the secrets of nature and his ownself. Rene Descarte's *cogito ergo sum* is the result of this questioning but much before the growth of Western philosophical tradition. Oriental seers and saints have discovered in their spiritual sublimity secrets of Being and Existence. Advaita Vedanta is the discovery of Indian seers and saints who experienced the truth as One Homogenous and Whole in their divine effulgence and meditative trance.

Advaita Vedanta is the discovery of Upanishadic seers who formulated Vedanta philosophy on the basis of their experience of transcendental nature of truth and reality in their spiritual sublimity. The Advaita Vedanta is a profound philosophy and sublime religion. Schrodinger while summarizing the quintessential teachings of the Vedantic vision writes "Hence this life of yours which you are living is not merely a piece of the entire existence, but is in a certain sense the whole; only this whole is not so constituted that it can be surveyed in one single glance. This, as we know, is what the Brahmins express in that sacred, mystic formula which is yet really so simple and so clear: *Tat tvam asi,* this is you. Or, again, in such words as 'I am in the east and in the west, I am below and above, I am this whole world'."[1] This is the answer of the quantum question, *Who am I.* Plotinus raised the same question *who are we.* The genesis of philosophy and religion is in search of this question. In the beginning man postulated the anthromorphic vision of god because he thought god must be like him. This relation of god and man manifested in mythology and metaphors in different religious scriptures in form of polytheism, henotheism, pantheism and monism. In the fifth century Xenophanes was the first philosopher who postulated monotheism in the Western tradition. He ridicules the anthromorphic conception of God. He has stated that if the ox or the horse or the lion would have hands they would have portrayed the forms of God like horse and lions.

However, we find a very deep philosophical thought in the earliest records of human civilization. In the beginning the man was part of nature and the environment had played a great role in formulating the philosophical and the religious doctrines. This is evident from the earliest writings of the Indian, Chinese, Egyptian and Persian. Mysticism is a genesis of cultural tradition of the Oriental and Occidental religious traditions. We find the appearance of this cosmic religious feeling from the very beginning of advanced human civilizations in Hinduism, Buddhism, Christianity Sufism and Pythagoreanism. Einstein while narrating the cosmic religious feeling as the profound form of philosophical and moral religion he talks about the social and the moral imperatives in the formulation of cosmic religion. According to Einstein in all the religious traditions we find the harmonious and the happy unification of social and the moral imperatives. Einstein considers cosmic religious feeling as the culmination of human search for the divinity and transcendality. However, he does agree that there are social and moral dimensions of religion also. The moral conception of God has given the concept of God of providence who functions as protector and awards and punishes those who cross the limits of social norms and behaviour as formulated by the social conditions of the respective social systems. From the religious concept of god of providence the moral dimensions of religion manifested. *The New Testament* is living example of primarily a moral religious order. The anthromorphic conception of god is present in these religious systems. According to Einstein there is no place of personal god in the true religion. The cosmic religious feeling is the only true religion. It is closer to Advaita Vedanta. Einstein writes "I shall call it cosmic religious feeling. It is very difficult to elucidate this feeling to anyone who is entirely without it, especially as there is no anthromorphic conception of god corresponding to it. The individual feels the futility of human desires and aims and the sublimity and marvelous order which reveal themselves both in nature and in the world of thought. Individual existence impresses him as a sort of prison and he wants to experience the universe as a single significant whole."[2]

According to Einstein saints and seers of all religious order have experienced the cosmic religious feeling which is evident from the scriptures which are free from dogmas and the anthromorphic conception of god. He mentions the names of Democritus, Francis of Assisi and Spinoza as true religious persons. St. Francis says, "That which is seeking is that which is being sought." The cosmic religious feeling would may provide the notion of god which would be like Brahman of Advaita Vedanta. Kepler and Newton have devoted their whole life in understanding the secrets of nature and true religious order. They have lived a life of solitary labourer in understanding the functioning of celestial bodies. Einstein thinks that "It is cosmic religious feeling that gives a man such in strength. A contemporary has said, not unjustly, that in this materialistic age of ours the serious workers are the only profound religious people."[3] Conception of the personal god which has given immense power in the hands of church, mosque and temples have always created fear psychosis and endanger the very existence of civilized society. Einstein strongly advocates the omission of doctrine of personal God from religion which is the source of fear and have given vast power in the hands of priests, *pandits* and *mullahs* who are the cause of great danger to the very existence of one world and one humanity. Advaita Vedanta and Einstein's cosmic religious feeling share the common understanding about the true religion which should be free from theology and it must be based on humanism. Religion is realization of god.

According to Nagarjuna, the absolute is beyond the four categories of *Bhava* (existence), *Abhava* (non-existence), *Ubhaya* (nor both existence and non-existence) *nobhay* (neither existence nor non-existence). All the views have been rejected because of the inherent contradictions. The Buddha's dialectics is used as *reduction ad absurdum.* Dialectic used by Buddha stands for the inability of reason to comprehend the absolute. The absolute is transcendent. It is *Sunya,* free from any kind of differentiation, change and metamorphosis. There is a great similarity between the philosophy of *Madhyamika* and Kant. Kant also considered criticism itself a philosophy. *Madhyamika* is a profound philosophical system. The whole Buddhist philosophy is based on Ontological mysticism. *Prajnaparamita* (perfection) is mystic experience of the truth and reality. It is *Nirvana.* T.R.V. Murti writes, "Metaphysics or true philosophy *(Prajna)* is non-dual knowledge-intuition of the real. The possibility of intellectual intuition is not only accepted but is taken to be very heart of reality. It is truth. In intuition, knowledge and the real coincide; essence and reality are identical."

Buddhism believes that we are all enlightened being like Vedanta, Buddhism also believes that Buddha-nature is the real truth and reality (*Boddhi Citta*). According to Advaita Vedanta all is Brahaman. Buddha-nature (*Bodhi Citta*) is a state of thoughtlessness and nothingness which is called in Taoism *Wu-wei*. Buddha-nature is a quintessence of one's own being and existence. It is because of dilution and false identification with non-self, one does not get the real experience of being which is state of *Nirvaṇa*.

Pythagoras was contemporary of Buddha. He was a great mystic and founding father of Arithmetic. He came from southern Italy. He was one of the most remarkable persons of Greece. He had supernatural powers and he was in knowledge of all the previous lives in his metampsychoses (the transmigration of soul). He had even proved by recognizing things and places which he had never seen before. Like Vedanta he did believe in the doctrine of rebirth which is one of the root concept of Vedanta. Cornford in his book *From Religion to Philosophy* writes "the school of Pythagoras represents the main current of mystic tradition which we have set in contrast with the scientific tendency." Like Shankar Pythagoras considered the phenomenal world as illusion and he believed in the one God and one reality. Like Buddha he believed in egalitarian society. The man and woman were admitted in his mystical society on equal terms and the property was possessed by all of them. Even Pythagoras held that scientific and the mathematical discoveries considered as the collective result of all. Burnet summarizing the teachings of Pythagoras writes "We are strangers in the world, and the body is the tomb of the soul, and yet we must not seek to escape by self-murder; for we are the chattels of God who is our herdsman, and without his command we have no right to make our escape. In this life, there are three kinds of man, just as there are three sorts of people who come to the Olympic Games. The lowest class is made up of those who come to buy and sell, the next above them are those who compete. Best of all, however, are those who come simply to look on. The greatest purification of all is, therefore, disinterested science, and it is the man who devotes himself to that, the true philosopher, who has most effectually released himself from the 'wheel of birth.'"[4] This speaks up the Vedantic truth and vision.

There is a great impact of Pythagoras on the philosophy of Plato.

According to some scholars Athenian schools were branch of Pythagoreans. The *a prioristic* idea and the concept is seen in the Platonism. Pythagoreans lived a life of mendicants like Indian saints in search of truth and salvation. Pythagoras was religious prophet and a mathematician. However, his philosophy and religion are based on Ontological mysticism.

The Good of Plato is the substance of Spinoza. To perceive the idea of *the good* is to know the reality. Russell does admit that "throughout Plato's philosophy there is the same fusion of intellect and mysticism as in Pythagoreanism but at this final culmination mysticism clearly has the upper hand."

If someone admits that Plato's philosophy is a culmination of mysticism then he should try to first understand what is mysticism and why Plato has been so much influenced by Pythagoreanism. The lack of this understanding of mysticism and Pythagoreanism does not justify Bertrand Russell's unwarranted criticism of Plato's mysticism occupying an upper hand as worst of philosophic sins.

Philosophy begins with Parmenides in the West. Bertrand Russell writes "What makes Parmenides historically important is that he invented a form of metaphysical argument that, in one form or another, is to be found in most subsequent metaphysicians down to and including Hegel. He is often said to have invented logic, but what he really invented was metaphysics based on logic." Parmenides propagated and propounded his philosophical doctrine in a poem *On Nature.* Like Advaita Vedanta he also considered pluralism as illusion. The true Being is "the One". According to him being is the ultimate reality like Brahman which is infinite, indivisible and whole.

Pythagoras' mysticism and Parmenides' *the Being* are the foundation of Plato's philosophy. Plato's theory of idea is based on the nature of eternal reality. Parmenides created a philosophical background by introducing to Plato, the concept of eternal and timeless reality which became the logical grounds of Plato's philosophy for rejecting the appearance and change as illusion. Plato derives mystical elements from Pythagoras.

This is clear from Plato's allegory of myth of cave in which there is an evident reference to the distinction between appearance and reality. Bertrand Russell writes "Plato like all mystics, has, in his beliefs, a core of certainty which is essentially incommunicable accept by way of life."

Plato's concept of *idea of the good* Spinoza's substance or God is nearer to Vedantic concept of Brahman. The controversy related to one and many resolved in mystical and metaphysical Vedantic thesis of a reality as a *whole.* Schrodinger writes "It is the view that all of us living beings belong together inasmuch as we are all in reality sides or aspects of one single being, which may perhaps in Western terminology be called God while in the Upanishads its name is Brahman." We are all aspects of one single being. This concept of single being which is the foundation of Vedantic thesis was formulated much before Parmenides. However, Pythagoras and Parmenides have exercised great impact on the Western philosophical and cultural tradition which is now being accepted by the quantum mechanics and Einstein concept of cosmic religious feeling. *Brihadaranyaka Upanishad* has stated "that there is no plurality. He who afflicted by multiplicity is ensnared from death to death."[5]

The quantum mechanics is coming closer to the Vedantic concept of truth and reality. According to Advaita Vedanta plurality that we experience is illusion (*Maya*) and not real. The ultimate reality which is called Brahman is cosmic consciousness. Erwin Schrodinger writes "the external world and consciousness are one and the same thing, insofar as both are constituted by the same primitive elements. But, we are then hardly even using a different formula whether we express the essential community of these elements in all individuals by saying that there is only one external world or that there is only one consciousness." The solution of the controversy regarding the appearance and reality lies in Vedantic philosophy. Schrodinger does accept in his celebrated book *My View of the World* where he asserts, "The only solution to this conflict, insofar as any is available to at all, lies in the ancient wisdom of the Upanishad." Even Bertrand Russell in "The Analysis of Mind" has accepted that the physical and the psychical consist of similar elements, with different combination. However, this view of Bertrand Russell does not go with his atheist outlook and belief. Philosopher and the scientist have been debating on the nature and the form of ultimate reality. According to quantum mechanics the form and the essence of nature and reality is contradicted. Pythagoreans took the help of harmony of vibrating strings to explain the secrets of nature. Heinsberg called it *atomysticism.* The other leading light of quantum mechanics Planck believes that religion and science are complementary. Erwin Schrodinger has stated that knowledge of nature can never reach its goal.

It is impossible to have so much as completely certain unambiguous mutual understanding between human beings, it is a goal for which we are for ever approaching but which we cannot reach. On this ground alone exact science is never really possible. This acceptance of scientists of Schrodinger status is the confirmation of Upanashadic teachings that reality "is beyond the reach of mind and senses" (*Taittiriya Upanishad*).[6] One of the greatest philosopher of last century, Ludwig Wittgenstein has also confirmed the findings of the scientists like Schrodinger and others. Wittgenstein says "there are things that manifest themselves. They are mystical." Mysticism is the genesis of philosophy and religion. We have to get liberated from the cobweb of obsession of reality based on Ontological materialism. Nature has not set any limit to the realization of human hopes and expression. Spirituality is the core of religion. It is a path of truth, virtue and salvation. Science gives us knowledge, spirituality provides wisdom. The Vedantic seers and saints have experienced in the state of spiritual sublimity and trance face to face with truth and reality. Integrating and mediating between these two planes of ratiocination and reflections given by science and spirituality could be the greatest intellectual and moral adventure and the most rewarding achievement of mankind. Albert Schweitzer writes "the essential nature of civilization does not lie in its material achievement, but in the fact that individuals keep in mind the ideas of perfecting man, and the improvement of social and political conditions of people, and of mankind as a whole." The mystics of all traditions have taken help of metaphors, allegories and myths in explaining the nature of truth and reality. Heisenberg writes "the fact that through the ages have spoken in images, parables, and paradoxes means simply that there are no other ways of grasping the reality to which they refer. But that doesn't mean that it is not a genuine reality and splitting this reality into objective and subjective side won't get us very far." Heisenberg does agree with Einstein's conception of religion. Einstein rejected the anthromorphic conception of god. He is of the opinion that religion must outrightly reject the doctrine of personal god which has given tremendous power in the hands of priests who have misused those powers and were greatest impairment in the cultivation of scientific temper. He thinks that the concept of personal God is the root cause of conflicts between science and religion. According to Advaita Vedanta, God is not a person but a principle. This doctrine of god as a principle is in agreement with the scientists like Einstein, Heisenberg, Schrodinger and Wolfangang. Heisenberg writes "Einstein's conception is closer to mine. His god is somehow involved in the immutable laws of nature. Einstein has a feeling for the central order of the things.... I don't believe Einstein is tied to any religious tradition and I rather think the idea of a personal god entirely foreign to him." But as far as his concern there is no split between science and religion. "The central order is a part of subjective as well as objective relm, and this strikes me as being a far better starting point."

The Advaita Vedanta believes that plurality is illusion. Phenomenal world is not real. Truth is one whole and homogenous. This fundamental doctrine has been clarified by analogy of the crystal which depicts the hundreds of little pictures what is in reality is a single existence which does not multiply. Ultimate truth is one and it gets manifested in many forms. In this sense we are all part, a piece, of ultimate reality, an aspect or modification of Spinoza's substance or god that the one substance or being is present in multiciplity. The Sufism which is mystical dimension of Islam also believes in one truth and one god.

The spiritual renaissance was the hall mark of Sixth century BC. In the world history it is known as era of mystical renaissance. The Buddha in India Lao-Tse and Confucius in China and Pythagoras and Parmenides in Greece brought a ethical and spiritual transformation.

Jesus and the Hassidic saints of Poland and Russia, Zen Masters in China and Japan brought a spiritual and mystical transformation in the life of the people. There was a dawn of new mystical era of Sufism from Eleventh to Fourteenth century in Persia. Abu Hamid Ghazzalin a Sufi saint of Eleventh century created a new religious awareness in Persia. He added an ascetic dimension of spirituality in his doctrine of Sufism. His works titled *"The Niche of Light"* makes an original contribution known as doctrine of illuminations. The mystic considers body as a prison with the soul as its real being and existence.

Jelauddin Rumi (1207-1273) is considered as the greatest Sufi saint. Rumi was born on September 30, 1207 at Mazar-I-Sarif in Afghanistan. In October 1244 he met Shams who was instrumental in awakening his dormant divinity. In December 1273 Rumi passed away. Rumi's mystical poems have been collected in sixth volumes known as *Mathnawi.* Mysticism is a philosophy of unknown reality which resides in our innermost being and existence. It is to be experienced and lived. It is a truth within truth. Being within being. Sufism is a mystic discipline for the interiorazation and intensification of divinity. Classical Sufism is based on asceticism and esotericism. It is a reaction against the attachment to the worldliness of the Caliphate. In the Arabic word Sufism is called *Tasawwuf.* This is the mystic aspects of Islam. This is a mystic discipline devoted to understand the reality as natural state of one's own being and existence. There is no difference between the God and the man. This state of mystic unification between God and the man is called enlightenment. There is a great similarity between Advaita Vedants, *Tattvamasi (Thou Art That)* and Rumi's *I am you.* Rumi says:

> "I am all orders of being, the circling galaxy,
> the evolutionary intelligence,
> the lift, and the falling away. What is,
> and what isn't. You know
> Jelaluddin, You the one
> in all, say who
> I am. Say I
> am You."[7]

Rumi was a great humanist. Humanism is the core of all civilizations and culture. Humanity is the highest truth. Human society is one and the indivisible. We find the affirmation of cosmic religious feeling in Rumi's *Masnavi.* Rumi says:

> "Not Christian or Jew or Muslim, not Hindu,
> Buddhist, Sufi, or Zen. Not any religion
> or cultural system. I am not from the East
> or the West, not out of the ocean or up
> from the ground, not natural or ethereal, not
> composed of elements at all. I do not exist,
> am not an entity in this world or the next,
> did not descend from Adam and Eve or any
> origin story. My place is placeless, a race
> of the traceless. Neither body or soul.
> I belong to the beloved, have seen the two
> worlds as one and that one call to and know,
> first, last, outer, inner, only that
> breath breathing human being."

Vedanta also does not believe in distinctions of caste, religion and ethnicity. *Astavakra Samhita* says "You do not belong to the Brahman or any other caste or to any ethnicity. You are not perceived by the senses. Unattached, formless, and witness of all are you. Be happy."[8] The central objective of Advaita Vedanta and Sufism is to attain enlightenment. Enlightenment is a natural state of being where all distinctions and differences are obliterated in mutual interpenetrations between god and the man. *Avadhuta Gita* one of the canonical literature of Advaita Vedanta says "The enlightened one, nude or clad in a patched garment made of rags gathered from roads, follows the path which is devoid of virtue and vice and stays in an empty abode, absorbed in the pure, stainless, homogeneous Being."[9]

The Sufi saints had experienced union with god. Sufi Persian saint of Thirteenth century Aaziz Nasafi has beautifully expressed his experience of union with god in these words: "On the death of any living creature the spirit returns to the spiritual world, the body to the bodily world. In this, however, only the bodies are subject to change. The spiritual world is one single spirit who stands like unto a light behind the bodily world and who, when any single creature comes into being, shines through it as through a window. According to the kind and size of the window less or more light enters the world. The light itself, however, remains unchanged."

The affirmation of the one god and one substance in the realization of Christian Trinity by a Spanish mystic saint Teresa who have had given a vivid experience of her divine effulgence. She has stated that at first illumination came to her as a dazzling cloud of Light followed by the manifestation of three Persons of Trinity. She experienced the vision of three Persons where all of one reality power and knowledge and were one god. This mystic experience and vision was not of the physical eye. It was mystic experience of sublimity and profundity of one god.

The central objective of Advaita Vedanta, Sufism and the mystic tradition of Christianity believe that truth is one homogeneous whole. In the state of enlightenment all distinctions and differences are obliterated in mutual interpenetrations between man and god. According to New Testament God is spirit.

Avadhuta Gita reiterates god as formless and all pervasive spirit. It says "The essence and the whole of Vedanta is this knowledge, this supreme Knowledge: that I am by nature the formless, all-pervasive Self."[10] Advaita Vedanta, Sufism and mystic tradition of Christianity are based on ontological mysticism. St. John speaks the same truth of non-dualism (Advaita) "You shall know the truth, and the truth shall make you free" (John 8.32).

I and my father are one.

I am in my father and you are in Me and I am in you. (Jesus—John 10:30; 14:20)

Father is in me and I in the Father. (John 10.38)

The Kingdom of God is within you. (Luck 17.21)

I am the Light of the world. (John 8.12)

I am He. (John 8.28)

I am the Gate for the sheep. (John 10.7)

I am the Way, the Truth and the Life. No one can get to the Father except by me. (John 14.6)

Anyone who has seen the me has seen the Father. (John 14.9)

Father, who lives in me, does his work through me. (John 14.10)

I am the resurrection and the life: he who believes in me will live, even though he dies. (John 11.25)

When I was hungry you gave me food, when I was thirsty you gave me drink, and when I was a stranger, you will welcome me into your home. When I was naked you clothed me, when I was sick, you visited me, and when I was in prison, you came to see me. (Matthew 25.35-36)

Be still, and know that I am God. (Old Testament, Psalm 46.10.7 Ecclesiastes.)

He is the Spirit of Truth. You know Him: He lives in you. (John 14.16-17)

That which is seeking is that which is being sought. (St Francis of Assisi).

Let me know my self, Lord, and shall know Thee. (St. Augustine)

Meister Eckhart was a great Christian mystic saint of thirteenth and fourteenth century. He didn't believe that god is person. According to him god is a principle which guides, controls the whole cosmos. God is a Deity. A divine entity distinguished from the persons. According to Eckhart god in the sense of deity does not call for any definitions as definitions limit the god as an anthromorphic person. God cannot be predicated. The Deity is absolute being and it is a negation of finite being. It is a negation of negation. It is one homogenous whole. Eckhart himself asserts that god is non-existence. He means that god is beyond the question of existence and non-existence. His statement about god speaks of Vedantic concept of Brahman. According to Upanishad god is beyond the reach of mind and of senses. Again Eckhart made a very mystical statement that god is not good. *Advadhuta Gita*, the canonical literature of Vedanta, also speaks out the same truth. There is no distinctions between virtue and vice. Brahman or god "The Supreme is the destruction of virtue and vice. It is the destruction of bondage and freedom from bondage. If there is only one indivisible, all-comprehensive Absolute, how can there be here any consciousness of sorrow and absence of sorrow?"[11]

Eckhart says the soul is an image of god. There is complete identity between the god and the man. He frequently refer god as a "spark" or "light". Here also we find the similarity between Vedantic vision of god and Eckhart's conception of god. According to *Katha Upanishad* the Brahman (the god) is the supreme light from which everything are illuminated. *Katha Upanishad* says "There the sun does not shine, neither do the moon and the stars; nor do these flashes of lightening shine. How can this fire? He is shining, all these shine; through his luster all these are variously illumined."[12]

Eckhart says that soul finds its perfection and bliss in the state of salvation. Spirituality is the core of all religions. In the state of salvation all existing distinctions and differences obliterated in mutual interpenetration of man and god. Everybody is an enlightenment being. To experience enlightenment one needs only to discard the dualism of subject and object. All of us are endowed with divine effulgence. Awakening is a natural state of our being. We are not living in harmony with our own true nature. This is called bondage. This is why we are not experiencing the bliss and beatitude of salvation. Essence of Religion does not contain in scriptures. Essence of religion is contained in our inner most being. The Buddha, the Lao Tse, Pythagoras, Jesus, Sankar, St. John, Kabir, Rumi, Eckharts are mystic seers. They have regenerated mankind by their propagation of spiritual humanism and non-dual metaphysical and mystical philosophy of inclusive oneness. They believe in the religion of man, devoid of all kinds of denominations. They are men of renaissance and makers of civilizations.

Brahman of Hinduism, Allah of Sufism, Tao of Taoism and Sunyata (emptiness) of Buddhism are ultimate reality. Reality is one homogenous and whole. It is a cosmic consciousness. It is substance and substratum of whole universe. Cosmic consciousness is cosmos.

Enlightenment is *summum bonum* of all religious traditions. The core concept of all religions are spirituality and mysticism. The non-dualism (Advaita) is the basis of all mystic religious traditions. It is pathless path.

Notes

1. Erwin Schrodinger, *My View of the World*, pp. 21-22, Ox Bow Press, Woodbridge, Connecticut.
2. *Cosmic Religious Feeling*, *Quantum Questions*, Edited by Ken Wilber, p. 104.
3. *Ibid.*, p. 106.
4. *Early Greek Philosophy*, p. 108.
5. मनसैवानुद्रष्टव्यम्, नेह नानास्ति किंचन।
   मृत्योः स मृत्यमाप्नोति य इह नानेव पश्यति ॥ 9 ॥

Bṛhadaraṇyaka Upaniṣad, iv.iv.19.

6. यतो वाचो निवर्तन्ते। अप्राप्य मनसा सह।
   आनन्दं ब्रह्मणो विद्वान्। न बिभेति कदाचनेति।
   Taitirīya Upaniṣad, 11.IV. 1.
7. *The Essentials Rumi*, New Expanded Edition, Harper One, Collins Publisher, 2004, p. 276.
8. न त्वं विप्रादिको वर्णो नाश्रमी नाक्षगोचरः।
   असङ्गोऽसि निराकारो विश्वसाक्षी सुखी भव ॥ 5 ॥
   Aśtavakra Samhitā, I.V
9. रथ्याकर्पटविरचितकन्थः
   पुण्यापुण्यविवर्जितपन्थः।
   शून्यागारे तिष्ठति नग्नो
   शुद्धनिरञ्जनसमरसमग्रः ॥ 1 ॥
   Advadhuta Gita of Dattatreya, Chapter-VII.1.
10. वेदान्तसारसर्वस्वं ज्ञानं विज्ञानमेव च।
    अहमात्मा निराकारः सर्वव्यापी स्वभावतः ॥5॥
    Advadhuta Gita of Dattatreya, I.V
11. ननु धर्मविधर्मविनाश इति
    ननु बन्धविबन्धविनाश इति।
    यदि चैकनिरस्तरसर्वशिव
    मिहदुःखविदुःखमतिश्रव कथम् ॥18॥
    Advadhuta Gita of Dattatreya, chapter vi. 18.
12. न तत्र सूर्यो भाति न चन्द्रतारकं
    नेमा विद्युतो भान्ति कुतोऽयमग्निः।
    तमेव भान्तमनुभाति सर्वं
    तस्य भासा सर्वमिदं विभाति॥ 5॥
    Katha Upaniṣad, II. ii. 15.

4
Kaśmīra Śaivism
An Analysis and Reflection

The *Śiva-Sūtras* form both the philosophical and esoteric basis of Kaśmīra Śaivism. According to the *Śivasūtravimarśinī, Sivasūtras* are the basis of all Āgamas. Lord Śiva revealed them to Vasugupta in his dream while he was residing in his hermitage below the Mahādeva peak. This view is supported by the *Spandavṛtti* of Kallaṭa. He is also of opinion that the *Sūtras* were directly imparted to Vasugupta in his dream.[1] According to Bhāskara, the *Sūtras* were composed by Śiva himself but were taught to Vasugupta by a *Siddha,* a realized soul with high spiritual attainments. Bhāskara often introduces the Sūtras with such phrases as *Śivasutram ariracat,* or *sūtram āha Maheśvaraḥ.*[2] According to this version, Vasugupta did not find the *Sūtras* inscribed on a rock as has been narrated by Kṣemarāja. Thus, there is a difference of opinion with regard to their authorship. In our view, because it is often said that esoteric secrets are imparted to a developed soul in dream, Vasugupta also received initiation from Śiva by means of a dream. *Śiva* is indeed considered as Ādi Guru (the eternal spiritual guide). Afterwards, Vasugupta stated his revelations in *Sūtra* form.

Kaśmīra Śaivism has acquired its distinctive name of Trika-Śāsana, Trika-Śāstra or simply Trika because it deals with the triple principles known as Śiva-Śakti-Aṇu, or Pati-Pāśa-Paśu, or Bindu-Nāda-Kalā. The phrase *naraśaktiśivātmakam trikam* occurs in *Pa-rātrimśikavimārśinī.* The Trika is known as a mystical school *(raha-syasampradāya)* which is quite different from other forms of Śaivism. It is an idealistic monism *(advaita),* but differs in fundamental principles from Śaṅkara's Advaita Vedanta. According to Kaśmıra Śaivism, Advaita means the eternal co-existence of Śiva and Śakti.[3] Paramaśiva is the fundamental reality.

He is indeterminable and transcendental existence, beyond all divisibility and separability. He is all-comprehensive.[4] The authorship of the entire manifest and unmanifest world lies with Paramaśiva. He is the nucleus of this cosmic cycle, the Supreme Controller of the world process. Kurt F. Leidecker says: "The difference of the Īśvarādvaya system from the Brahmavādins consists herein that the Cit-like Exalted One always retains the authorship of the fivefold world process."[5]

Kaśmira Śaivism accepts *Māyā* as *Brahmamayī, Nitya* (eternal) and *Satyarūpā* (Truth). In this school of Advaita philosophy, *Brahman* and *Māyā* become one and co-existent. By accepting the principle of *Māyā as a reality, Kaśmīra Śaivism agrees on the Absolute as all-embracing unlike Śaṅkara's Brahman* which is based on the principles of renunciation and elimination.

Paramaśiva

Paramaśiva of the Āgamaśāstra is the perfect and profound principle of oneness. The plurality and diversity of the cosmos represent the essential spiritual oneness of Paramaśiva. He is the Absolute of Kaśmīra Śaivism, unsubjectivated Transcendentality. He is *Pūrṇāhantā,* self-luminous and pure consciousness. Just as light and heat co-exist in fire, in the same way Śiva, the universal I-ness *(ahantā)* and Śakti co-exist in pure consciousness. To make any real distinction between Śiva and Śakti will be a logical abstraction. Paramaśiva is unaffected by the limitation of time, space and causality, and unrestricted by his Vimarśa Kriyā who is identical with himself. By virtue of his Power he is described as the Free Agent. Freedom is the essence of consciousness.

Paramaśiva is the Supreme Reality. He is of the nature of bliss and complete in Himself. He holds in Himself the unmanifested universe as an idea. At the same time he transcends this ideal universe. He is Pure Intelligence as well as the one all-including Supreme Experience. J.C. Chatterjee says: "He is logical first principle but not in time".[6] He is beyond the categories of existence and non-existence. He does not come within the scope of the thirty-six *tattvas* of Śaivism.

Paramaśiva is both transcendental and immanent. His transcendental aspects is called Śivatattva while Śaktitattva is the immanent principle. The duality involved in this admission of Śiva and Śakti is due to the analytical approach of mind. Kaśmīra Śaivism maintains the spiritual monism of Śiva and Śakti. Śakti is identical with Śiva as salt is with the sea-water.[7] Śiva is consciousness as statis (*cit*), Śakti is consciousness as dynamis *(Cidrṇpiī).*

Paramaśiva is further called Mahābindu. He is without colour *(avarṇa)* and formless *(nirākāra)*. Bindu has position but no magnitude. This means: Paramaśiva exists but He cannot be conceived. He-is-logically indemonstrable, beyond the reach of speculative mind and thought. He is the composite form of Śiva (consciousness) and Śakti (operative principle). To separate Śiva and Śakti is as impossible as to separate moving wind from the steadfast ether in which it blows. Paramaśiva is, therefore, Yãmalarupa. In this way, Kaśmīra Śaivism resolves the philosophical dilemma of monism and dualism. It resolves the scientists' enigma of mind and matter and the Vedāntin's problem of *Brahman* and *Māyā*.

The inalienable concomitance of Śiva and Śakti is called Avinābhāvi. The word Avinābhāvi means "inseparable", i.e. the existence of the one cannot be proved in the absence of the other. There is no Śiva without Śakti and no Śakti without Śiva.[8] Paramaśiva in His transcendental aspect is beyond all manifestations; in His immanent aspect, He pervades the universe. The universe with all its infinite diversity of objects is nothing but a manifestation of the immanent aspect of Paramaśiva. This is called Śakti (operative principle), which is not in any way different from, or independent of, Paramaśiva.

All things of the universe are made of the same cosmic consciousness *(caitanya)*. The transcendental aspect (Śiva) of Paramaśiva is the fundamental stuff of the cosmos. Śakti, the creative matrix, is the cause of multiplicity. She is the Vimarśa aspect of Paramaśiva. Śiva is witnessing consciousness. Śakti is the binding principle.

The material cause and the efficient cause are the cardinal principles of creative idealism. Every object has these two causes. Over and above these, there is a conjunctive principle which acts as a catalytic agent between the material and efficient cause. Śiva is the material cause. Śakti is the vital force. As the efficient cause, Śiva is the primary and Śakti the secondary factor.[9] Śiva is consciousness-force and all-pervading entity. Śakti is always merged in Śiva. She activates the process of creation only when Śiva offers an opportunity and grants divine permission. Hence, the doership lies with Śiva. Paramaśiva, however, remains the fundamental stuff and supreme doer, the nucleus of all the nuclei, the soul of the soul and life of life. He is described as one because He can be realised by making the mind apexed or one-pointed. An apexed mind realizes Paramaśiva in the state of deep meditation, in which Mind is dissolved into Divine Consciousness. This state is called the mystic oneness of Śiva and Śakti, Kuṇḍalinī and Para-bindu. Paramaśiva is attainable with the awakening of the serpent power (Kuṇḍalinī Śakti).

Ābhāsavāda

According to Śaivism, the entire creation is Ābhāsa. Creation is the result of self-movement (*spanda*) on the part of Śiva-Śakti. The world of waves and vibrations, things and beings, is the self-manifestation of the non-dual cosmic consciousness. The Supreme Reality splits itself spontaneously into two: subject and object, and again coalesce into one undivided unity of transcendentality. The former is the Illuminating (*Prakāśa*) and knowing entity, the latter is the Veiling (*Vimarśa*) and Activating entity. So long as Śakti remains merged in Śiva and does not get any scope for her activation, Śiva is unqualified and objectless. This theoretical dualism of Śiva and Śakti is symbolically represented by a grain of gram having two seeds closely joined and covered with a sheath which is Māyā. Creation starts only when they come apart. When Śakti starts acting and reacting, differentiation is started. This differentiation between Śiva and Śakti is the cause of creative ideation (sṛṣṭikalpanā). By differentiation is meant objectivation of the supreme Subjectivity.

In *Pratyabhijñāhṛdayam* it is said[10] that Śiva, animated by the desire of having a manifest universe which is one with Himself, first of all shines forth as the one *Cit* which is the very void detached from *Māyā*. This state of isolation of *Cit* is known as *anāśrita* Śiva (Śiva who is attached to nothing). Thereafter he is metamorphosed in the totality of suchness: worlds, entities and *Tattvas*.

Kaśmīra Śaivism expounds the philosophy of thirty-six *Śaiva-Śākta Tattvas*. *Tattva* means the created being.[11] The stages of creation are the stages of what might be called involution of the macrocosm and evolution of the microcosm. In the process of involution, consciousness is metamorphosed into subtle and gross *Tattvas*. J.C. Chatterjee says: "The process of the production of the *Tattvas* may, therefore, be spoken of as it indeed is, as one of involution, the Reality of Paramaśiva being more and more involved, until it reaches a stage at which it appears as the physical.[12] Involution is the process of analysis: the one, Infinite Self, is transformed into innumerable entities. Each *Tattva* remains involved in its lower *Tattva*. The cruder *Tattva* is developed from the subtler *Tattva*. The subtler *Tattva* has a wider scope for the manifestation of the Spirit, the cruder *Tattva* has increasingly greater restrictions. Even in the crudest *Tattva* all the causal, subtle, ideal and spiritual principles are present. "That is to say", remarks J.C. Chatterjee, "whenever there exists a lower *Tattva*, i.e. a *Tattva* of greater restriction... there are also all the other and higher ones, in full manifestation and holding the lower, as it were, in their bosom, they existing as so many concentric circles of gradually, decreasing extent —or, from another point of view, standing like a number of mathematical points occupying the same position and yet somehow maintaining their individuality, in the heart of the lower as its very life and soul."[13] The whole creation is the unfolding and manifestation of consciousness *(citi)*. Consciousness gets itself transformed into the following thirty-six *Tattvas:*

1. *Śiva.* Śiva is a consciousness-force *(citiśakti)*. Consciousness is the very cause of the universe which is the process of becoming perfect. Kurt F. Leidecker says: "When the universe is in the process of becoming perfected means as much as when (all suchness) from Sadāśiva to the earth emerge."[14] We observe that the process of becoming perfected means mergence or re-absorption of the world process into Śiva. When all our loves and longings, aspirations and desires are directed into Him, we attain perfection by becoming one with Him. According to the Śivādvaita school, the original cause of the world must be the unity of male and female principles as all beings are constituted of *he* and *she* parts. The Śivādvaita system forms the basis of the Sāṁkhya conception of *Puruṣa* and *Prakṛti.* However, according to the Svacchanda Tantra and its commentator Kṣemarāja, Śiva-tattva is *Aprameya* "Immeasurable"[15] and hence He does not come within the purview of logical thinking and metaphysical speculation.

2. *Śakti.* Śiva is *Jñāna-tattva* and Śakti is *Kriyāśakti.* Śakti is a primordial force. She is the immanent principle of Siva[16]. Reality is one and eternal, but due to the activation of Śakti, Śiva appears to have taken different forms. However, notwithstanding the operation of Śakti, Śiva does not lose his transcendentality. Although Śakti exists at all levels of manifestation and unmanifestation, even in the state of Paramaśiva, the transcendentality of Śiva always remains uncontaminated. When Śakti is merged into Śiva, She is called *Mūlaprakṛti.* Śakti or *Prakṛti* is a combination of three attributes or *guṇas,* i.e. *Sattva* (Sentient), *Rajaḥ* (Mutative) and *Tamaḥ* (Static). In the state of *Mūlaprakṛti,* all the three *Guṇas* remain in equilibrium and hence Śakti is unmanifested. But the moment the equipoise is disturbed, due to the belligerent nature of the three *Guṇas,* Śakti is transformed into *Māyā,* the creative matrix. This is why in Śaivism She is addressed as cosmoform Mahāmāyā. The phenomenal world is the manifestation of her heterogeneous forms. It is nothing but her playful motivation.

3. *Sadāśiva.* From the state of Śiva-Śakti there emerges, in this *Tattva* the experience of "Being begins" *(ahamidambhāva).* It is a state *of I-ness* in which the notion of being is experienced as "*I am*" and therefore it is called Sādākhya[17]. It is the state in which the Icchā aspect of the Divine Śakti is predominant. In common parlance this state of 'I-ness' is a state of individualization, of self-awareness.

4. *Īśvara.* From the state of I-ness the next stage of *I exist (ida-mahambhāva)* is developed. *Īśvaratattva* is dominated by *Jñāna-śakti. Īśvaratattva* is quite different from Īśvara, the Lord. First there is "I am" and then only "I exists" (I in third person).

5. *Sadvidyā.* The Sadvidyā is dominated by *Kriyāśakti.* It is a state of co-ordinated cooperation between *Aham* and *Idam,* a state in which two aspects of the relation of identity are established. It is also called Śuddhavidyā — a state of cognition in which the true relation of things is realised. In this state of Sadvidyā, every individual being experiences his body, thoughts and feelings as at once diverse and different from and yet identical with himself. It is a state of pure manifestation.

6. *Māyā.* Bondage is due to the erroneous identification of the Self with the non-self which is the product of *Māyā.* Due to *Māyā's* force of obscuration, the Self identifies himself with the object of experience, i.e. the non-self. From this moment, the five typical forms of perfect relation become imperfect and limited. *Māyā* limits the true nature of both subject and object, the Self and the universe. The supposition of *Māyā* as a principle of obscuration is both necessary and logical. For, if the ultimate Reality possesses all the five powers — *Cit, Ānanda, Icchā, Jñāna* and *Kriyā* — and so is perfect in every way, and the universe is identical with it, the question remains: where does the plurality of selves with all their limitations come from, and what is the cause of the limited creation which forms the object of experience of the limited beings? Due to *Māyā,* the Self becomes the victim of *Svarūpākhyāti. Māyā* creates the five principles or powers known as *Kañcukas* (sheaths) which limit the knowldge and power of the Self. These five are as follows: 7. *Kāla,* 8. *Vidyā,* 9. *Rāga,* 10. *Niyati,* and 11. *Kalā.* With these powers, *Māyā enwraps Puruṣa.* The microcosm goes into a deep slumber and forgets its divine nature and origin. According to Śaivism, every microcosm is a hybernated macrocosm. This is why Śaivism lays down detailed principles of intuitional practice to arouse the dormant divinity (Kuṇḍalinī) in man and to make him realise that he is Śiva, the Absolute.

12. *Puruṣa.* The *Puruṣa* of Śaivism is somewhat different from the *Puruṣa* of *Sāṁkhya*. According to Trika, *Puruṣa* is a reflection *(ābhāsa)* of the Supreme Reality.

13. *Prakṛti* or Bhogya-sāmānya[18], the equipoise of the three *Guṇas.*

14-16. *Manas, Buddhi, Ahaṁkāra.*

17-26. Five sense organs and five motor organs.

27-31. Five *Mahābhūtas (Pṛthivī, Āpa, Tejas, Vāyu* and *Ākāśa).*

32-36. Five *Tanmātras (Gandha, Rasa, Rūpa, Sparśa* and *Śabda).*

According to Trika, the entire creation is Ābhāsa. The phenomenal world is real in the sense that it is a manifestation of Paramaśiva. Creation is the result of spontaneous movement *(Spanda)* on the part of Śiva. *The world of-waves and vibrations, things and beings, is the manifestation of the non-dual cosmic consciousness with which Māyā* is in essence identical. Gopinath Kavi-raj says: "when the universe comes into being, it does so as only an image within the unique Self. The universe as such is varied but underlying it is the pure and simple unity of Caitanya.... The manifestation of the universe, due to the Free Will (*svātantrya)* of the Absolute, is then a process of Ābhāsa and for the initiation of this process nothing beyond the play of the will is needed."[19] The world of appearance is real in the same way as an image is real but it has no existence apart from the consciousness in which it is manifested. Its existence is only the existence of the Absolute.

According to the Śivādvaita school of Kaśmīra Śaivism, Supreme Reality is of the nature of pure consciousness, self-luminous and all-pervading. Its mystic experience is characterized by vividness, directness and bliss. Śiva is *Sat* (Being), Śakti is *Satī* (Being as a power). Śiva is *Cit* (Consciousness), Śakti is *Citi* (consciousness as force). Śiva is *Ānanda* (Bliss), Śakti is *Paramananda-sandoharupā* (Soul of Bliss). Śiva is *Brahman,* Śakti is *Brahma-mayī.* Some say that Truth is Advaita (non-dual), some others speak of it as Dvaita (dual) but it is, in the Śivādvaita view, Dvaitādvaitavi-varjita: neither the one nor the other. It is beyond dualism and non-dualism.

Notes

1. *Lahdhamahādevagirau maheśasvapnopadiṣṭāc chivasūtrasindhoḥ.* See J.C. Chatterjee, *Kashmir Shavism*, Srinagar, Research and Publication Department, 1962, p. 27.
2. BHĀSKARA, *Śivasūtravārttika,* pp. 5, 9.
3. *Śivaśaktisāmarasyamayajagadānandarūpam ity artham,* Jayaratha on

Abhinavagupta, *Tantrāloka* 29, 116.
4. *Paramaśivapuniṣottamaḥ, viśvasya kendram. Ānandasūdram,* p. 4.
5. *Pratyabhijñāhṛdayam,* Madras, Adyar Library, 1938, p. 50.
6. *Kashmir Shaivism,* p. 63.
7. *Saklimadaikyatmyalakṣaṇal lavaṇāranālavat parasparamelanāt.* Jayaratha on *Tantrāloka* 3, 198.
8. *Na śivaḥ śaktirahito na śakiiḥ śivavarjitā.* Quoted by Jayaratha on *Tantrā-loka* 3, 67.
9. *Ānandasiram,* p. 3.
10. *Pratyabhijñāhrdayam*, ed. K.F. Leidecker, p. 30.
11. *Tasya bhāvaḥ tattvam. Iśvarapratyabhijñāvimarśiṇī,* II, p. 219 (ed. K.A.S. Iyer and K.C. Pandey).
12. *Kashmir Shaivism,* p. 148.
13. *Ibid.*
14. *Pratyabhijñāhṛdayam,* p. 20.
15. *Apraṃeyam tato jñeyaṃ śivatattvaṃ varānane. Svacchandatanlram* 10, 674; Vol. V, Part B, (ed. Kashmir Series of Texts and Studies, 1933), p. 281.
16. *Śaktiḥ sā sivasya śaktih. Ānandasūtram* 2, p. 3.
17. *Sadākhyāyaṃ bhavaṃ yataḥ prabhrti sad iti prakhyā. Pratyabhijñāvimar-śini,* III, 1.2.
18. *Tantrasāra, Āhnika,* 8.
19. *Tripurārahasyam,* p. 11.

5
The Mysticism of Wittgenstein and the Upanishad

The purpose of this chapter is firstly to determine the nature of Mysticism as it may be discovered in the *Tractatus* and secondly to try to make a comparative study of this Mysticism and the Upanisadic Mysticism. According to Wittgenstein the sense of a proposition is completely determined by the statement of the conditions under which the proposition is true or false. On this view, all other factors including feelings, emotions or such other subjective factors which may happen to accompany one's understanding of the proposition, are excluded from the sense of the proposition. Wittgenstein says that logical propositions are tautologies. In the 2^2n truth function of n atomic propositions there are two limiting cases of importance in logic, namely *tautology* and *contradiction*. A tautology has no truth-conditions for, it is unconditionally true; and the contradictions are degenerate forms of propositions in the sense that "they are not pictures of reality". They present no possible state of affairs. Wittgenstein rejects the Kantian theory of synthetic proposition *a priori*. "There is no order of things *a priori*."[1] Thus logic does not deal with the world of facts and hence logical propositions lack sense.

The analytical approach and treatment of logical propositions as tautology was appreciated by Russell. Bertrand Russell after receiving the M.S. of *Tractatus* sought certain clarifications from Wittgenstein who was languishing in some Italian prison as a war prisoner. In reply to Russell's letter Wittgenstein made the following observation, which demarcates the areas of science and mysticism. Wittgenstein says, "Now I am afraid you have not really got hold of my main contention to which the whole business of logical proposition is only corollary. The main point is the theory of what can be expressed by proposition—i.e. so by language ...and what cannot be expressed by proposition, but only shown which, I believe is the cardinal problem of philosophy."

According to Wittgenstein all propositions are either elementary propositions or truth—functions of elementary propositions. An elementary proposition depicts an atomic fact or state affairs. The world is a totality of facts and not of things. My book on the table is a fact, but neither the book nor the table are facts. Wittgenstein goes further and says that nothing significant can be said about the world as a whole. That the world is my world; shows itself in the fact that the limits of language (the language which only I understand) mean the limits of my world. What we cannot think, we cannot think. To say that such and such objects do not exist is to be based on the observation of facts. That alone can be negated whose existence is a possibility. On the basis of the logic of language existence of some such things cannot be denied which does not come within the scope of language or thought. It some one does it, he transgresses the limits of language and thought and says what is unsayable and thinks what is unthinkable. The language depicts the fact. The world in its totality cannot be described because the world is a totality of facts but itself is not a fact. Explaining the central thesis of his book, Wittgenstein says, "The sense of the book might be summed up in the following words, 'what can be said at all can be said clearly, and what we cannot talk about we must pass over in silence.' " The Central theme of the *Tractatus* is to set a limit of thought and language. We cannot set the limit of thought because we do not know the limit of the thinkable and the unthinkable. Thus to say that there cannot be any proposition about the whole world as there cannot be any thought regarding the whole world, only means that we are attempting to think about the unthinkable. Thus philosophy sets the limits to the much disputed sphere of natural science. It sets the limit to what can be thought, and in doing so, also to what cannot be thought. It sets the limit to what cannot be thought by working outwards through what can be thought. Thus, according to Wittgenstein, there are only two world, of science and of mysticism, the totality of true proposition constitutes the world of science and silence is the domain of Mysticism.

We can examine the Mysticism of Wittgenstein on the basis of isomorphism of language and knowledge. There are two kinds of knowledge (*jnana*), i.e. Cognitive (*Apara*) and Intuitive (*Para*). The structures of Cognition and intuition are quite different. Cognition gives knowledge known as relational understanding as it entails the two terms—relation of the sign and the signified which is expressed in language. But intuition is an experience of a different kind. It is direct, vivid and immediate. It speaks the language of silence. In meditative insight reality is intuited directly and this experience of the whole cannot be divided into signs and reference—this is called in Vedanta—revelation (*Saksatkara*) and in Buddhism enlightenment (Buddhi-Jnana). Cognition is expressible and communicable while intuition is inexpressible and uncommunicable. Wittgenstein's Mysticism is an outcome of his philosophical analysis of language and thought. There is something which is beyond the scope of language and thought. There is a reality which can be intuitively experienced, which can reveal itself, but which cannot be expressed. Wittgenstein says, "There are, indeed, things that cannot be put into words. They make themselves manifest. They are what is mystical."[2] But according to him, what we cannot speak about exists. Here we find a striking similarity between the teachings of the Upanishads and Wittgenstein. According to Taittiriya Upanishad. "Reality is beyond the reach of mind, speech and senses."[3] For Wittgenstein also Mysticism can be expressed by the language of silence only. Like a true mystic he says "whereof one cannot speak thereof one must be silent".[4] Buddha and Sankara also uphold some such views when they are confronted with the philosophical problem regarding the nature of Reality. They try to explain this intricate problem with the help of parables but in their ultimate analysis they come to the same conclusion, namely that it is inexplicable. Buddha calls such metaphysical questions unanswerable (*Avyakatani*).[5] Sankara tries to explain the nature of reality through metaphors, but he also comes to realize that this process has its own limitation and so he ends up finally by saying that 'silence is Brahman'.[6] What is meant here actually is that the exact nature of reality cannot the expressed by words, and that silence succeeds in conveying what words fail to convey. This is why Wittgenstein rejects metaphysics because it is impossible to formulate metaphysical propositions. Wittgenstein believes metaphysics to be impossible because it is impossible to formulate metaphysical propositions, not because such propositions would be about something that did not exist, but because language cannot make metaphysical assertions.[7] The Upanishadic seer also facts the same difficulties while formulating metaphysical assertions and takes recourse to neti, neti (not this, not this) and thus finally describes the reality as inexpressible.

Mysticism is a philosophy of oneness. It takes man to the world of reality which is beyond the dualism of the subject and the object. In the mystic experience 'the one' or 'the whole' is felt and realized. This realization, however, cannot be clearly expressed and communicated. It is experienced through the inner transformation of consciousness. It is, but it cannot be said *what it is*. This unique experience is a kind of realization of the 'totality'. This mystic experience is a rare experience. Wittgenstein has dealt with the age-old philosophical problem of knowledge that is communicable and the knowledge which lies beyond the domain of language and thought. He has succeeded in setting the limits of language, thought and reason. However, he holds that there is something which is beyond the reach of language and thought which he calls '*the mystical*'. Here Wittgenstein speaks in the language of the Upanishads. It is some such spirit that reflects itself in Wittgenstein's suggestion that a successful philosopher is like a fly which succeeds in escaping from a bottle in which it is somehow trapped. It is perhaps not very far-fetched to suggest that, according to Vedanta, the man in bondage the embodied individual is more or less like Wittgenstein's 'fly' in the bottle, and that the ultimate aim of philosophy is to show him the out of it.

What is the way out of it? It is nothing but the realization that there was no genuine problem, or, in other words, that there was no genuine bondage. Thus, Wittgenstein's conception of intellectual illness and its cure has a striking resemblance with Upanishadic conception of bondage and liberation.

Wittgenstein is perfectly right when he says, 'And it is not surprising that the deepest problems are in fact not problems at all.'[8] Thus, we can say that the Mysticism of both Wittgenstein and the Upanishadic seer can be said to have arisen from the feeling of a deep concern—a sort of a restless buzzing at not being able to discovery the way out, and also that according to them both philosophical redemption consists in the realization that there never was a puzzle—that there never was a bondage. Although the 'Puzzle' has been dealt with by Wittgenstein at the linguistic level and 'bondage' has been dealt with by the Upanisadic seer at the metaphysical level, there appears to be a striking similarity between the two both in tone and spirit. This point appears to be very vital, almost central to out thesis; but there are some other points also with respect to which the two philosophies appear to have a similarity of spirit.

Anscombe is of the opinion that 'Wittgenstein had been much impressed by Schopenhauer as a boy; many traces of this influence can be found in the *Tractatus*.'[9] Possibly Wittgenstein might have been influenced by the Upanishads through Schopenhauer. Wittgenstein's style of writing is mysteriously aphoristic like that of the Upanishads. The element of mysticism of Wittgenstein is a puzzlement to many of his great admirers. Rusell and Ramsey, who are otherwise very sympathetic to Wittgenstein, are very critical of his mysticism. However, his mysticism is an integral part of Wittgenstein's philosophy. Wittgenstein in course of his philosophical analysis and insight became fully aware of the limitation of language and thought. After years of philosophising he came to the conclusion that there is something which is beyond the reach of science and language. This according to him, is the realm of the mystical. In his exposition of mysticism, Wittgenstein talks of a new concept, the concept of a 'limited-whole'. Although, apparently the concept of a limited whole seems to be self-contradictory the Indian tradition does not find any difficulty with this. In fact this concept can be given a plausibility and a sense by every type of idealistic metaphysics. According to both Bradley and Sankara we cannot have the knowledge of Absolute or *Brahman* through discursive reasoning. There cannot be any limitation of the 'whole'. But the 'whole' or Absolute appears limited like *Iswara* of Sankara on the intellectual plane. Now Wittgenstein also says that we experience the world as a 'limited-whole'. The notion of a 'limited whole' is itself mystical. It is in this context that Wittgenstein makes a distinction between 'what can be known' and 'what can be shown'. The concept of a limited whole has a relevance for the former and that which is described as the 'mystical' has relevance for the latter. Thus, Wittgenstein's reference to the limited whole, and the two levels of its apprehension roughly correspond to similar views held by Sankara in the metaphysical context.

When Wittgenstein is faced with any philosophical problem his inter seer starts talking in the language of mysticism like the Upanishadic seers. He holds the view that one cannot make real evaluation of the world so long he lives in the world of dualism of the knower and the known. He admits that the problems which he has dealt with is otherwise unanswerable. The value of the *Tractatus* lies in its realization that it is non-sensical. Wittgenstein says [one] must transcend there proposition and then he will see the world aright[10]. Thus, according to Wittgenstein also truth is beyond the reach of language and thought. According to the Upanishads also reality is beyond the reach of sermon, reason, and philosophical enquiry. We can have the experience of anything because of the form but the form itself is not an object of cognition but of intuition.

After a close examination of Wittgenstein's philosophy we come to the conclusion that his philosophy begins with empiricism but it culminates in 'rationalistic mysticism'. Wittgenstein discovers mysticism after analyzing the structure and form of language and thought. Indeed Upanishadic Mysticism has its roots in meditative insight. Even so, one is constrained to feel that both Wittgenstein and the Upanishadic seer have a definite affinity of spirit which forces them both turn towards Mysticism.

Notes

1. *Tractatus*, 5.634.
2. *Tractatus*, 6.522.
3. यतो वाचो निवतन्ते अप्राप्य मनसा: स:
4. *Tractatus* 7.
5. *Saniyutt Nikaya*
6. मौन ब्रह्म
7. Justus Hartnack, *Wittgenstein and Modern Philosophy*, p. 43.
8. *Tractatus*, p. 37.
9. *As introduction to Wittgenstein's Tractatus*, p. 168.

6
Philosophy and Quantum Mechanics
An Analysis and Reflection

Ludwig Wittgenstein is considered as most original and one of the greatest thinkers that Europe has produced. He has made a great impact on contemporary Western philosophical movements. His two books—*Tractatus Logico-Philosophicus* and *Philosophical Investigations* exercised great influence on the recent philosophical movements especially of Europe and America. I shall confine myself mainly to the impact of mysticism on Wittgenstein's earlier philosophy as formulated in Tractatus. Wittgenstein by making a difference between sayable and unsayable created a theory of Solipsism. His theory of meaning which is the fundamental of the *Tractatus* is known as the picture theory. He says that "A proposition is a picture of reality for if I understand a proposition I know the situation that it represents. And I represent the proposition without having had its sense explained to me."[1]

Language is a picture of reality. Reality stands here as a fact. Fact means state of affairs. There is a structural similarity between the world of language and the world of facts. The ultimate unit of language is elementary proposition and the ultimate unit of world is atomic facts. This is known as isomorphic relations. He considers that limit of thought is the limit of language.

"We cannot think what we cannot think; so what we cannot think, we cannot say either."[2]

This remark provides the key to the problem, how much truth there is in Solipsism. For what the solipsist means is quite correct, only it cannot be said but makes itself manifest. The world is my world: this is manifest in the fact that the limits of language (of that language which alone I understand) mean the limits of my world.[3]

According to Wittgenstein proposition does not actually contain it sense but does contain the possibility of expressing it. Proposition contains its form but not the content of its sense. Wittgenstein accepts like Upanishadic seer that truth and reality cannot be expressed in words because it is indescribable. In place of Upanishadic dictum '*indescribable*' and Buddhist '*unspeakable*' (*avachya*) Wittgenstein uses *unsayable*. He accepts that, "There are indeed, things that cannot be put into words. They make themselves manifest. They are what is mystical. It is not how things are in the world that is mystical but that it exists."[4]

It is very evident from *Tractatus* that it does not deny the existence of the mystical reality and accept that it is beyond the reach of our thought and language. Wittgenstein concludes in formulating the seventh and the last proposition in *Tractatus* "Whereof we cannot sayeth thereof we must consign to silence." In Philosophical Investigation Wittgenstein says that language depicts the cultural form of life. Meaning of word is determined in a cultural context. This is why it becomes difficult to express Oriental ethos in Western language because Oriental tradition is mystical and spiritual whereas Western tradition is dominated by ontological materialism and rationalism. Oriental language faces the same problem in describing the Western scientific and technological terminology. However, with the fusion of two traditions and impact of globalization in recent years easing out this problem to great extent. Moreover, language as a means of communication has its own limitations. This is why Wittgenstein makes a bold declaration that concept of language cannot be defined. After analysis and close examination of the structure of thought and language—both Kant and Wittgenstein draw a line between sayable and not sayable.

Kant talked about two realities—*phenomena* and *noumena,* whereas Wittgenstein made a distinction between the worlds of sayable and mystical. Thus, I come to this conclusion that whole Western philosophy is also essentially and basically based on ontological mysticism.

Stephen Hawking in the beginning of his book entitled '*The Grand Design*' writes, "How does the universe behave? What is the nature of reality? Where did all this come from? Did the universe need a creator? Most of us do not spend most of our time worrying about these questions, but almost all of us worry about them some of the time.

Traditionally these are questions for philosophy, but philosophy is dead. Philosophy has not kept up with the modern development in science, particularly physics."[5] Philosophy is not dead, rather science has become a philosophy. Problem of *'why'* has been the fundamental issue of philosophy since its very inception and the problem of 'how' comes within the domain of scientific investigation and discovery. Now science is trying to understand, reflect and solve the problem of *why.* It is a welcome step. Scientist propagating their theories on foundation of ontological materialism. Coming out of Plato's cave to new awareness f Truth and Reality scientists have become aware of truth and reality postulated by ontological mysticism (ontological spiritualism). There is a convergence of science and philosophy today. Philosophy is not only alive and vibrant but it has made science a living subject. The problem whether the matter is wave or particle is rooted in misunderstanding and the wrong notion of wave and particle. Matter is neither wave nor particle it is a consciousness. Whole cosmos is the modification of cosmic consciousness (*Brahman, Ataman*), Emptiness (*Sunyata* or *Tao*). Whole cosmos is the modification of cosmic consciousness. Consciousness is the *Reality* and the sole *Truth.* Science and philosophy are the quest for truth and reality. The classical science was concerned with the objective truth. The theory of relativity and quantum mechanics have transcended the boundary of classical science in search of the understanding and knowledge of true nature of reality and entered into the subjective domain of philosophy. If science would not have entered and made inroad into the *"subjectivity"*, it would have become dead and would have lost charm, beauty and relevance. Unless we understand the true nature and structure of truth we would become the victim of such dilemma. Einstein has revolutionized the science by his famous formulation of $E = mc^2$. He was the first scientist who came face to face with truth. For him matter is not dead but it is energy and alive. By this formulation he rejected the aged old scientific dogma of dead matter. The universe is vibrating with life. It is a living reality because it is a modification of consciousness. Consciousness is the quintessential nature and structure of the cosmos. Both science and philosophy culminate in spirituality. It is the goal and the end of the quest for science and philosophy. This is ontological mysticism. According to Spinoza the human body is a modification of infinite substance (God). Insofar as it is expressed in attribute of extension. According to him the material world is a modification of God. Hence, it follows from Spinoza's philosophy that there is consciousness which corresponds to the vital processes of our body. Ervin Schrodinger, one of the founding fathers of Quantum Mechanics, writes, "And then, on the other hand, we say that consciousness is that by which this world becomes manifest, by which indeed, we can quite calmly say, it first becomes present; that the world consists of the elements of consciousness—this world within which we have just discovered the emergence of the brain as a highly specialized phenomenon, something which has emerged but which might quite well have remained non-existent and which is; in any case, by no means *sui generis*. And now we are asked to believe that this special modification in the evolution of the higher mammals had to happen in order that the world should dawn on itself in the light of consciousness; whereas, if it had not emerged, this world would have remained nothing but a drama played to an empty house, not present to anyone and hence not in a real sense present at all. If this is really the ultimate wisdom to which we can attain in this question, then to me it seems to be utter bankruptcy of our picture of the world. And we thought at least to acknowledge it, and not act as though it did not matter to us, or jeer, in our rationalistic wisdom, at those who try to find a wayout, however desperate."[6] Danish physicist Neil Bohr (1855-1962) came out with a new theory of complementarity to explain the dilemma of wave and particle. The concept that a single model may not be adequate to explain all observations made of atomic or sub-atomic systems in different experiments. For example, 'electron diffraction is best explained by assuming that electron is a wave, whereas the photoelectric effect is described by assuming that it is a particle. The idea of two different but complementary concepts to treat quantum phenomena was first put forward by him.

Wave and particle dilemma is due to incomplete understanding of reality. The reality is beyond wave and particles. The nature is not governed by whims and caprices. There is some system, some rules, some principles, behind the movement of the phenomenal world. The uncertainty principles which explains certain natural functions like Newtonian Classic Physics which also explains gravitational movement some natural bodies but which does not give scientific explanation of particles and waves, but it has some limitations. The principles of uncertainty entail absence of our proper knowledge and understanding of the movement of particles and wave which has given rise to the principles of uncertainty. The movement of particles and waves would be explained by some law. Einstein didn't agree with the Copenhagen interpretation of Quantum mechanics. Einstein's rejections of Bohr's doctrine of complementarity are based on some scientific thinking and reflection.

It is to be ascertained whether Einstein is right in his assertion that God does not play dice with the world. If we accept the theory of complementarity then the logical doctrine of principles of identity and contradiction will have no place in science.

Washington Post writes, "In science, revolutions take time. So, the day after news broke of a possible revolution in physics 'particles moving faster than light'—a scientist leading the European experiment that made a discovery calmly explained it to a standing room only crowd at CERN the giant particle acceleration straddling the Swiss-French border. The physicist, Danrio Anterio made no sweeping claims."[7]

In the *Washington Post* of 25th September, 2011 highlighted the new discovery by science which has almost falsified the findings of Einstein that nothing travels higher than light. Some particles according to the report travel faster than the speed of light. It is called the "God Particle". However, I believe that the cosmic consciousness has got the speed of infinity. It may be called in mathematical terms that the cosmic consciousness travels with absolute speed and at the same time it has a zero speed. The whole cosmos exists in between zero and infinite speed. The cosmic consciousness which is called in Hinduism as a Brahman, Tao in Lao Tzu metaphysics and *Sunyata* (emptiness) in Buddhism is the ultimate reality. It has got absolute speed and absolute stillness (pause). From philosophical perspective we can say that the consciousness has got infinite speed and from other perspective it may be called that it has a zero speed. Conceptually there is no dilemma between absolute speed and absolute pause. The root of knowledge is spirituality. The trunk is science. And the branches are all other schools of social sciences and humanity. Knowledge bereft of ontological mysticism is Pyrrhonism. In mystical experience knowledge and wisdom become one. Monism is true philosophy and ultimate basis of science.

Oneness with reality is the goal of spirituality and the proper understanding of the reality is the end of scientific journey. I feel the convergence of science and spirituality will herald a new era of ontological mysticism. Science and spirituality is the integral form and part of human existence.

French mathematician Marquis de Laplace (1749-1827), has made a very logical and rational assertion that all our knowledge is problematical. And in that background we have to examine the different scientific doctrines. I think that the Einstein's assertions about the speed of the travelling light is the fastest, i.e. it is a relative truth. So there is every possibility of its limitation and falsifications. As I have already asserted that the phenomenal world exists between the zero and infinity and hence, any scientific formulation which has not reached infinity has every possibility that it would be falsified by other scientific formulation.

Scientific formulation being relative in nature it does not entail that the Einstein's assertion was totally wrong. As I have already stated every scientific postulations are relative and subject to being corrected, improved and modified by another scientific postulation. Marquis de Laplace writes, "Strictly speaking it may be even said that nearly all our knowledge is problematical; and in the small number of things which we are able to know with certainty, even in mathematical sciences themselves, the principle means for asserting truth—induction and analogy, are based on probabilities; so that the entire system of human knowledge is connected with the theory set forth in the essay. Doubtless it will be seen here with interest that in considering, even in the eternal principles of reason, justice and humanity; only the favourable chances which are constantly attached to them, there is a great advantage in following these principles and serious inconvenience departing from them; their chances like those favourable to lotteries, always end by prevailing in the midst of the vacillations of hazard."[8]

There has been a constant debate between the domain of philosophy and science. We have been making arbitrary distinction between philosophy and science, between speculative and logical aspects of science. However, it would be wrong to assume that philosophy must develop into logic of science, which has been asserted by A.J. Ayer. He writes in his concluding celebrated book '*Language, Truth and Logic*' that, a person who is engaged in understanding the logical relationship of the different hypotheses and defining them in form of symbols. According to him it is one and the same thing to address such people who are engaged in logical relationship of hypothesis to address such person as a philosopher or a scientist. He concludes with this sentence that "What we must recognise is that it is necessary for a philosopher to become a scientist, in this sense, if he is to make any substantial contribution towards the growth of human knowledge."[9]

A.J. Ayer being a positivist is biased for science. He could not comprehend the whole gamut of philosophical thinking and speculation. There is no necessity of philosopher becoming a scientist, when scientists are becoming philosophers in pursuit of truth, beauty and reality. The pure physics and pure foundation of mathematics are branches of philosophy. The root of knowledge is ontological mysticism, the trunk is philosophy and science and other forms of knowledge are different branches.

Karl Popper is of the opinion that scientific knowledge and all other theories are open to be proven false. However, mediating between two planes of perception and reflection given by science and philosophy would be greatest intellectual adventure and most rewarding of our times.

I would analyse, examine and evaluate the findings and the postulations of classical physics, theory of relativity and quantum mechanics in the larger background of philosophical reflection and ontological mysticism.

According to classical physics the universe is governed by laws that are susceptible to rational understanding. And the chief purpose and objective of the classical physics has been application of those laws for extending our knowledge about the phenomenal world. Newton was a deeply religious man. He considered these laws as the manifestation of God's perfection. However to a great extent the classical physics became a tool for understanding the laws that governed the phenomenal world. However, the classical physics failed to explain some problems that govern the events on sub-atomic level. It failed to make enroots into some atomic phenomena with any certainty.

Strictly speaking the quantum physics does not believe in the world of waves and particles, of position and velocity. We enter into world of inconsistency and contradictions when we try to explain quantum world in the language of classical science.

Actually the measurement of the object measured and the subject doing the measuring are inexplicably involved. David Lindley in the introductory remark of Werner Heisenberg's celebrated book '*Physics and Philosophy*' writes, "In stressing the inadequacy of either the wave or the particle picture alone, Heisenberg tells us that 'by playing with both pictures by going from one picture to the other and back again, we finally get the right impression of the strange kind of reality behind our atomic experiments.' This, I fear, will strike a good many readers as a bit of dodge. That's all very well, Professor Heisenberg, these readers might say, but can you spell out for us just what this 'strange kind of reality' consists of? Alas, that is ultimately what we cannot do, at least not in a very satisfactory way."[10] On the basis of the analysis of different concepts of classical physics, relativity and quantum mechanics, we come to the conclusion that the physics of today have not been able to formulate any satisfactory doctrine of the reality. Schrodinger and Heisenberg both accept the role of consciousness and subjectivism in formulating the concept of reality. I shall deal with this problem in detail later on. Before that I would like to give the brief historical account of development of science in the West. It is necessary to understand the development of the doctrine of reality in course of the scientific development which ultimately culminates to my mind in ontological mysticism.

The modern Western science begins with Thales, who stated that 'everything is made of water'. Thales was born in Miletus, in Asia Minor. However a lot of other writers consider Thales as the founding father of philosophy. I consider Galileo as the father of modern science. His greatest contribution in the field of science is his doctrine that the object in absence of resistance falls at the same rate. It is considered that he made this experiment from the Leaning Tower of Pisa. However, some consider it as a myth. But this laid down the sound foundation to the classical physics. He was a son of music, theorist and luteinise. He was the first scientist who used technology to explore and uncover the mystery of nature. He was the first to use telescope to explore the strange world of stars. This application of technology in exploring the mystery of the universe was a great revolution in the field of science. He discovered the stars which have never been thought of before. His observation of the movement of different stars leads him to believe that the Copernicus was right and thus he made a historic observation that the earth is not the centre of the universe. Earth moves around the sun. It is the sun which is the centre of the galaxy around which all planets move. For this discovery Galileo was severely punished by the Church because Galileo's discovery went against the Biblical doctrine under the pressure of the Church.

In 1632 Galileo opines, "Take note, theologians, that in your desire to make matters of faith out of propositions relating to the fixity of sun and earth you run the risk of eventually having to condemn as heretics those who would declare the earth to stand still and the sun to change position—eventually, I say, at such a time as it might be physically or logically proved that earth moves and the sun stands still."[11] In 1663 Galileo's good friend became the Pope and he tried his level best to get the 1616 decree revoked. His book dialogue concerning the two chief world systems was published in 1632 which had become very famous throughout the Europe. In this book Galileo had come out with strong argument in favour of heliocentric world as propagated by Copernicus.

The Pope became very angry though he was his friend and he had sentenced Galileo to house arrest for the rest of his life and asked him to make public announcement of the falsification of Copernicanism. Before his death in 1646, Galileo succeeded in smuggling his another manuscripts which was published as entitled '*Two New Sciences*' in Holland and this had become the foundation of the classical physics.

In 1609 when Galileo Galilei was scanning the night sky with a telescope he observed that planet Jupiter was having several small satellites or moons that revolved around it and it went against the Aristotle and Ptolemy who had thought that everything orbit directly around the Earth. It was a Polish priest Copernicus, who had propagated this heliocentric doctrine that earth is not the centre rather the sun is the centre around which all other planets revolve. Kepler a German scientist made some improvement in the Copernicus theory by introducing a new concept that planets do not orbit in circles but in ellipses. This was the end of the Ptolemy's theory that earth is the centre. The sound foundation of classical physics was laid down by Isaac Newton. He published his book entitled, '*Philosophaie Naturalis Principia Mathematica*'. It is considered as the greatest single publication which has revolutionised the scientific world. He came out with rational and scientific explanation for the planets orbiting the sun by introducing a path breaking doctrine of gravitation. In Principia, Newton presented a law that all objects are by nature in the state of rest until some external forces work upon to move or change the movement. Newton gave a scientific explanation that why any object fall to earth instead of remaining at rest and he called this force gravity. Newton was of the opinion that this law of gravitation was applicable to all objects of the universe from the falling of an apple to the stars and planets. It was a great change and revolution in the scientific thinking because it was for the first time that the theory of gravitation explained the movement of the planets and other objects and he laid down the foundation for classical modern physics and modern astronomy. According to the modern classical physics matter was considered as the fundamental reality. The phenomenal world of things existed in space and time. The matter would be produced and it could be acted upon by forces. Every event is the result and cause of other events and it is all because of the interaction between the matter and the forces. Galileo observed the interplay of the things and events that provided the basis of scientific materialism.

According to classical physics the universe is governed by a set of laws. These laws could be analysed for better understanding. With the application of these laws that govern the universe we could exert change and influence our environments. Newton was a deeply religious person. He considered these laws as the manifestation of God. The understanding of these laws enhanced the dignity and honour of man which were reduced to the cog of a machine during the middle ages by the birth of Western natural philosophy. The success and importance of any scientific theory depends upon the strength of predictability of events and providing a rational model of the universe. The Newton's theory became very famous because of his doctrine of gravitation, which could predict the motion of the sun, moon and other planets of our galaxy with higher degree of certainty.

According to the theory of gravitation each body attracts other with the force proportional to the quantity (mass) and universally proportional to the distance between them. This is a very simple scientific model. But all theories howsoever important it may be it is based on degree of probabilities. Marquis de Laplace says, "It is remarkable that science, which commenced with the consideration of games of chance, should be elevated to the rank of the most important subjects of human knowledge."[12]

According to Newton's Law of Gravitation, it was predicted that with great amount of certainty about the movement of the earth, moon and other planets. Ever since the birth of civilization the philosopher and the scientist have been grappling with the problem of the single theory that would explain the whole universe. Though it is very difficult to formulate a theory that would provide a proper scientific and rational doctrine which would explain universe in one go. In the process of understanding the mystery of nature we develop and discover a number of different theories to explain and predict certain events. One of my central objectives is to search for a new theory which would explain the universe in terms of science and philosophy. Stephen Hawking writes, "But ever since the dawn of civilization, people have not been content to see events such as unconnected and inexplicable. "We have carved an understanding of the underlying order in the world. Today we still yearn to know why we are here and where we came from. Humanity's deepest desire for knowledge is justification enough for our continuing quest. And our goal is nothing less than a complete description of the universe we live in."[13] Modern science today is trying to discover a basic law from which the motion of matter and all elementary particles and their properties could be mathematically understood. Thales was the first who considered that water is the material cause of all things. And with this postulation of Thales science took birth in the West. The German philosopher Nietzsche formulated three basic philosophical principles to understand the mystery of the universe. The first condition was that to find out the material cause of all things. Secondly, the analysis and postulation must be based on logic and rationality. And these fundamental laws should be reduced to one principle. This has been the search from the beginning of human civilization.

Werner Heisenberg one of the greatest physicists of last century observes, "The constant element in physics since Newton is not a configuration or a geometrical form, but a dynamic law. The equation of motion holds at all times, it is in this sense eternal, whereas the geometrical forms, like the orbits, are changing. Therefore, the mathematical forms that represent the elementary particles will be solutions of some eternal law of motion for matter. Actually this is a problem which has not yet been solved. The fundamental law of motion for matter is not yet known and therefore, it is not yet possible to derive mathematically the properties of the elementary particles from such a law. But theoretical physics in its present state seems to be not very far from this goal and we can at least say what kind of law we have to expect. The final equation of motion for matter will probably be some quantized non-linear wave equation for a wave field of operators that simply represent matter, not any specified kind of wave or particles."[14]

The basic difference between the classical physics and the quantum mechanics are that according to classical physics there is an objective world which exists apart from us. We can measure, observe and experiment about the external world without changing it.

The whole idea of external objective world depends upon the postulation of "*it is outthere'*. The new physics believe that the reality goes under change in the process of our observation. Gary Zukav writes, "According to quantum mechanics there is no such thing as objectivity. We cannot eliminate ourselves from the picture. We are a part of nature, and when we study nature there is no way around the fact that nature is studying itself. Physics has become a branch of psychology, or perhaps the other way round."

Quantum mechanics as a theory was developed to explain electromagnetic waves and atomic structure. Classical physics failed to explain both the electromagnetic waves and atomic structure. At the beginning of the twentieth century the atomic structure puzzled the physicists in explaining the emission of electrons from the surface of the metal illuminated by light. Einstein was the first scientist to realize that the classical description of light as a wave on an electromagnetic field does not explain the photoelectric effect. The experiments have proved that electrons could be emitted only if the incident light was of a sufficient wavelength while the intensity of light appeared to be not relevant.

Einstein postulated that photoelectric effect, light behaves as a shower of particles, E with the energy given by Planck's expression, E = hf. Here 'f' stands for light frequency and 'h' is the Planck's constant. However, in non-relativistic quantum theory particles are assumed to be neither created nor destroyed, to move slowly relative to the speed of light, and to have a mass that doesn't change with velocity. This postulation is applicable to atomic and molecular structure and which is considered as an aspect of nuclear physics. The relativistic quantum theory applies to particles that travel at or near the speed of light. Quantum mechanics is replaced by classical mechanics and Maxwell's electromagnetic theory. It was a new revolution in the world of pure physics.

Max Planck (1858-1947) laid down the foundation of modern quantum physics by postulating the theory that nature is not continuous but it is marked by discrete packets or quanta. He was awarded Nobel prize in Physics in 1918. He published his quantum postulation in December 1900. The Planck's theory of heat radiation and the postulation that energy is emitted or absorbed only in discrete energy form called quanta was inanalogous with the traditional classical physics of Newton. Light can be interpreted in terms of electromagnetic waves propounded by Maxwell's theory or it could be interpreted in terms of light quanta, i.e. energy packets passing through space with higher velocity.

Werner Heisenberg writes, "This time it was the young Albert Einstein, a revolutionary genius among the physicists, who was not afraid to go further away from the old concepts. These were two problems in which he could make use of the new ideas. One was the so-called photoelectric effect, the emission of electrons from metals under the influence of the light. The experiments, especially those of Lenard, had shown that the energy of the emitted electrons did not depend on the intensity of the light, but only on its colour or, more precisely on its frequency. This could not be understood on the basis of the traditional theory of radiation. Einstein could explain the observations by intercepting Planck's hypothesis as saying that light consists of quanta of energy travelling through space. The energy of one light quantum should, in agreement with the Planck's assumptions, be equal to the frequency of the light multiplied by the Planck's constant."[15]

The theory of uncertainty initiated by Heisenberg in 1927 and Bohr's doctrine of complementarity are the fundamental basis of quantum mechanics. According to Heisenberg, electron does not occupy any fixed location in atoms as has been the basis of classical physics. One can know and ascertain the average position of an electron. But any measurement of the movement of the electron is work under the principle of uncertainty.

According to the new postulation of quantum mechanics we can have proper understanding of movement of electrons only at quantized levels. And it was assumed that the laws of classical physics do not apply at the quantized movements of electrons in an atom. This paradigm of quantum mechanics is applicable at the atomic scale. It only throws light on the limitations of classical physics in the interpretation of nature. At the macroscopic level of nature or material world, the laws of the classical physics are operated. But at the microscopic scale of atom classical laws breaks down. Newton's work entitled '*Philosophiae Naturalis Principia Mathematica*' postulates that the all objects at rest remain in that state unless it is moved by some external force. And he explained the movement of the planets around the sun in the elliptical orbits in terms of force of gravity.

Now the universe is described and explained in terms of two fundamental theories of general theory of relativity and quantum mechanics. The general theory of relativity is capable of explaining the macrocosmic level of universe. Quantum mechanics deals with microscopic level of phenomena. However, these two doctrines one which works at the macroscopic level other with microscopic level of nature are analogous to each other. Now the scientists and the philosophers are in quest of a doctrine which could resolve this ambiguity and provide a doctrine which Einstein dreamed of as 'theory of everything'. However, one should be conscious about the limitation of the rational thinking. It is an impossibility to discover and arrive at some absolute truth with the help of rationality. Heisenberg writes, "The philosophic thesis that all knowledge is ultimately founded in experience has in the end led to a postulate concerning the logical clarification of any statement about nature. Such a postulate may have seemed justified in the period of classical physics, but since quantum theory we have learned that it cannot be fulfilled. The words "position" and "velocity" of an electron, for instance, seemed perfectly well defined as to both their meaning and their possible connections, and in fact they were clearly defined concepts within the mathematical framework of Newtonian mechanics. But actually they were not well defined, as is seen from the relations of uncertainty."[16] "The essence of substance" is beyond the reach of our mind and senses. James Jeans (1877-1946) has dealt with this problem in his celebrated work the *Mysterious Universe.* According to him the objective reality exists because they affect our consciousness. But we believe that that objective reality is either real or ideal. He explains everything in mathematical language. According to him, "God is a mathematician and the universe begins to look more like a great thought than a great machine." There is an echo of Pythagorean mysticism in his thought. However, he rejects the Humean thesis of solipsism, i.e. "All this is creation of my own mind, and exists in no other mind." Rationality has a limitation. He says, "A mathematical formula can never tell us what a thing is, but only how it behaves; it can only specify an object through its properties. And these are unlikely to coincide *in toto* with the properties of any single macroscopic object of our everyday life." The modern science is trying to discover some basic law of motion for matter from which all elementary particles and their properties could be deduced mathematically. This elementary particle is being postulated to basic substance which is known as energy or matter. Energy is considered as the basic substance. Elementary particles and all atoms are made from this basic substance. But the greatest problem before the modern scientists is to ascertain the mathematical forms of elementary particles which could be a solution of the eternal laws of motion for matter. Heisenberg says that the fundamental law of motion for matter is not known and therefore, it is not possible to drive mathematically the properties of elementary particles from such a law. The concept of matter has undergone great change and metamorphosis. According to Aristotle matter is in itself not a reality but only possibility "*a potentia*". Matter exists through the means of form.

Matter according to Aristotle is not a specific matter like Thales water or anything else. It is a kind of indefinite material substratum which is the basis of possibility of passing and transforming into actuality with the help of forms. As for example the statue is potentially in the stone before it was transformed into a splendour or beauty in form of statue by the sculpture. According to Heisenberg this concept of *Potentia* could be compared with the modern concept of energy. The division between matter and form does not exist in the modern physics.

Elementary particles are not only producing some force and is activated by some force, it represents a certain field of force. According to Copenhagen interpretation matter and force are the appearance of waves and particles. However, the theory of special relativity and quantum mechanics presents two different concepts and throws light on two different aspects of nature. Theory of special relativity deals with the space-time continuum which is quite analogous to classical physics. According to Einstein, the maximum velocity of light cannot be surpassed by any other moving objects. The theory of special relativity which postulates the structure of space and time put infinitely the boundary between the regions of simultaneousness.

On the contrary quantum theory of uncertainty put a definite limitation on the position and momenta, i.e. time and energy which could be measured simultaneously. Heisenberg writes, "Therefore any theory which tries to fulfil the requirements of both special relativity and quantum theory will lead to mathematical inconsistencies, to divergencies in the region of very high energies and momenta. This sequence of conclusions may perhaps not seem strictly binding, since any formalism of the type under consideration is very complicated and could perhaps offer some mathematical possibilities for avoiding the clash between quantum theory and relativity."[17]

Copenhagen interpretation of quantum theory has thrown a new light on the elements of subjectivism into theory. According to the Copenhagen interpretations of quantum mechanics our knowledge of the position of the particle is complementary to our understanding of velocity. Space-time postulation of atomic events is complementary in providing the proper description of the structure of space-time. This has been formulated from the epistemological and ontological stand points. Here epistemology and ontology help each other in having a proper understanding of nature. Quantum mechanics presents a two analogous picture of waves and particles. The complementary doctrines of waves and panicles has initiated a great debate between Einstein and Neil Bohr. While Einstein and Schrodinger criticising the doctrine of complementarity advocated by Copenhagen interpretations of quantum theory and formulated by Neil Bohr and supported by Heisenberg and the others. The misunderstanding of the dualism between the two descriptions of reality in the form of waves and particles posed another serious problem about the actual happenings in atomic events. It is believed that the results and mechanism employed in observation can be formulated in classical concepts. But mathematical formulations of the combined statements about the possibility and our knowledge of facts cannot be described what happens between this observation and the next. Heisenberg writes, "This looks as if we had introduced an element of subjectivism into the theory, as if we meant to say: what happens depends on our way of observing it or on the fact that we observe it. Before discussing this problem of subjectivism it is necessary to explain quite clearly why one would get into hopeless difficulties if one tried to describe what happens between two consecutive observations."[18] In the theoretical explanation of any experiment involves two steps. For example the experiment of source of monochromatic light that radiates towards a black screen with two small holes.

The wavelength of the light and the diameter of holes create the problem. Distance behind the screen of a photographic plate which witnesses the events of light can be explained in the experiment in terms of wave picture one may observe that the primary wave penetrates through two holes and there is a possibility of secondary spherical waves that begins from the holes that interfere with one another. This interference would create a pattern of varying intensity on the photographic plate. If the experiment is multiplied the light quantum that has gone through the first hole blackening of the plate due to, would correspond to the probability distribution. Heisenberg writes, "This example shows clearly that the concept of the probability function does not allow a description of what happens between two observations. Any attempt to find such a description would lead to contradictions; this must mean that the term 'happens' is restricted to the observation."[19] If we enumerate this interpretation of an experiment which has been started with two steps, we in the first deal with the arrangement of the experiment in the light of classical physics which is being explained in terms of probability function. This is a very important factor which throws light on the probability function of laws of quantum theory. In the second step it could be measured in the initial condition. Heisenberg writes, "The probability function combines objective and subjective elements. It contains statements about possibilities or better tendencies ("potentia" in Aristotle philosophy). These statements are completely objective, they do not depend on any observer; and it contains statements about our knowledge of the system, which, of course, are subjective insofar as they may be different for different observers in ideal cases the subjective element in the probability function may be practically negligible as compared with the objective one. The physicists then speak of a pure case."[20] The Heisenberg's theory of uncertainty is based on the probability function which is the combination of objective element of tendency and the subjective element of incomplete knowledge. This has been the basis of Heisenberg postulations that the result of observation cannot be normally being predicted with certainty. We can only predict of the probability of certain results of observation which could be about the repeated confirmation by repeating experiments. According to Quantum mechanics our observation of the knowledge of system undergoes change which does not have continuity and with thc result the mathematical also undergoes discontinuous change which is termed as *quantum jump*. This speaks of a very significant development in quantum physics of transition of events from the *possible* to the actual which happens during the process of observation. The quantum mechanics throws a new light on the events that takes place in atomic experiments. The events are related to the observation and not to the state of affairs between two observations. The psychological act of observation does not apply, while it does apply to the physical events. In other words while we can summarize that transition from the *possible* to actual happens as soon as the interaction of the object with the measuring device takes place. And thereby it entails that the rest of world also takes place in the drama of this place. Heisenberg comes to the conclusion that in the objective description of the world especially in the reference of the atomic world in the classic physics science starts with belief or may be termed as from the illusion; the description of the world or the parts of the world without any reference to the observer. Quantum theory does not contain the real subjective element. However, it does divide the world into the object and the rest of the world. The Copenhagen's interpretation of quantum theory starts with the paradox. The starting point of formulation of quantum experiment is in terms of classical physics. At the same time from the knowledge that these concepts do not adhere to nature accurately. This is the root of the paradox which speaks of the statistic character of quantum theory. This paradox leads to the uncertainty in relation to the macroscopic behaviour of the world, when it enters into the quantum theoretical system.

Heisenberg writes, "Therefore that a part of matter or radiation which takes part in the phenomenon is the natural "object" in the theoretical treatment and should be separated in this respect from the tools used to study the phenomenon. This again emphasizes a subjective element in the description of atomic events, since the measuring device has been constructed by the observer, and we have to remember that what we observe is not nature in itself but nature exposed to our method of questioning."[21]

While understanding and describing the harmony in the cosmic drama of nature we are both a choreographer and the spectator. In describing and understanding the laws of nature and our scientific relations we become very important when we enter into dialogue with parts of nature with the help of nature by using most effective, scientific tools. The introduction of the *"subject"* in postulating the quantum physics. Heisenberg writes, "It is understandable that in our scientific relation to nature our own activity becomes very important when we have to deal with parts of nature into which we can penetrate only by using the most elaborate tools."[22]

To my mind Heisenberg's acceptance of active role of subject in understanding nature opens new vistas in modern science and philosophy. I postulate that the Einstein's four dimensional world of subject, space-time does not provide the proper scientific and philosophical understanding and knowledge of the world without introducing and accepting the role of the subject. And hence I feel *space-time-subject* does provide the true and the real picture of nature and reality. As subject being a conscious element it has a singular function. When the four dimension world is subjectivised in the prism of subjective consciousness of an observer it becomes multidimensional world. Subject is definitely one of the most important and relevant fifth dimensions of the world and in the spectrum of this *space-time-subject* world becomes multidimensional.

Werner Heisenberg's formulation of uncertainty principle put limits on our ability to predict the future in terms of scientific laws. It follows from the principle of uncertainty that concept of determinism does not hold well. According to quantum theory even one quanta of light could disturb the structure of particles. According to this principle, there is an uncertainty in the position of particle times and uncertainty in velocity times. The concept of uncertainty of position and velocity of particles is the quintessential nature of atomic structure. The theory of uncertainty is fundamental principle on which the whole quantum mechanics has been founded. Heisenberg, Erwin Schrodinger and Neil Bohr are the founding fathers of this new and revolutionary scientific postulation of quantum physics. The application of uncertainty principle entails the dualism of waves and particles. The nature is explained in terms of either particles or waves from one perspective and from other's perspective it is a particle. This has been enunciated by Neil Bohr which is called concept of complementarity. Though Quantum theory has been very successful especially in the field of life science and creating the technological wonder in form of electronic device like television, computers etc. but it has failed in the large scale structure of universe. Quantum physics provides a new concept of reality. The classical physics was to great extent successful in providing a concept of reality which has been successful when applied to macroscopic level. In one of the root concepts of waves-particles dualism, when applied it does explain the microscopic mystery of atomic structure. According to this new scientific postulation of quantum mechanics in spite of all our knowledge and understanding the physical events cannot be predicted with certainty, because it is not deterministic in nature. The future course of nature according to quantum mechanics is basically uncertain and unpredictable.

Stephen Hawking writes, "Quantum physics might seem to undermine the idea that nature is governed by laws, but that is not the case. Instead it leads us to accept a new form of determinism: given the state of the system at some time, the laws of nature determine the probabilities of various futures and pasts rather than determining the future and past with certainty. Though that is distasteful to some, scientists must accept theories that agree with experiment, not their own preconceived notions."[23]

The refutation of Copenhagen interpretations led by Einstein is based on ontological spiritualism. There has been great debate between Einstein and Bohr, on the validity of Quantum mechanics. Bohr observes, "There is no Quantum World. There is only an abstract mechanical description. It is wrong to think that the task of physics is to find out how nature is. Physics concerns what we can say about." Einstein differing with Bohr based his assessment of Quantum Mechanics on his belief in the existence of a causal, observer-independent reality. Einstein observes, "What we call science has the sole purpose of determining what is." Einstein believed in the observer independent reality, whereas Bohr believes that Quantum Mechanics considers that there is no possibility of having knowledge of nature without getting it modified and tinged in the process of observation and experimentation. Manjit Kumar writes, "For Bohr the theory came first, then the philosophical position, the interpretation constructed to make sense of what the theory says about reality. Einstein knew that it was dangerous to build a philosophical worldview on the foundations of any scientific theory. If the theory is found wanting in the light of new experimental evidence, then the philosophical position it supports collapses with it."[24] Einstein reiterates, "It is basic for Physics that one assumes a real world existing independently from any act of perception." However, he admits but "This we do not Know"[25]. Einstein's refutation of Copenhagen's interpretation of Quantum Mechanics is based on his implicit faith in God that doesn't play dice with the world. However, Einstein does not reject the whole theory, only that it does not provide complete picture of physical reality at the Quantum level. However, Einstein accepts his profound ignorance about the world as it is. Science has its own limitation. It cannot comprehend the transcendental nature of reality.

The whole debate between Einstein and Bohr is about the kind of Physics that is acceptable as a theory which speaks of the nature of reality in its self. It does not provide a complete picture of reality. Einstein has been working throughout his life to provide a complete picture of worldview in form of unified theory. In the absence of proper understanding and knowledge of "reality as it is" which is beyond the reach of scientific rationalism, it is not possible to enunciate any philosophical or scientific doctrine to explain the reality in its totality and wholeness. In the ultimate analysis of the whole philosophical pursuits and scientific experiments and reflections divorced from ontological mysticism is incomplete. To my mind the ontological mysticism is only possibility to fulfil the dream of Einstein's formulation of unified theory. But a new discovery has postulated a theory which is called sting theory which claims that sting is the fundamental particles. However, this theory is also being questioned and a new concept known as M-theory which has been formulated by scientists like Stephen Hawking in his famous book '*The Grand Design*'. Hawking claims that this could fulfil the dream of Einstein and it could be considered as the theory of everything. To me M-theory as postulated by Hawking seems to be more of a scientific fiction than a scientific doctrine. Hawking does claim that this new theory would explain the problem of quantum gravity.

We shall examine, analyse and evaluate the veracity of whether it is a scientific fiction or a scientific doctrine. Heisenberg is honest and forthright in accepting that the experiments carried out about atomic structures but "the atoms or the elementary particles are not as real; they form a world of potentiality or possibilities rather than one of things or facts."[26] Einstein's dream of having unified theory of matter has become a deep concern for scientists of all hues. The unification of theory of relativity and quantum mechanics may provide a foundation for future scientific investigation and discovery. Hawking had postulated the theory of quantum gravity on the basis of the unification of the above two lines of scientific thinking, postulations and formulations. In spite of all the knowledge and development in the realm of mathematical formulations, the scientists do accept that we fail to provide an unambiguous behaviour of an electron in the interior of an atom. Heinrich Hertz (1857-1894) has formulated the limitation of scientific thinking and postulations in his introduction to the principles of mechanics published in 1876, states that natural science is one whose proposition on limited domains of nature can have only a corresponding limited validity; that science is not a philosophy developing a worldview of a nature as a whole or about the essence of things. The proposition of science does not have the task or the capability of unfolding the inherent essence of nature. The conclusion derived from our scientific investigation and observations does have any valid causal relationship on the basis of which we can make a prediction about the truth and veracity of scientific proposition. Science must be conscious about its own limitations otherwise it would make nonsensical assertions in the name of scientific truth and revelations. Eddington states that "We have found that where science has progressed the farthest, the mind has but regained from nature that which the mind has put into nature. We have found a strange footprint on the shores of the unknown. We have devised profound theories, one after the other; to account for its origin. At last, we have succeeded in reconstructing the creature that made the footprint. And Lo! It is our own." Heisenberg's formulation of scientific proposition speaks of his deep understanding and knowledge of not only physics but of philosophy too. His whole formulations and postulations of scientific propositions are a philosophical treatise dealing with the most profound philosophical issues and problems. He says, "The philosophical content of a science is only preserved and science is conscious of its limits. Great discoveries of the properties of individual phenomena are possible only if nature of the phenomena is of generalized *a priori.* Only by leaving open the question of the ultimate essence of a body, of matter, of energy etc., can physics reach an understanding of the individual properties of the phenomena that we designate by these concepts, an understanding which alone may lead us to real philosophical insight."

Heisenberg speaks about a third constant which would be able possibly to determine the masses and other properties of elementary particle. Scientists have engaged in determining the third hypothetical constant which would give an approximate accuracy about the function and nature of atomic interior structure and function of the atoms. Heisenberg does admit that this is for future research and investigation in the field of atomic physics. He writes, "But all these problems will be a matter of future research atomic physics. One may hope that the combined effort or experiments in the high energy region and of mathematical analysis will someday lead to a complete understanding of the unity of matter. The term "complete understanding" would mean that the forms of matter in the sense of Aristotelian philosophy would appear as results, as solutions of a closed mathematical scheme representing the natural laws for matter."[27] Before Edwin Hubble an American astronomer discovered with his advanced and sophisticated telescope on Mt. Wilson in California that universe was expanding.

There are lots of stars and galaxies and Milky Way in the terrestrial paradise of cosmos. The scientists believed that earth is static. Hubble discovered that the galaxies are moving with faster speed going beyond our solar system. This forced Einstein to reject his own postulation of cosmological constant because he believed in static universe. His postulation was based on the mutual attraction of all the matter which entails according to him the static universe. The concept of cosmological constant on the other hand speaks of a new anti-gravity force which is responsible for maintaining balance in the universe. Stephen Hawking believes that the Einstein's concept of cosmological constant is true and proper theory to explain the expansion of the nature of stars, galaxies and milky ways while maintaining the balance and equilibrium of the cosmos. Hawking writes, "He later disavowed the cosmological constant, calling this fudge factor his "greatest mistake". As we'll soon see, today we have reason to believe that he might have been right to introduce it after all. But what must have disappointed Einstein was that he had allowed his belief in a static universe to override what his theory seemed to be predicting: that the universe is expanding. Only one man, it seems was willing to take this prediction of General Relativity at face value. While Einstein and other physicists were looking for ways of avoiding general relativity's non-static universe, the Russian physicist and mathematician Alexander Friedmann instead set about explaining it."[28] Friedmann's formulation of universe was based on a very clear postulation that if the universe would have been static it would have looked same and identical from every direction. And he concluded that the universe was not static. This was much before the Edwin. Hubble's discovery of the expanding universe. The Friedmann's postulation that the universe looks same from different directions, it entails that the universe would look identical in all directions as looked from other galaxies also. However, there is some limiting factor in Friedmann's postulations which is the nature of all scientific postulations, and theories. The recent observations have proved that the different galaxies and stars movement are speeding up rather than it is slowing down. Hawking further writes, "no one is sure yet, but it could be an evidence that Einstein was right about the need for the cosmological constant (and in antigravity effects) after all."[29] In fact Einstein's theory of General Relativity entails the nature of expanding universe. However, he didn't believe that his theory of General Relativity speaks of the expanding universe because nobody before had any inkling about the expanding universe and this is why in 1930, he declared his biggest blunder while postulating the cosmological constant. Lisa Randall writes, "After Hubble's measurements, Einstein dispensed with the fudge he had made, calling it "his biggest blunder". This modification was not entirely erroneous, however. We will soon see that more recent measurements show that the cosmological constant term he added is actually necessary to account for recent observations—although the measured magnitude, which accounts for the recently established acceleration of its expansion, is about an order of magnitude bigger than the one Einstein proposed to merely stall it.

The expansion of the universe was a nice example of a convergence of top-down and bottom-up physics. Einstein's theory of gravity implies that the universe expands, yet only with the discovery of the expansion did physicists feel confident they were on the right track."[30] Planck laid down the foundation for quantum mechanics as stated earlier. If we go through the development of quantum mechanics then we find that it has been used first time in 1900 by Max Planck while explaining the black body radiation. However, its physical significance and importance in the scientific world was not very clear.

In 1905 it was the genius of Albert Einstein who examined, evaluated and clarified the Planck's theory in the background of understanding the nature of light. The nature of light has been explained in terms of both as a wave and a particle. In the scientific formulation a particle known as photon is considered massless, which has the speed of light 'c' and it is denoted by energy 'E' and it has been formulated that $E = h\nu$. When the scientist started examining the nature and the structure of a photon and it was considered that a photon has energy, it must be associated with momentum. In 1923 Louis de Broglie came out with a new concept that the electron which was considered as particles are waves. In Neil Bohr's concept of atomic structure electron orbiting is an integral multiple and the quantity denoted by letter 'h' which played a significant role in postulation of the modern quantum mechanics in which 'E', 'h' plays a significant role. Heisenberg's doctrine of uncertainty put limitation on the accuracy in explaining the structure of atom.

There is another enigmatic scientific concept known as *cosmological concept* which is being debated. And it is being discussed by almost all the modern scientific minds dealing with the pure physics and cosmology. It is now equated with dark energy which constitutes seventy two per cent of total energy. Quantum mechanics does accept the existence of cosmological constant with very high energy density. This energy density is so high that it does not come within the purview of scientific observation. And hence cosmological constant has become one of the greatest enigmas of physics. To examine and evaluate the scientific significance of cosmological constant is one of the greatest searches for understanding and ascertaining the veracity of this concept.

To my mind the cosmological constant that maintains the harmony and balance in the universe is the result of interaction between two aspects of the same Ultimate Reality known as cosmic consciousness (*Siva*) and cosmic matrix (*Sakti*). The cosmic consciousness and the cosmic matric are two facets of the same coin. They coeternally exist and it could not be separated from one another. The cosmic matrix may be in modern scientific terminology being able to be called as Cosmic Energy. In fact, the whole universe is the reflection of this ultimate reality (cosmic consciousness) which is called Paramsiva in Kashmir Saivism. Abhasavada of Kashmir Saivism provides both the scientific and philosophical explanation of origin and development of the universe in form of innumerable galaxies, milky ways, supernova, stars and other celestial bodies.

Quantum mechanics postulation of dark energy and the vacuum with no permanent particles present are the greatest enigma. It is present in a paradox that in the presence of density of dark matter and dark energy which are the source of origin and development of the universe is rooted in ontological mysticism. In the modern scientific world the concepts of dark matter and dark energy is posing a greatest problem in explaining the mystery of the universe. Scientists do accept that they are unable to provide and resolve this problem in the realm of scientific postulation, discovery and experiments. It has been accepted now that there are innumerable universe with multi-dimensional structure and functions.

Lisa Randall writes, "Why is there matter in the universe at all? Our equations treat matter and antimatter on the same footing. They annihilate when they find each other, and both disappear. Neither matter nor anti-matter should remain when the universe has cooled." [31] The existence of the asymmetry of matter and antimatter is another enigma for the scientists and the cosmologists.

According to Kashmir Saivism, Vedanta and Buddhism, there is existence of non-zero vacuum. The whole universe is pervaded by cosmic consciousness and its modification due to the activation of cosmic matrix energy. Ultimate reality is known as *Param Siva* or *Brahman* in Hinduism and Emptiness (*Sunyata*) in Buddhism and the *Tao* in Taoism.

This different terminologies used by Hinduism, Buddhism and Taoism speak of the same reality and truth. There is inherent limitation and difficulties in expressing and communicating the real and ultimate nature or reality. Even the common experiences of colour red and blue cannot express the true nature of what is in reality colour red or blue as has been postulated by Heisenberg. It is the domain of ontological mysticism as has been accepted by even Schrodinger and others. Scientists are facing this problem and showing their inability to resolve this mystery because their whole postulation is based on ontological materialism. Planck accepts that science cannot resolve the ultimate mystery of nature. And that is because, in the last analysis, we ourselves are part of nature and, therefore, part of the mystery that we are trying to solve. Twenty first century will usher a new era of spiritual renaissance. This renaissance would come in which mankind would discover the ethical and spiritual truth are highest truth and highest practicality and it would liberate mankind from the miserable obsession of the reality which is based on ontological materialism. The integration of multi-dimensional kaleidoscope in depth of nature of science with monastic and spiritualistic kaleidoscope is ontological mysticism. East is monastic and the West is theistic. East is mystical and the West is dualistic.

East is spirituality and West is science. Ontological mysticism is the happy and harmonious blending of the East and West and science and spirituality. Nature has not set any limit to the realization of human hopes and aspirations. Spirituality is a path of truth, virtue and *nirvana*. Science gives us knowledge, spirituality brings wisdom. In the state of spiritual sublimity we are face to face with truth and reality. Integrating and mediating between two planes of ratiocination and reflections given by science and spirituality would be greatest intellectual and moral adventure and most rewarding achievement of today. The impact of ontological materialism which has disastrous impact on our civilization is that it is far more developed materially than spiritually. With the scientific and technological advancement the forces of nature at our command in such an unprecedented way it has polluted the very civilization which was born out of love and compassion. We value material achievements and we do not keep in our mind the importance of ethical and spiritual values. Albert Schweitzer writes, "The essential nature of civilization does not lie in its material achievements but in the fact that individuals keep in mind the ideals of the perfecting of man, and the improvement of the social and political conditions of people, and of mankind as a whole. And that their habit of thoughts is determined in living and constant fashion by such ideals."[32]

The modern science has succeeded in revealing some of the mysteries of the nature and in course of their penetration deeper into the knowledge of natural harmony they have got a glimpse of awareness that there is harmony and order which rules the universe. And this harmony and order are beyond the realm of scientific ratiocination and experiments. This natural harmony and order is the result of the activation of some hidden reality which I consider as cosmic consciousness. However scientists do accept the existence of an *ontological order* which is beyond the reach. Prince Louis De Broglie considers that the truth is that humanity has been able to adapt itself to live in this world in which there is some isomorphic relation with our mind. If there would not have been so, perhaps humanity would not have been able to survive. He writes, "How remarkable is the harmony between the resources of which our mind disposes and the profound realities which conceal themselves behind natural appearances. To bring this harmony more completely into the light, to glimpse yet more the ontological order of which Duhem spoke—such appears to be the true mission of pure science. Removed from all utilitarian preoccupation, solely devoted to the search for truth, it appears to us as one of the noblest activities of which we are capable.

By the wholly ideal nature of the goal it pursues, by the intensity and the disinterested character of the efforts that it demands, it possesses a moral value which cannot be denied."[33] I am in complete agreement with the observation of Schrodinger, "Briefly stated, it is the view that all of us living beings belong together inasmuch as we are all in reality sides or aspects of one single being which may perhaps in Western terminology be called God while in the Upanishads its name is Brahman. A comparison used in Hinduism is of the many almost identical images which a many-faceted diamond makes of some *one* object such as the sun. We have already conceded that we are here dealing not with something logically deducible but with mystical metaphysics—just like the acceptance of a real object—world (usually called an external world, but it includes one's own bode)."[34]

For proper understanding and comprehension of reality one will have to equip himself with proper frame of mind, cultivated by mystical and moral discipline of non-attachment, discrimination and the longing for the realization of truth in its wholeness. Without proper understanding and study of philosophy and science in a dilettante fashion will land him in confusion and contradiction. The path of spirituality and ontological mysticism is like walking on the razor's edge. The Upanishadic seers have rightly stated "Arise, awake, and learn by approaching the excellent ones. The wise ones describe that path to be impassable as a razor's edge, which when sharpened, is difficult to tread on."[35]

From the ontological mystical perspective ultimate reality is non-dual and homogenous being and existence. It is cosmic consciousness. From the conventional point of view reality is multi-dimensional and from the transcendental perspective. It is *Advaitam* (non-dual). The cosmic consciousness is neither singular nor plural. It is *Advaitam.* It cannot be expressed in any linguistic formulations. There is only one consciousness. The world and the reality are constituted of this cosmic consciousness. It is beyond the reach of both philosophy and science. Neither exact science is really possible nor can any philosophical knowledge comprehend the nature of reality. It is mystical and metaphysical.

Notes

1. *Tractatus* 4.021
2. *Ibid.,* 5.61
3. *Ibid.,* 5.62
4. *Ibid.,* 6.522
5. Stephen Hawking & Leonard Mlodinow, *The Grand Design,* Bantam Press, London, 2010.

6. Ervin Schrodinger. *My View of the World,* Ox Bow Press, Woodbridge, Connecticut. 1983, p. 40.
7. *Washington Post*, 25th September, 2011. *Faster than Light: Revolution or error.* Particles burst Einstein's Speed Limit by Brian Vastag.
8. Marquis De Laplace. *A Philosophical Essay on Probabilities,* Dover Publications, Inc., New York, 1951, pp. 1-2.
9. A.J. Ayer. *Language, Truth and Logic,* London, Victor Gallanez Ltd. 1936, p. 248.
10. Werner Heisenberg. *Physics and Philosophy, The Revolution in Modern Science,* Harper Perennial Modernthought Publishers, New York. 2002, p. XIII.
11. Galileo, 1632. *Science and Religion: Opposing Viewpoints,* ed. Janelle Rohr, Greenhaven Press, 1988, p. 21.
12. Marquis De Laplace. *A Philosophical Essay on Probabilities,* Dover Publications, Inc. New York, 1951, p. 195.
13. Stephen Hawking & Leonard Mlodinow. *A Briefer History of Time,* Bantam Press, London. 2010, p. 18.
14. Werner Heisenberg. *Physics and Philosophy, The Revolution in Modern Science,* Harper Perennial Modernthought Publishers, New York. 2002, p. 46.
15. Werner Heisenberg. *Physics and Philosophy, The Revolution in Modern Science,* p. 6.
16. *Ibid.,* p. 59.
17. *Ibid.,* p. 136.
18. *Ibid.,* pp. 24-25.
19. *Ibid.,* p. 26.
20. *Ibid.,* p. 27.
21. *Ibid.,* pp. 31-32.
22. *Ibid.,* p. 32.
23. Stephen Hawking & Leonard Mlodinow. *The Grand Design,* Bantam Press, London, 2010, p. 72.
24. Manjit Kumar, *Quantum, Einstein,* Bohr and *the Great Debate About the Nature of Reality.* Hachette UK Company, 2008, p. 320.
25. *Ibid.,* p. 320.
26. *Ibid.,* p. 160.
27. *Ibid.,* p. 140.
28. Stephen Hawking & Leonard Mlodinow. *A Briefer History of Time,* Bantam Press, London. 2010, pp. 58-59.
29. *Ibid.,* pp. 66-67.
30. Lisa Randall. *Knocking on Heavens Door,* Harper Colin Publishers, p. 355.
31. *Ibid.,* pp. 375-376.
32. Albert Schweitzer. *Philosophy and Ethics, The Philosophy of Civilization,* A & C Black Ltd., 4, 526 Soho Square, London, W. 1, 1929, pp. 2-3.
33. *Quantum Questions, Mystical writings of the World's Greatest Physicists,* p. 123.

34. Erwin Schrodinger, *My View of the World,* p. 95.
35. *Katha Upanisad I. Hi.* 15, Verse 14.

7
Some Modern Critiques and the Indian Archetypal Evidence

The history of man and his civilization is, in a sense, a history of the concept of man. Much of the modern critique and challenge—from anthropology, biology, psychoanalysis, Marxism, phenomenology, existentialism and science—do not really apply to the perennial tradition or the eastern context, but a brief mention of these positions is called for. In my short survey, I shall try to show that the modern critique notwithstanding, the basic insights of Indian Culture—theistic as well as non-theistic—have still a part to play.

Anthropologists suggest a three-way paradigm, i.e. (i) individuals, (ii) culture, and (iii) situations, to explain the complex human behaviour. As C. Kluckhohn says, "Culture does not 'behave', only individual behaves. Concretely, the influence of Culture is always and everywhere mediated by specifiable individuals."[1] A psycho-spiritual process of *development* in which man's behaviour is reflected and manifested, is as if the basic pattern of culture. It must be reflected in the internal structure of each individual person, as if the individual was in some sense a microcosm and the culture to which he belongs a macrocosm. Each individual, like the Leibnizian monad, "reflects" the culture of his world from his own point of view and with varying degree of clearness and confusion.[2] Ruth Benedict's *Patterns of Culture* introduced a new methodology. According to her the psychological coherence of the individual personality is isomorphic with the psychological coherence of the culture.

Sooner or later one comes up against the imponderable questions of human essence and manifestation. Is man by nature divine, amoral, or evil? Is he free or determined? These are more fundamental issues than merely determining whether men are classic or romantic, mystic or Marxist, conservative or liberal, and behaviourist or existentialist, idealist or realist. For most people, there is nothing to speculate. Life is factual, objective and patent. There is no concept of man or the subjectivity of consciousness. For them Nietzsche's assertion that life is determined by one's perspective hardly carries any meaning. But, there is no existence free from conflict and contradiction. Existence, from existential agony, is antithesis of Buddha, Marx, Freud and Nietzsche. As James E. Royce says, "Perhaps the biggest problem here is the matter of perspective, the point from which we view man. In the micro-universe of sub-atomic particles, the organized bundle of molecules we know as man is a giant. In the macro-universe of galaxies beyond our Milky Way, man is tinier than an amoeba in our solar system."[3] Man is an enigma which few can understand and fewer resolve. However, everybody who is interested in exploring the hidden depths of human nature and looking for the meaning of life has had to confront and speculate on such metaphysical problem. At any rate, man is not an arithmetical constant. He exists in inverse proportion to his problem. Man's existence is sociological, but his being is philosophical. Man is not a machine; he is an evolving being.

Social scientists consider biological heredity, situation and culture as general categories for understanding human behaviour. Each category is an aid but no category in itself is sufficient to explain the complex phenomenon of human nature and behaviour. The concept of the total man is wanting in our sciences, knowing more and more about less and less.

Man is more than a biological organism. Of course, certain biological heredity of *Homo sapiens* determines some of the parameters of human behaviour. A person with gene for juvenile amaurotic idiocy will behave in similar ways in whatever physical environment and social interactive situation he is placed. Yet man does not behave simply as a biological organism. His response to stimuli and situation is not wholly mechanical. Culture plays an important role in shaping human response to stimulus. "Actually, when we look at any complex assemblage of events it is clear that culture (the precipitate of history, situation, and the idiosyncracies of individuals determined, in turn, by unique combination of biological, experiential, and cultural influences) are intricately intertwined."[4] The study of Balinese by Margaret Mead and

F.C. Macgregor has shown that even the motor habits can be culturally patterned. We see things not as they are but as we are. Childe has shown how Babylonian conception of space is as different from Euclidean as the latter is from Riemannian; at a higher level too he has shown that there is absence of the principles of identity, non-contradiction, and causality of the Kantian type in the ancient thought of Egyptians and Sumerians. "Human minds are not...mass produced machines into which uniform experience has only to be fed for them to turn out uniform thoughts."[5] Recent study and researches have suggested the inadequacy of simple biological analogy of "organism and environment" in explaining human behaviour. Pan-determinism is passe.

According to Szasz and Laing, mental illness is a myth. According to these applied-behaviour analysts, to diagnose some one as schizophrenic is useless and often harmful. We must believe that situation and social interaction determine human behaviour. If anybody behaves abnormally or exhibits "deviant" behaviour it is the society that is responsible and not the individual. Now Skinner has become the talk of the day. He wants as well as claims to control human behaviour and to create a model man and new Utopia. In his engineered society there is no place for dignity or freedom. For him and others of his persuasion freedom is a myth. He says, "As man *qua* man, we readily say good riddance." Obviously, such a view poses a serious problem to the traditional values and norms. His "operant conditioning" is no doubt an achievement. But is environment the only factor which determines human behaviour? Skinner has himself said that "a person's behaviour is determined by a genetic endowment traceable to the evolutionary history of the species and by the environmental circumstances to which an individual has been exposed." Here there is precisely agreement amongst the psychologists. The further study of man and society takes up to the world where two principles are working: (i) the principle of conflict, and (ii) the principle of co-operation and harmony. Freud, Marx and Darwin are the advocates of the principle of conflict. According to Freud, man is against himself. Eros (Love-Sex) and Thanatos (Destruction-Aggression) are universal, hereditary and fixed. These instincts are based on maturation and not acquired by learning. Eros and Thanatos taken together are called Libido, which is considered to be the life-force. According to Freud conflict is like an *a priori* category of human existence and there is no escape from it. Hence, man is against him. Like sex, war is inherent in human nature. Darwin too is an exponent of the principle of conflict, red in tooth and claw. According to him, one species is against the other and survival goes to the fittest.

Freud says that desire or pleasure is basic to man. He writes, "Our entire psychical activity is bent upon procuring pleasure and avoiding pain, is automatically regulated by the pleasure principle."[6] But the conscious self which is governed by the principle of reality adjustment is always in conflict with the pleasure principle. Neurosis, dream and other hallucinatory satisfactions such as fantasy and Utopian thinking are substitutes for the pleasure-principle denied by reality, hence repression.[7] In this view, as Norman O. Brown has pointed out, Neurosis is the name of civilization and culture.[8] Freud simply reaffirms the view of Nietzsche about "disease called man". But, he is distinguished from the animal not simply because he is in possession of a supra-biological apparatus known as culture but because of his desire to change culture so that he can change himself. Gorden Childe rightly says that in making history "man makes himself".

But the problem is not solved here. The important question is whether and really man makes himself or unmakes himself in process of making history. Freud's view of universal neurosis of mankind which is rooted in Oedipus Complex may not be palatable for many but it is his most original and revolutionary contribution, even if it is an analogue of the theological doctrine of original sin.[9] Marxism points a different picture of man. According to Marx, history of man is history of class struggle. As against Hegel's doctrine in which man is regarded as a subjective spirit, Man believes in a concrete man. "In direct contradistinction to German philosophy, which descended from heaven to earth", Marx and Engles wrote "we here rise from earth to heaven, i.e. we start out not from what people say, imagine, picture to themselves; nor do we start out from imagining people, who exist only in words, in order to go from them to real people; for us the starting point is really active people, and from their real, vital process we also deduce the development of ideological reflections and the echoes of this vital process."[10]

Against the principle of conflict, universally acknowledged, we have, however, the principle of co-operation of harmony. In the process of evolution man finds and identifies himself with a higher consciousness. *Homo religious* represents the "total man".[11] It does not deny the other aspects, but fuses them into a higher whole. To understand the concept of man, more than psychology, anthropology, sociology and biology philosophical anthropology is required.[12] The phenomenological approach to religion helps us understand the meaning of the religious data and historical approach is an attempt to unfold the meaning of the religious data which have been "lived" and "experienced" by man in various moments of history in different cultures and civilizations. It throws light on the origin and growth of different civilizations in terms of time and space dimensions of those "lived" and "experienced" religious myths and symbols which have enriched, transformed or impoverished the human race. Eliade calls "this history of religious meaning" as "the history of the human race".[13] For the sane and sensitive thinker the evidence is convincing.

The theory and thesis propounded by Darwin, Marx, Freud, Skinner and company are original, profound and (if you like) revolutionary but they are not wholly acceptable, not the last word. Their criticism and outright rejection of the spirit in man is justified neither by scientific evidence nor sociological researches. Sri Aurobindo, Lecomte Du Novy, Kropotkin and Mircea Eliade have come out with a brighter thesis and new hope for mankind. Kropotkin's "Mutual Aid" is a classic reply to the school of the "survival of the fittest"! Contradicting the evolutionary thesis of Darwin and Lamarck, Lecomte Du Novy argues that when "the fittest" is forced to face a change in environment or driven out of it as a result of some geological or climatic convulsion, finds out itself under such conditions the characters which assured it a superiority, become useless, troublesome, and even harmful.[14] Du Novy gives a vivid picture of evolution and he comes to the conclusion that the future of human society depends upon the further conscious evolution of man.

It is interesting that in the evaluative sense, death is the greatest invention of nature. The asexual cell does not know death. What in the sudden appearance of sexual regeneration a revolution in the process of evolution heralded is the school of a totally new cycle of birth and death. According to Novy up to the advent of conscience man differs from animal morphologically but with the advent of conscience evolution witnessed the birth of a new species of the religious man.

Self-identification, original ideas and convictions are the categories which differentiate man from machine. The computer is amazing, inevitable, but we cannot enter into any dialogue with it as with another man because it lacks the self-actualizing quality with which man is endowed. James E. Royce says, "we may anthropomorphically attribute loyalty, excitement, perfectionism, and other reactions to computer but we have no evidence that it actually experiences such emotions or has any sense of value. Quite the contrary, we know that it reacts only in accordance with the way we built it. Man's spirit shows a contrasting independence of what others may try to make him. He is an individual, not a product. His creativity and appreciation of beauty far transcends the artificial poetry or music a computer might crank out. Most important, he had a sense of his own dignity and responsibility, his historical roots and immortal dignity, which no machine can experience because it has neither these to know nor the means of knowing them."[15] Thus though Skinner's pigeons may play ping pong and his rats press the right levers to get their food, we have reason to believe that the process of evolution has not ended with ping pong and the levers. There are miles to go. In the words of Jaspers, "Man is mind, and the situation of man as man is a mental situation."[16] Today's existential crisis is due partly to the fact that man exists but he is not living. Crisis is due to the conflict between existence and being. The crisis can be resolved and an answer and alternative to Darwin, Marx, Freud and Skinner can be found in the higher religions re-interpreted. Here is the task for the religious thinker.

The criticism of Marx and Freud may be valid in relation to Christian theology but hardly with regard to Hindu philosophy and religion. If Christian theology and Western capitalism are the thesis, Marxism is its anti-thesis and what we need is a new synthesis, a reformulation in terms of a new religion of man. What is the Indian evidence? The Freudian concept of pleasure-principle is not new in the Hindu culture and life style. *Kāma* (sex) is one of the four *Puruṣarthas* of man according to Hinduism and the very basis of *Dharma* is happiness. The difference between Hinduism and Freud is that the Freudian concept is confined to sensuous pleasure. The Hindu concept of happiness points to eternal bliss *Ananda,* a synonym of Brahman, the supreme godhead. This may be related to the discovery of the grand equation of *Tattvamasi.* (Thou art that). There is a sublimation beyond the reach of Freud.

It is sometimes said that the Hindu view of life-style is puritanical. Nothing can be further from the truth. The *Tantra* for instance considers sex as a primal force. Sex in itself is or can be an amoral act. In a socio-cultural context it may become moral or immoral. Again, it depends upon the perspective and the nature of the person. In *Tantra* the same sexual act when performed with spiritual discipline becomes sacramental. Behind its many aberrations, the modern world is perhaps moving towards this aim and realization. According to *Tantra*, as well as other Indian *sadhanas* and philosophy, man is a divine being. He is a cosmic being. He is a Śiva. Man, universal self *(atman),* is possessed of five powers—*Cit*, *Ānanda*, *Iccha*, *Jñāna* and *Kriya*. Due to the limitation and obscuration of *Maya*, the self becomes a victim of *Svarupakhyāti.*

Due to *Mala* (impurities) and *Kancukas* (sheaths) the knowledge and the power of the self (*Jiva*) get limited. The bondage of individualization *(anavika mala)* and, the fetter of *Maya (mayika mala)* obscure and limit the transcendental character of the self. *Kāla, Vidyā, Rāga,* and *Niyati* are known as the five *Kancukas*. These five principles obscure the interest, knowledge, power, space and time. *Kāla* produces the limitation of time and makes the individual mortal. *Niyati* snatches the freedom, the will to do everything and anything. *Rāga* creates a sense of attachment to the mundane objects. *Kāla* limits the omnipotent powers of self and reduces the power of man to doing only a few things. The transcendence, omniscience and omnipotence of the self are circumscribed by *Mala* in purities and the *Kancukas* (sheaths) and the self is reduced to but a little "doer" and "knower". The religious philosophical and esoteric practices of *Tantra* are directed against the removal of the unreal character of the self *(Svarupakhyāti)* and the restoration of his original spiritual consciousness. The *Tantric* and *Yogic* practices are religious and sacred acts because they lead man from mundane existence to spiritual reality. *Tantra* combines *Yoga* with *Bhoga* (enjoyment). *Tantra Sādhanā* is based on the cardinal principle that the Absolute is to be realized in and through the human body. Everyman is a potential divine. *Sādhanā* awakens his dormant divinity with the clear assurance that the truth which is realized within it is the same truth as pervades the whole universe. The concepts of *Bodhisattva, Tattvamasi* and *Purnahantā* are the cornerstones of Indian culture and phenomenology. The concepts are part of living experience and are still not on the wayout. Here alone is a hope for man. In this age of science and technology, we are in search of our identity and destiny, in search of what Tillich calls the New Being.

There is no need to pooh-pooh the triumphs of science, its methods or its findings. But in the end its image of man has not been a success. Contemporary history shows that mankind is reaching almost the journey's end, the triumph of death-in-life. History has brought us to that point of no return where a total abolition of man has become at last a practical, if not immediate possibility. For a true and lasting peace, as Toynbee has suggested, religious revaluation is a *sine qua non*. For this religion itself will no doubt have to undergo profound changes. We cannot discuss the details of the adjustment here and now. All that we can say is that the opposition between self and civilization, class and class, nation and nation, science and spirituality may not be the last word. In the new order to which we look forward we have to get rid of the mutual rejections—the naturalist thinker's denial of religion and religion's denial of the world. In spite of their apparent differences, Vedanta, Tantra, Yoga, Buddhism and Vaishnavism bring the same evidence, an evidence with which the latest tendencies in the science seem to agree. Looking back, we can echo the insights of the Indian thinker; "Indian culture recoginzes the spirit as the truth of our being and our life as a growth and evolution of the spirit. The rhythmic lines of this culture have already passed through two complete external stages—the early Vedic and the Purana-Tantric—while a third has taken its initial step and is the destiny of her future."[17] While we live forward we understand backward.[18]

Notes

1. Kluckhohn, *Handbook of Social Psychology,* Vol. II (Culture and Behaviour), p. 924.
2. *Ibid.,* Grace do Leguna.
3. *Man and Meaning,* p. 21.
4. Kluckhohn, *Handbook of Social Psychology,* Vol. II, p. 922.
5. V.G. Childe, *Social Worlds of Knowledge,* In Hobhouse Memorial Lectures 1941-1950 p. 18, London: Oxford University Press, 1952.
6. J. Riviere and J. Struchey (ed.), *Collected Papers,* Vol. V, p. 339.
7. *A General Introduction to Psycho-Analysis,* Tr. J. Riviere, p. 27, 310.
8. *Life Against Death,* pp. 3-10.
9. *Life Against Death,* p. 6.
10. K. Marx and F. Engels, *Works,* Vol. III, p. 25.
11. Mircea Eliade, *The Quest,* p. 8.
12. Eliade and Kitagawa (ed.), *The Supreme Being: Phenomenological Structure and Historical Development in History of Religion,* p. 66.
13. *The Quest,* p. 8.
14. *Human Destiny,* p. 71.
15. *Man and Meaning,* p. 290.
16. *Man in the Modern Age,* p. 11.
17. Sri Aurobindo, *Foundations of Indian Culture.*
18. Kierkegaard.

8
Some Reflections on Truth, Consciousness and *Samadhi*

I propose to speak today why truth, consciousness and *Samadhi* have been the core of Indian philosophy, how each is correlated to the other and why they have fascinated our saint-philosophers. Let us first understand what truth or *Satya* is all about. *Satya* embodies *Chitta* and *Anand*, i.e. consciousness and bliss. In other words, it is a state of spiritual sublimity and enlightenment. While pursuing *Satya*, our seers discovered the transcendental nature of being, which lit the path for them to lay down the philosophical foundation of Hinduism, defined also as *Dharma* traditions.

According to the *Dharma* or *Dhamma* tradition, the only truth of being is cosmic consciousness which our ancient philosophers refer as *Brahman* or *Atman* and *Bodhi Chitta*. *Brahman* is undifferentiated and undivided consciousness of bliss, enlightenment and realization of self, as the only reality. It can be experienced in salvation where one feels nothing but Cosmic Consciousness (*Brahman*). The *Ashtavakra Samhita* explains that because self is pure consciousness and a witnessing entity, it could survive the pillage of time and plunder of history and helped our subliminal seers provide a sound spiritual and moral foundation of India's culture and civilization.[1] Endorsing it, Mircea Eliade, the Romanian Indologist, writes that, "The great discoveries of Indian thought will in the end be recognized, despite the philosophic jargon they are expressed in. It is impossible, for example, to disregard that consciousness freed from its psychological structures and temporal conditioning is subliminal reality and that the liberated man possessed with such consciousness is someone who has succeeded in emancipating himself from temporality and who knows the true, inexpressible freedom. The conquest of this absolute freedom has been the goal of all Indian philosophies and is realized through various mystical techniques, Yoga being one of them. It may have many forms but it substantially helps in achieving the ultimate reality of consciousness."[2] Let me dwell a bit more on the concept of Cosmic Consciousness (*Brahman*). No reality or truth exits apart from Consciousness. It undergoes no change or transformation as the world evolves. Its transcendentality is supreme and all pervasive. The world is simply its expression. The philosophers and commentators of the *Śruti*, however, view this narrative differently. They argue that there are difference—(*Bhed*)—between Brahman and the world. The world, they maintain, is a higher entity of which Brahman is only a transcendental manifestation.

This difference is a grave error of scholastic judgement. Madhav rightly observes that the mention of *Bhed* and *Abhed* negates the very philosophical fundamentals of ultimate truth of being, which we know as Cosmic Consciousness (*Brahman*). These differences also find no place in Vedas in which Brahman is accepted as the ultimate reality. For Madhav, every act that affects the cosmos, derives from Brahman which he perceives as the supreme orchestrater of events around individuals. It is an Advait concept, that is complete and paramount in its nature and form. He further points out that the belief that individuals determine the course of our reactions and achievements is sheer illusion. It is actually *Brahman* that shapes the substance and substratum of our whole existence. For this reason, Madhav finds Sankara's *Mayavada* as unacceptable and a rejection of moral and philosophical principles, amounting to Nihilism.

In understanding world vis-à-vis *Brahman*, it is important we refresh ourselves with the teachings of *Astavakra Samhita*, *Avadhuta Gita* and *Nirvana Sataka*. These three classical works illustrate the essence of Vedanta. The greatest challenge before the *Advaita Vedanta* had been to provide a rational and spiritual exposition of the existence of world. It had also been a quest for scientists and philosophers, since ages, to find out what should constitute absolute reality to satisfy the scrutiny of their respective scientific and philosophical tempers. *Advaita Vedanta* has no ambiguity about it and does not admit any kind of reality or truth apart from *Brahman*. However, for the sake of practical convenience it propounds three kinds of truth, i.e. *Paramarthika, Vyavaharika* and *Pratibhasika*. *Brahman* is *Paramarthika satya*, world is *Vyavaharika satya* because it defines the objective aspect of the world and *pratibhasika Satya* relates to those who are wrapped in the bondage of ignorance but perceive their existence as truth. To sum it up, *Vyavaharika Satya* of the world is the cumulative illusions of believers in *pratibhasika Satya.*

The Advaita Vedanta's basic thrust is to falsify anything that presents an alternative to cosmic consciousness. For it, *Brahman* that defines cosmic consciousness, alone is real whereas the world is appearance and its *Jivas* are conventional reality. The illusion about truth exists when individuals erroneously identify self with non-self that is still bonded to ignorance. This bondage is neither of ideas nor of metaphysics. As the skeptics slowly step out of their psychological handicaps and rational limitations and begin freeing themselves from non-self, they experience the real nature of self and realize that *Brahman* is the only ultimate reality. *Astavakra Samhita* elucidates this crisply in these words. "I am neither in bondage nor I have freedom. Having lost both, my illusion has ceased. Oh! the universe that I thought was existing in me, does not exist but exit in reality."[3]

Avadhuta Gita echoes the same views. It concedes that, "All truth is about accepting the absolute self. Distinction and non-distinction between *Brahman* and self are irrelevant. How can I say, it exists, when it does not exist. The essence of Vedanta lies in the knowledge that *Brahman* by nature, is formless and an all pervasive Self."[4]

The Advaita Vedanta also rejects a world that is viewed in terms of sense and intellect, that is embedded in the philosophy of dualism and does not have any logical or ontological justification. All philosophical attempts to give a rational justification of ontological materialism are more likely to end in rejection of all religious and moral principles in the belief that life is meaningless. Logic or rationality has limitations and it cannot offer a complete comprehension of the ultimate reality which is *Brahman* or the Self. However, Vedanta does not ignore the rational or philosophical pursuit. In fact, it supplements the understanding acquired by the intuitional science that does not go disagree with the fundamental rational approach to Self by science or philosophy. Coming to *Samadhi*, it may be pertinent to first explain the philosophical phenomenon of God. It is generally believed that under the Vedantic and the mystical devotional school, the concept of God was introduced in Yoga system to attain *Samadhi*.

This is not entirely valid. Yoga is also practiced in different other systems without God becoming a necessity for the attainment of *Samadhi*. Buddha and his contemporaries and *Tirthankaras* of Jain systems attained *Nirvana* or *Kaivalya* respectively without help of God.

The controversy of God in the context of *Samadhi* was actually created by Patanjali. As Mircea Elliade explains, "Patanjali had to introduce *Isvara* into Yoga on an experimental basis. Yogis appealed to God as a starting point to move towards *Samadhi* although this could have been obtained by simply following the techniques of Yoga."

As explained earlier, cosmos and the Self or the cosmic consciousness is the only reality. In fact, this in itself is a form of meditation and can be realized by practicing *Dhyana*. *Tripura Rahasya* mentions, "That the oneness of the Self is the same as identification of the transcendence over all diversities of the world, known to individuals. This identification destroys the root of ignorance, instantly and completely. *Dhyana* signifies many sides of consciousness whereas *nirvikalpa* signifies its unitary nature. When mind does not create any picture due to crowding of thoughts, it is in an unmodified state, primal and pure. *Dhyana* is like pictures on a wall. Even if they are erased, the original wall, i.e. cosmic consciousness still remains. No other work is necessary to restore the wall's original condition."[5]

According to Patanjali's *Yoga Sutra*, there are two kinds of *Samadhi*—*Sampranjnata Samadhi* (*Savikalpa Samadhi*) and *Asamprajnata Samadhi* (*Nirvikalpa Samadhi*). *Sampranjnata Samadhi* consists of five stages that lead to final and ultimate realization of the Self. These are *Salokya, Samipya, Saujya, Sarupya* and *Sasti*. In *Salokya*, Yogin feels that he is on the course to reach the cosmic consciousness. In the second stage, he experiences *Samipya*, i.e. closeness to the ultimate reality. In *Saujya*, he realizes that the Self and *Brahman* are the same.

Visistha Advaitavada of Ramanujam believes that *Saujya* is the ultimate goal of life, based on devotion. By referring to devotion, he brings out the difference between the devotee and God and hints at the existence of dualism.

Sarupya, the forth stage, is almost the same as *Saujya*. It is only in the last stage of *Sasti*, that yogin finally realizes that he is both God and *Brahman*, though not completely merged in the cosmic consciousness.

Patanjali also explains *Sampranjnata Samadhi* in terms of *Vitarka*, *Vicara*, *Ananda* and *Asmita*. According to Vijnanbhiksu, these terms are purely technical and they are mentioned to define different forms of realization. They can be called *Samapattis* (coalescence) in which various elements merge together or *Beeja Samadhi* as they retain in themselves future manifestation of the metempsychosis and the full potential of the *karma* in the seed form. Explaining the state of seedless *Samadhi* in the last verse of Chapter I, Patanjali mentions that, "In this state, impressions of mind are wiped out and seeds of all thought, attachment, craving and desires are burnt. It is a state of unqualified, unequivocal unification of *Atman* and *Brahman* wherein there is no trace of any vestige of duality but have only illumination and eternal bliss. It is a state in which yogin is fully awake, but he is free from all *vrittis* or tendencies. He may possess the physical body but remains united with *Brahman* and lives in the world of infinity and transcendence. He may be conscious, but he retains his godliness, realizing that his real Self is only being *Brahman* and everything else is a manifestation of the same reality." Patanjali claims that in the *Sampranjnata Samadhi,* yogin acquires the faculty of absolute knowledge (*Ritambharaprajna*) by meditation that he is the Self and not body. This state is called *Dharma Megha Samadhi*.

However, in *Asamprajnata Samadhi* (*Nirvikalpa Samadhi*) there is no trace of individuality. Ramakrishna Paramhansa succinctly explains this phenomenon by using metaphor of a doll of salt. He says that when a doll of salt goes to fathom the depth and the sublimity of the ocean, it gets dissolved the moment it enters into the ocean. That state of the doll is like the state of *Asamprajnata Samadhi* in which there is no knower and no knowledge that is unknown. It is actually the final state of self-realization, a state when mind gets transformed into *Atman* (cosmic consciousness).

Nirvikalpa Samadhi also has two stages for Yogini to realize his Self. These are *Sabija Nirvikalpa* and *Nirbija Nirvikalpa*. There are instances when after attaining *Nirvikalpa Samadhi*, some Yogis take a vow to retain their physical body to serve the suffering humanity and help each and every *Jiva* obtain his final release from the fetters of ignorance though still retaining their *Satvika* metempsychosis. In Buddhism, such Yogis are called Bodhisattvas while others describe them as *Paramahamsa*.

The living example of this kind of great yogis are Swami Ramakrishna and Raman Maharsi. Ramakrishna Paramahansa attained *Nirvikalpa Samadhi* after receiving initiation from his *guru* Totapuri. Totapuri was surprised to notice that Ramakrishna had attained *Nirvikalpa Samadhi* immediately after getting initiated into a kind of *Dhyan Yoga* that he had mastered. However, even after attaining *Nirvikalpa Samadhi,* Ramakrishna Paramahansa retained his physical body to serve humanity by awakening the dormant spirituality in men and women. Both Ramakrishna and Ramana Maharsi, however, remained throughout inwardly in the state of *Samadhi*. Such Yogis are referred to as *Videhamukta*. Rajarishi Janak, foster father of Sita, is also known as *Videhamukta*.

When a yogin like Swami Ramakrishna Parmahansa enters into *Nirvikalpa Samadhi,* his *Atma* or *Sutratma* may be connected to his physical body with the thread of his consciousness but he remains *Jivanmukta* and completely liberated in life. He lives neither in time nor in history. Patanjali defines this state of yogin as pristinely pure. Agreeing with this exposition, Mircea Elliade writes, "The Yogin, through *Samadhi*, transcends opposites and in a unique manner, unites emptiness and superabundance, life and death and being and non-being. Like all paradoxical situations, *Samadhi* is equivalent to a reintegration of different modalities of the real in a single modality — the undifferentiated completeness of pre-creation and the primordial Unity. The Yogin who attains *Asamprajnata Samadhi* realizes a dream that has obsessed the human spirit from the beginning of its history to coincide with all, to recover unity, re-establish the initial non-duality and to abolish time and creation. The dream is also about attaining the multiplicity and heterogeneity of the cosmos and abolishing the two fold division of the real into object and subject".

For Samadhi, Yoga is both critical and integral. Yoga is a branch of *Tantra Shastra*. Its central objective is to awaken the dormant divinity which is known as *Kundalini*. With the awakening of the *Kundalini* and the piercing of the different *chakras* (*Padmas*), yogi attains extraordinary psychic power which is known as occultism. In this process, he also becomes conscious of the cosmic vision and its power. Yoga is a powerful technique that helps him attain salvation. Swami Vivekanand writes, "During internal meditation, when the vast mass of energy stored up inside, travels along the *Susumna* and strikes at the nerve centre, the reaction is tremendous, immensely superior to the reaction of dream or imagination and more intense than the perception of senses. And when it reaches the crescendo, all sensations in the brain react and the result is full blaze of illumination which is the real face of the Self. As the Kundalini force travels from centre to centre, layer after layer, the mind opens up and the Yogi is able to perceive universe in its finest form."[6]

In the Yoga system, *Dharana, Dhyana* and *Samadhi* are known as *samyama*. After practicing *samyama,* Yogi acquires *Siddhi*. It is a miraculous power that enables Yogi to realize his true nature and his being. Vivekanand writes, "Wherever there is a manifestation of what is ordinarily called supernatural power or wisdom, it can be is reasonably assumed that a little current of *kundalini* has found its way into the *Susumna*. In the majority of cases, people ignorantly stumble on one or the other practices that sets free a tiny portion of the coiled up *Kundalini* inside them to experience their self. In fact, all forms of wsorships consciously or unconsciously lead to this end."

Samadhi is an inevitable outcome of meditation, when mind becomes objectless. The property of mind is to remain always with some object. But when mind becomes objectless with long practice of meditation, it loses its properties and with it, ceases to exist and then gets transformed into consciousness. This transformation of mind into consciousness (*Atman*) is called salvation. Salvation or *Samadhi* is nothing but establishing oneself in his own true nature.

Siddhi is the closest step towards salvation. Chapter III, Verse 16 to Verse 56 (*Bibhutipada* of *Patanjali Yoga Sutra*) deals with different kinds of *Siddhi*.

Verse 51 deals with giving up all the occult powers and Yogi becoming free from all evils and attaining *kaivalya*. This is called burning of seeds of all wrong doings. When Yogi rids himself from feelings and ideas of omnipotence and omniscience, he rejects all kinds of temptations and pleasures emanating even from celestial beings. When Buddha was practicing meditation under the Bodhi tree, different celestial beings known as *mara* tried to allure Him by offering different kinds of *Siddhi*, but He did not pay any attention to their allurements until He attained supreme knowledge and became Buddha from Siddhartha. This journey to spirituality is like walking on the razor's edge[7].

A yogi who has attained *Samadhi*, lives permanently in a state of divinity and supreme blessedness. Even though he is conscious of his *Siddhi*, he is not under its control, but *siddhi* is under his control. Sometimes he has to demonstrate his *Siddhi* but not for the sake of power, prestige, name or fame, but to acquaint the common man with the glory of God. Jesus Christ is believed to have demonstrated several *siddhis*. The *New Testament* throughout shows Christ showing his omnipotent and omniscient power. Yoga, however, views the exhibition of *Siddhi* differently. According to it, the power generated by *Siddhi* is not alien to man. It believes that man is essentially a God and a Brahman. Vivekanand points out that, "The man who thinks that he is receiving response to his prayers does not know that the fulfilment comes from his own nature, that he has succeeded by his prayer in waking up a bit of his infinite power which is coiled up within himself. What man worships under various names ignorantly out of fear or tribulation, the Yogi declares it to the world to be the real power coiled up in every being as the mother of eternal happiness. The only problem is that common man is unaware of how to approach her. Yoga in essence is the science of religion and the rationale of all forms of worship, ceremonies and miracles."

The cosmic consciousness or Brahman also find an elaborate mention in Kashmira Saivism. In *Agamamshashtra*, it is emphasized that Param Shiva is the perfect and profound metaphysics of oneness who embodies the plurality and diversity of the cosmos. He is absolute, fathomless transcendence, *Purnahanta*, self-luminous and undiluted consciousness. Just as light and heat coexist in fire, in the same way, universalness (*ahanta*) and Shakti co-exist in pure consciousness. To make distinction between Shiva and Shakti is nothing but a logical abstraction.

Param Shiva remains unaffected by the limitation of time and space and, unrestricted by his *Vimarsa Kriya*. By virtue of his power he is described as the Free Agent.

Kashmira Saivism is the most profound and sublime form of non-dualistic philosophical school. It is called *Shivadvaita* system. Behind its Tantric and Yogic mystical culture and practice, there is an evolved philosophical system of thought which provides the intellectual support for the theocratic culture. Kashmira Saivism believes that reality is nothing but Param Shiva, a state of pure consciousness, self-enlightening and all pervading. It is the indeterminable and transcendental existence, beyond all divisibility and separability, also described as Advaitam, meaning supreme unity. In his immanence, Param Shiva is manifested in the universe within confines of sixty four Tattvas. He is consciousness *stasis* (*Chitta*) while Shakti is consciousness dynamics (*Chidrupini*). Their absolute reality is *Prakasa-vimarsa-Samarasyarupini*.

Prakasa is the cosmic effulgence without which nothing can appear. *Prakasa* is Shiva while *Vimsara* is Shakti. The latter is the mirror in which Shiva experiences his own grace, power and beauty. It is the creative matrix around which the supreme reality Shiva revolves. Kashmira Saivism considers the world as real in the same way as the supreme reality. Rejecting the *Vivartavada* of neo-Vedanta that world is unreal and has a fundamentally false appearance, M.M. Gopinath Kaviraj argues that the world is real in the same way as an image is real and has no existence apart from the medium in which it is manifested....

Similarly, the ignorants believe that world is *Maya* and materialistic and not identical with *Brahman*. On the other hand, for a *Tantrika*, the world is not only real but also an expression of the *Chit-Sakti* or Free will of the Lord and in a spiritual sense, like the Lord himself." According to *Pratyabhijnahridaya,* Shiva manifests the cosmos where all beings live and co-exist. Consciousness that is Shiva, is the substratum on which the cosmos that is Shakti is supported. In spite of this apparent dualism, they are essentially one and indivisible. Actually, Shakti forms the ultimate substance of Shiva's own being and by the power of her will, she unfolds the universe in Shiva's image.

The *Chit-Sakti* is referred in Buddhism as a philosophy of mind *(chit-darshan).* Theravadins, the oldest and most conservative followers of Buddhism, reduce the mind into a set of thoughts and feelings and seek deliverance from ignorance through detachment. Mahayana, another stream of Buddhism, considers mind as a seed of enlightenment (*Bodhi Citta*) and as *Kalpa Vriksh* and *chintamani.* They believe that all living beings have the nature of Buddha. This nature remains unpolluted and pure in spite of defilement and cravings and represents ultimate consciousness and infinite bliss (*maha sukh*).

The cosmic consciousness has also drawn interpretations from various other schools of philosophical thoughts. *Madhyamika* school talks of its subliminal emptiness while *Vijnavada* emphasizes that all elements (*dharmas*) are consciousness which is the only reality. *Vasubandhu*, the commentator of *Vijjnavada* considers men and the world as a unique reflection of consciousness. Asanga, the founder of *Vijjnavada*, has explained the concept of consciousnesses in his treatises known as *Vimsatika* (twenty verses) and the *Trimsika* (thirty verses). *Vasubandhu* has also written a commentary known as *Trimsika – Karika* pointing out that consciousness is the only reality.

There is a great similarity between the views of Vedanta and the Buddhism on this subject. Both propound that consciousness is the only truth and truth is the only consciousness, that the attainment of enlightenment is the *summum bonum* (highest good) of our life, that bliss is the quintessence of transcendental reality and that transcendental reality is realized when men experience reality as cosmic consciousness, *Brahman* or *Bodhi chitta*.

The modern science is coming closer to accepting the Vedantic and Buddhist concept of truth and reality that both are singular. Joining the issue, Ervin Schrodinger, the Austrian physicist writes that, "The external world and consciousness are one and the same thing, in so far as they are constituted by the same primitive elements. But then, we are hardly even using a different formula to express the essential community of these elements in all individuals by saying that there is only one external world or that there is only one consciousness."[8]

We thus notice a convergence of science and spirituality. Admittedly, consciousness is the only truth and reality. It is beyond the reach of senses and mind. Neither the exact science nor any metaphysics can comprehend its true nature. One of the greatest philosophers of the last century Ludwig Wittgenstein beautifully sums up the predicament of scientists in the following words. He writes that, "there are indeed things that cannot be put into words. They make themselves manifest. They are what may appear mystical....If we cannot define or explain them, then we must consign ourselves to silence."

Notes

1. *Astavakra Samhita,* Chapter 1, verse 3.
2. Mircea Eliade, *Yoga Immortality and Freedom*, Bollingen Series/Princeton, New York, 1952, p. xx.
3. *Astavakra Samhita*, Ch. 2, verse 18.
4. *Avadhuta Gita*, Ch. 1, verse 4.
5. *The Mystery Beyond the Trinity: Tripura Rahasya,* Sri Ramanasramam, Tiruvannamalai, 2011. Ch. XVII, Verses 70–73.
6. Swami Vivekanand, *Raja Yoga*, Advaita Ashram Publications, 2012, pp. 59–60.
7. *Katha Upanisada*, 1. iii. 14.
8. Erwin Schrodinger. *My View of the World*, p. 37, Ox Bow Press, Woodbridge, Connecticut, 1983.

9

Reason and Religion

Crisis of Civilization

The conflict between reason and religion is called challenge. When the challenge becomes intense, it is called crisis. Every civilization has faced this challenge at the different periods of history. The civilization which resolves this crisis comes out victorious and it heralds an era of glory and achievement. The twentyfirst century is facing the same crisis but it has entered into the period of intense clash and crisis, which has never been experienced in the annals of human history. On the resolution of this crisis depends the very survival of mankind.

I propose to analyze, examine and evaluate the concept of reason and religion for better and deeper understanding of the present crisis. The reason without moral content becomes dangerous and religion without rational metaphysics becomes demonic. Religion becomes breeding ground of superstition and dogmatism, fanaticism and fundamentalism and hatred and violence. This is the hypothesis of this chapter.

The reason is considered as human capacity for seeing, forming, investigating and examining cognitive relations. Reason is an instrument than as supreme defining characteristic of human being. It is a faculty or process of ratiocination of drawing logical inferences. Kant considers reason as power of synthesizing into unity with the help of the comprehensive principles and concepts that are provided by intellect. According to him there are two kinds of reasons—pure and practical reasons. "Pure Reason" is based on *a priori* principles, which is distinct from "Practical Reason". Practical reason is concerned with the performance of action.

Nagarjun is of the opinion that reason has four categories—*Bhava* (positive), *Abhava* (negative), *Ubhaya* (neither positive nor negative), *Nobhaya* (nor both positive and negative). According to him, the thing cannot be said to be either real or unreal, or both real and unreal. According to him, there are two truths on which Buddha's philosophy is based, one is empirical (*samvṛti satya*) and stands for the ordinary people, another the transcendental (*paramartha-satya*). When Buddha was asked about the transcendental nature of truth, he kept silent. Buddha maintained silence not because he did not know the answer, but because he was aware of the antinomical character of the reason. The resolution of antinomical character of reason paved the path for the discovery of dialectic. The knowledge is a dialectical process.

On the question of cosmic origins or the first principle as why is there something and not anything has occupied human enquiry since the dawn of civilization. The reason and religion have been trying to understand universal and historical principles of reason by which to speculate on matters of ultimate reality.

Reason and the social system are epigenetic. In a socio-economic system, this epigene manifests in a linear cumulative and quantitative form. In this process of growth and differentiation, man is becoming more and more independent of nature. Only man possesses the rational power and spiritual vision to create a society of his own imagination and requirements, yet man does not enjoy absolute freedom. He is strained by the axial facts that each social system has a different realm of change. All social changes are not compatible with one another. Our analysis and examination from prehistory to modern time view that our perception of time, space and causation has undergone a great change.

With the publication of a research paper by Heisenberg in 1927, "On the principles of uncertainty" causation has ceased to be an ontological reality. The power that we possess today to transform nature and the range of socio-political life are on a scale, which no civilization howsoever great might have been able to comprehend. This is the achievement of man's power of reason. The reason is instrumental in creating a scientific temper in the modern times. Science and technology are products of human intellect. However, the scientific and technological advancements are getting out of balance without our moral and social performances. We are in need of social engineering and spirituality, to arrest the decline of moral values, by giving religious and moral content to reason. Arnold Toynbee is of opinion that the constituents of society are not individuals but their relationship. Unless society is based on sound moral foundation, it will not remain harmonious. This is a classic question on which the philosophers have been speculating from the time immemorial. The difference between the reason and religion has been reflected in Plato's myth of the cave. Karl Jaspers is right in formulating this problem. He says: "Morality is rooted not in internal scales or value or in the moral practices of any given society, but rather in the decisions of moral individuals." Further he says, "Whatever else we may know there is no knowing how to live." The society is a promise or hope. The role of man is very important in creating a just society. However, man has not been part of the universe. Man has been considered as a unique creation, distinct from physical things.

We live in the universe that contains both matter and consciousness. Matter and consciousness are salient constituents of universe. Matter and consciousness have been regarded as strange partners. Both are contained in reality which is the inner aspect of the web of the Universe. At present our understanding of reality is undergoing a great change. The scientific worldview is making room from rationalism to complimentarity. The foundation of logic is ratiocination that any logical proposition must be either true or false. Logical reasoning does not accept any middle ground for partial truth or falsity. It follows from the above that if any proposition confirms that if a single logical statement and its negation on both simultaneously true, and then nothing can be ascertained. Complementarity rejects both these proposition on the basis of observations of physical phenomena. We observe a single electron behaving both as a particle and as a wave. The logical propositions are true in logic, but not in physical world. It follows from the above that Universe in a limited circumstances only adhere the proposition of logic.

Kant has long before stated that we cannot know things in themselves. He was the first systematic thinker to challenge the objectivity, the ideal that we know the things as they are because the concepts with the help of which we know the things are our concepts come out of our own understanding which pass through *a priori* categories of sensibility. Everything we know has subjective element. Therefore, absolute objectivity is impossible. We now know that dilemma of appearance and reality cannot be resolved by reason. Wittgenstein is nearer to truth when he says "whereof we cannot sayeth, thereof we must consign to silence".

Let us now analyze, examine and evaluate the concept of religion. Rudolf Otto considers awareness of *awe* a mixture of fear and fascination before the divine as the quintessence of religion. He speaks of a kind of experience of *Mysterium tremendum* the wholly otherness of divine being. Otto has made great contribution in philosophising religion. However, he commits a mistake when he emphasizes that this was the prototype of all truly religious experience. This conception of the essential nature of religious experiences may be acceptable in the context of Western theism. This definition of religion, nay this kind of placation and use of spirits and powers and different forms of rites and rituals speaks of Western theism.

Sociologists and anthropologists have always put over-emphasis on socio-cultural contents of religion. Emile Durkheim says that "a society has all that is necessary to arouse the sensation of the divine in minds, merely by the power that it has over them." (*Elementary Forms of the Religious Life,* p. 207, New York, 1926). According to him the gods of religion are nothing more than society in disguise.

The *Encyclopaedia of Religion* says that "religion is a unity of life based on esoteric experience. It speaks of depth of dimensions of mystic experience—harmonious in form, divine effulgence and clarity in accordance with different cultural milieu." Thus, some kind of esotericism forms the basis of all religion. However, different religious traditions have some salient features but the subterranean spiritual flow is the same. Hinduism and Buddhism emphasize immanence rather than transcendence. Both of them believe in continuous rather than discontinuities both of theory and experience but underlying spirit is marked by spirituality.

Though, Buddhism denies the existence of transcendental creator-god in favour of an indefinable, non-personal absolute sources or dimension that can be experienced as the depth of human subjectivity. However, there is a presence of transcendence. In Zen Buddhism and Advaita experience of Satori and realization of Brahman speak of deeper spirituality. This kind of experience is wholly other than or wholly transformative of ordinary awareness.

It is true that transcendence cannot be defined. In Jaspers words, "Everything thinkable is rejected as invalid by transcendence. Transcendence can be defined by no predicate, objectified by no representation, and attained by no inference, although all categories are applicable as means of saying that it is not a quality or a quantity, it is not a relation, and it is not one, not many, not being, not nothing etcetera. (Philosophic III, pp. 38-39). Karl Jaspers only affirms the traditional wisdom of almost all religious scriptures. Soren Kirkegaard also speaks the same language. He says "God is altogether other than man and man's world. His existence, therefore, cannot be proven nor His nature conceived."

Religion is a way of divine life. Religion is a spiritual technique to move man and woman from the mundane to supermundane existence, from the dualism of subject and object to the higher and sublime state of oneness of infinity and divine being. Religion has undergone great change and transformation and has provided moral and spiritual anchorage to mankind. The aim of religion is to make person free and this is possible by man's establishing relation to what Jaspers calls "authentic being". According to him the independence of man as an individual free from everything that happens in the world comes from establishing a deeper integration to transcendence. In Upanishad it has been stated that it is Truth that wins (*Satyamev Jayate*). Truth wins against untruth and falsehood because it is truth.

Philosophers have gone beyond an investigation of things in being to a systematic knowledge of being itself. We have been trying to understand the reality, which has been hitherto appeared in different forms of metaphysics—materialism (everything is matter), spiritualism (everything is spirit) and hylozoism (cosmos is a living spiritual substance). In every case being has been defined as something existing in the world from which all other things originated. But, this kind of investigation has been rejected by Karl. Karl has shown that being *per se* unlike things in being, is not an object and can never become one. That is to say those things are those appearances of phenomena with the help of categorization; appear as clear, distinct, and thinkable. Man can become an object only in part as physical existence. However, it does awaken in us a faculty of sensing what authentically is in the phenomena. Philosophy's search for reality or being is to secure a sound foundation for rational metaphysics of religion. Philosophy does change our entire consciousness of being and reality. It is at the heart of every philosophy. Religion based on such vision and philosophy succeeds in arresting the decline of moral values and enthroning it once again to the wills and minds of the people. True religion is that which provides sound rational metaphysics to seek to live in organic harmony with the reality; the highest religious experience is characterized by mystical oneness. It is a quest to seek such transcendence within human self. Religious life is one of harmony with both mental and human orders. It is a religious act of submersion of individuality in an organic relationship and in a mystic experienced oneness with reality.

Man is a spiritual being. In the words of St. Augustine, man is a spiritual substance. Transcendence is the essence of man. However, man is in a state of hibernation. He has forgotten his true being and transcendentalist. In the words of T.S. Eliot "Where's the life we have lost in living." The task of religion is to awaken the dormant divinity and to take man to the state of spiritual sublimity.

The present crisis of civilization presents distinctive challenges to both Reason and Religion. Reason is the human capacity for seeing, forming and investigating cognitive relations. Reason when employed in the process of ratiocination it becomes the basis of science. There can be three ways of relating Reason and Religion: conflict, cooperation and harmony. We can find examples of all three in the present and past. The conflict between Reason and Religion is because of the misunderstanding about their role and function. Reason is the greatest gift of creation but it is the two-edged sword. It can help in cutting as under the trammel of ignorance and provide religion much needed rational metaphysics. But, when it is devoid of moral content it can unleash the forces of destruction.

Reason and religion move by making models. These models are put to test. Differences in testing the models is based on the distinctions of objective (scientific) and subjective (religious) truth. Our life and culture are guided by both objective and subjective truths. There are limitations for both reason and religion, each of which deals with different aspect of reality and being. When Kant says that "the territory of pure understanding" is "an island enclosed by nature itself within unalterable limits", he wanted to convey that "land of truth" is "surrounded by a wide and stormy ocean, the native home of illusion." It is an attempt to restrain the concepts of understanding in favour of the ideas through which reason begets and diverts moral conviction and religious belief. However, when reason is bereft of moral content, it creates weapon of mass destruction with its scientific and technological tools. Again, when religion is divested of its rational metaphysic, it looses its universal character and appeal and becomes institutionalized and denominational.

The cooperation of reason and religion is to live as a part of universe, in alignment with reality. In the convergence of reason and religion the very concept of being and reality demands the unity and harmony. We can take spiritual humanism as far as it can go. This possibility of co-operation and convergence of reason and religion is based on the complimentarity. It is a scientific known fact as the essential involvement of the observer in what is being observed.

The universe is diverse and apparently it is full of contradictions. In spite of these apparent contradictions, we postulate a unity and harmony. We live in the world which contains matter and consciousness. The matter and consciousness have been considered as strange partners. However, both are contained in reality or being, which is the transcendental aspect of the web of universe. Our scientific worldview is undergoing great change and transformation from rationalistic reductionism to complementarity. The rationalism is discovering the hidden dimension of non-rational character of physical reality. Erwin Schrodinger claims to resolve the dilemma of wave/particle in favour of wave remains still a dilemma to be solved by reason. Rational metaphysics provides a philosophical foundation for the possibility of freedom and intuitive experience of reality and being. Routledge Encyclopaedia of Philosophy writes, "... Jaspers understands Jesus as one of the 'exemplary man' in human history alongside Confucius, Buddha and Socrates. Because of the paradigmatic way that Jesus realized existential possibilities, such as the ability to love and capacity for suffering, he is relevant to human beings at all times. In place of any religious faith grounded on a revelation of God, Jaspers holds out the conception of philosophical faith. This sort of faith has no objectively guaranteed proof of the existence of transcendence and is not bound to rituals, churches, priest and theologians, who claim to be the interpreters of God's revelation."

The harmony and integration of reason and religion would pave the path for spiritual humanism. This kind of religion would foster the feeling of non-violence and compassion. Dalai Lama and some prominent Christian fathers have initiated an inter-faith dialogue to provide a rational understanding of different religious traditions. Religion has been greatest civilizing force. However, the wrong interpretation of religious texts is posing great danger. Cultivation of love and non-violence is a historical necessity for the preservation of moral health of mankind. The solution of the crisis of civilization lies in radical changes in human behaviour. To change one's behaviour and life style is not easy task but is one area where religions have something special to offer—for dawn through the history, religions have track record success in changing people. Convergence and integration of reason and reality may herald an era of spiritual renaissance and save the mankind from holocaust of nuclear war.

10
Reciprocity
A Human Value in a Pluralistic World

The creation of Pluralistic International world is a historical necessity for the preservation of ethical health and the very survival of mankind. The political and economic systems are at variance to each other. There is an emergence of new global economic system within the existing nation-states. It is ushering in a new civilization and a new value system. The reciprocity in different cultural values like tolerance, peace, love, respect for other belief systems would create a new human value system.

According to Kant moral law springs from our rational nature which binds us with one another. Aristotle introduced *phronesis* or special capacity of reasoning about what one should do in the *Nicomachean Ethics*. Kant formulated the laws governing free action in "Metaphysics of Morals". Augustine says that God of Christianity is the basis of unity and goodness. Nietzsche argues against Kantian moral theory in his book *Beyond Good and Evil* and says that the transvaluation of values would liberate mankind from not only the perversity of evil but from the perversity of morality also. The basic question of metaethic is whether it is possible to drive an *"ought"* from an *"is"*?

We are living in multipolarity of value and contradictory realities. Today we are facing a grave threat from the spread of weapons of mass destruction, environmental depredations and genocidal practices.

In the light of the present explosive situation which has threatened the very existence of mankind a new value system based on Buddhist compassion, Christian's love, Confucian filial piety, Islamic brotherhood, Marxist socialism, Western liberal democracy and Gandhian non-violence is historical necessity. The reciprocity between these value systems is a historical mandatory for creation of a new international social order. The reciprocity of these value systems would result into a new pluralistic world based on spiritual humanism. The spiritual humanism would be the basis of new pluralistic world and future metaethics.

11
Eastern and Western Metaphysics
A Study in Philosophical Postulation

In the history of Metaphysics I find two distinct schools of thought, i.e. monism and dualism. The Oriental school is dominated by monism and mystical schools and Western Metaphysical School is predominantly dualistic and doctrinaire. Monism and mysticism are fundamental and basic philosophical thought of East and dualism is the salient feature of Western rationalism. The Oriental monism culminated in mysticism and dualism became the basis of Western scientific rationalism. The origin and development of science and spirituality can be traced to these two metaphysical schools and traditions. Conquest of nature is the hallmark of Western scientific rationalism and conquest of self is the goal of Eastern mystical and spiritual tradition. The scientific materialism became the dominant culture of Western Metaphysical school and spiritual humanism became the cornerstone of Oriental school of thought and tradition. Man became the author and choreographer of drama of nature in Western culture and nature became living and pulsating poetry of divinity in Oriental tradition. Nature is all divine in Oriental culture and tradition.

Greece is the birth place of Western metaphysical school of dualism. Matter and form became the guiding principles of Aristotelian metaphysics and *Brahman, Sunyoto* and *Tao* were pronounced as the ultimate reality by Indian and Chinese metaphysical thinkers.

Thales is considered the father of Western Philosophy. According to Thales, "*Water is ultimate reality*". He tried to ascertain the basic principle that governs the multiplicity of the world. Thales says, "it is water", Anaximander 'indefinite matter', Anaximanes 'air', the Pythagoreans 'number', and Parmenides of Elea calls it 'Being'. I consider Parmenides as the founding father of Western philosophy because he was the first who postulated that ultimate reality is *Being*. Not-Being loses its truth and reality. He identifies not being with becoming. The world which is known to us by means of our mind and senses is changing and fleeting. It does not have permanent existence. The world of sense perception is unreal and an illusion. The world of not-being is only an appearance according to Parmenides. Only Being is ultimate reality. *Ex nihilo nihil fit* is the kernel of philosophy of Parmenides. Being is neither existence nor non-existence, it does not come out of nothing nor something out of nothing, being does not come out of not being.

We cannot explain Being in terms of past, present and future. The past, present and future is bound by limitation and hence Being is eternal and timelessness. It is undivided, individual and absolute. It is absolutely self-identical. If we analyse the common features of the universe we come to the strange conclusion that what is common in all is simply *"being"*. It is a concept. It is a thought and not a thing. Thus Parmenides can be said as the founding father of Western philosophy. Zeno who is considered as a founder of dialectics tried to justify Parmenides philosophy of Being by destroying the multiplicity of the world.

There is another great Greek thinker who has played an important role in formulation of scientific and metaphysical thinking of the modern times. His name is Heraclitus. He was a mystic. He considered 'fire' as the basic substance. According to him "All things come out of the one and the one out of all things". However, all other realities are less than God. His doctrine is based on the concept of "perpetual flux", "all things are flowing". There is a very famous saying of Heraclitus, "We cannot enter into the same river, we go down and we do not go down; but into the same river no man can enter twice; ever it flows in and flows out." He further rejects the relative permanence of things as an illusion. Nothing remains identical from one moment to another. Appearance of any kind of permanence is an illusion.

Plato summarized the whole of doctrine of Heraclitus as "nothing ever is" and Aristotle as "nothing steadfastly is".

Socrates is another great philosopher that the Greece has produced. His impact on Western metaphysics is monumental. He was a mystic. Socrates was guided by some mystic experiences. It is called an oracle or *daemon*. This mystic experience was a guiding principle of Socrates life. The Western mind does not have the proper understanding of the deeper and the profound meaning and richness of such spiritual experiences, because it is analogous and antithesis to Western mechanistic and materialistic Western tradition.

Plato is the first Western thinker who is considered as a founder of metaphysical system. In the latter part of *The Republic* Plato formulates his philosophy. Plato makes a difference between knowledge and the opinion. According to him knowledge is certain and infallible while opinion suffers from mistakes and error. Opinion is both *is oris not,* because the things posit the opposite characters. A thing could be cognised as both beautiful and ugly. According to Plato opinion is related to the phenomenal world and knowledge is related to transcendental. I find a great similarity between Plato and Kant. For Kant *thing in itself* is unknown and unknowable. Kant makes a distinction between *phenomena* and *noumena.* Only difference between Plato and Kant is that according to Kant *thing in itself* is beyond the reach of human knowledge and understanding, but according to Plato knowledge of reality is a possibility. Opinion is related to particular things, knowledge is concerned with universal. This is the basis of Plato's theory of ideas. Thus reality is a concept. Knowledge by concept is real knowledge. Sensation does not provide the proper background of true knowledge and understanding of the facts in existence.

There is a great similarity between the Buddhist and Hindu concept of spirituality which pervades the whole life of a man and that of Socrates and Plato's view on moralism. According to Socrates and Plato wisdom alone brings liberation of soul from the thraldom to the body. Soul is eternal and only in contemplation of transcendental in which its essence becomes harmonies in life and thought, soul when it is used as an instrument of sense perception it gets rooted in the world of change and becoming. Soul attains the eternal bliss in company of gods when it is liberated from the attachment of senses. Plato does believe in rebirth, this is the clear and unquestionable impact of Hinduism on the philosophy of Plato. Like a mystic Plato advocates for keeping oneself away from the life of lust and cravings in which soul becomes attached and glued with body. According to him a philosopher "is conscious that the soul is simply fastened or glued to the body—until philosophy received her, she could only view real existence through the bars of the prison, not in and through herself... and by reason of lust had become the principal accomplice in her own captivity." The man of wisdom is aware that "each pleasure and pain is a sort of nail which nails and rivets the soul to the body, until she becomes like the body, and believes that to be true which the body affirms to be true." There is happy and harmonious blending of precept of Virtue and Transcendence in the philosophy of Plato. Aristotle is a philosophical system builder. His writings are systematic and creative. His philosophy is free from the mystic elements of Plato. The Doctrine of matter and form is the foundation of Aristotle's philosophy. The form in its essence is primary substance. He makes a difference between substance and universal. According to him *form* is a substance which universal lacks. Aristotle's metaphysical doctrine has grown out of his polemic against Plato's doctrine of ideas. According to Aristotle, matter and form are inseparable. We cannot think of form without matter or matter without form. Every object is composed of matter and form.

Most of Western philosophers introduce the concept of God as first principle to explain the world. Aristotle's first principle is also God, thus God or absolute is the ultimate cause and the world as its effect. However, God is not related to the world as caused to effect. The relation of cause and effect in context of God does not depend on time; it is rather a logical relation. According to Aristotle God is logical premise from which the world is deduced just like the syllogistic reasoning. In Aristotelian logic the conclusion is deduced from the first premise. However, the concept of premise is not in time but it is in thought. God is a thought, God is spirit, and He is form of form. Aristotle defines God as "the thought of thought". No dualism of subject and object exist in God. Aristotle while enumerating the concept of God as he is essentially self-consciousness. God embodies in himself the principle of form that contains formal, final and the efficient causes. God is totality of all these. While propagating the theory of causation Aristotle it seems landed himself in the pitfalls of mechanism. W.T. Stace while summarizing Aristotle's doctrine of causation writes, "This last argument sounds as if Aristotle is now thinking in terms of mechanism. It sounds as if he meant that the first mover is something at the beginning of time, which, so to speak, gave things a push to start them off. This is not what Aristotle means. For the true efficient cause is the final cause. And God is the first mover only His character as absolute end. As far as time is concerned, neither the universe, nor the motion in it, ever had any beginning. Every mechanical cause has its cause in turn, and so *ad infinitum.* God is not a first cause, in our sense, that is, a first mechanical cause which existed before the world, and created it. He is a teleological cause working from the end."[1]

Whatever may be the shortcomings of Aristotle's metaphysics but he has raised some philosophical issues which subsequent generations have been trying to solve. Here lies the greatness and originality of Aristotle's metaphysics. Though God of Aristotle is not a subjective thought but a pure thought which is objective and real. Here Aristotle makes a radical departure from the Plato's theory of idea. For Plato thought is real and objective only when it is an existent. Absolute thought is absolutely real for Aristotle's but he does not ascribe existent status to God. Here Aristotle's metaphysics ends with the concept of God.

Friedrich Nietzsche's monumental work *Thus Spoke Zarathustra* created a great debate in the world of philosophy and religion by declaring, "God is dead". There is a saint who talks about songs that he composes and sings which makes him to laugh and cry. The whole song is devoted to the praise of God. After hearing the saints narration about God Zarathustra made a farewell to the saint "What should I have to give you? But let me go quickly lest I take something from you!" and thus they separated, the old one and the man, laughing as two boys laugh. But when Zarathustra was alone he spoke thus to his heart: "Could it be possible? This old saint in the forest has not yet heard anything of this, that *God is dead!*"[2]

Nietzsche put on himself the mask of the Persian prophet Zoroaster. The life of Zoroaster has been of suffering in a sublime form of wisdom and enlightenment. I personally feel that Friedrich Nietzsche's philosophy which dominated the entire philosophical world of Nineteenth century has been misinterpreted and misunderstood. He introduced three main doctrines in *'Thus Spoke Zarathustra'*, i.e. the doctrine of God is dead, Superman and Eternal Recurrence. We have to take into account these three basic concepts of Nietzsche while evaluating and understanding his philosophy. He declared the God of religion as dead. There has been historical religious and cultural milieu prevalent at that time which has created a great misunderstanding and notion about God. Moreover it is accepted view that concept of personal God as has been propagated in most of the semitic religions which does not satisfy the rational mind of modern times. The God of theistic religion have outlived its utility. People are in search of a real God which could satisfy both the rationality and spirituality of modern man.

While enumerating the teachings of Friedrich Nietzsche, Graham Parkes who has translated *Thus Spoke Zarathustra* into English says in his introduction while enumerating the teachings of Nietzsche in following words:

> "Since it seems that a condition for the possibility of the appearance of the Overhuman is 'the death of God', it's often

> assumed that this advent heralds the disappearance of the Divine. The book's First Part does indeed end with the resounding cry, *'Dead are all Gods: now we want the Overhuman to live'*—but this is only a provisional teaching of Zarathustra that will soon be superseded. Rene Descartes is considered as the father of modern Western philosophy. After Aristotle, Rene Descartes is the first eminent philosopher who developed a system of philosophy. Apart from his contribution to philosophy he was a mathematician and man of science. His greatest contribution to science was the discovery of co-ordinate geometry. His concept of *Cogito ergo sum, I think therefore I exist is the basis and foundation of his whole philosophical superstructure.*"

After discovering a strong foundation in the form of *Cogito ergo sum* from which he deduced the concept of God and the soul, Descartes says, " 'God is positively infinite, that is, he exists everywhere etc.' 'I do not agree with this everywhere'. For here you seem to locate God's infinity in the fact that he exists everywhere; I do not agree with this view but think that God is everywhere by reason of his power. But he has no relation at all to any place by reason of his essence. Since power and essence are not distinguished in God, I think it is more satisfactory to reason about such things in the case of our mind or the angels, as realities that are more suited to our perception, rather than in the case of God."[3] I think 'therefore I am' with this aphorism Descartes tried to establish in a single indubitable truth in certainty. Descartes' views have been refuted by many. Hume's arguments against certainty of relation have been of great philosophical importance. However, Descartes' diffusion of his doctrine of God as transcendental reality occupies an important position in the history of philosophy and religion. He says, "the feebleness of human understanding and the arrogance that masks, it is most apparent when we try to reduce transcendent reality of God to limits of Human concept, but the uncertainty of human knowledge is not limited to speculation about God. Our senses frequently deceive us."[4]

Spinoza is one of the most respected, lovable and great philosophers that the world has produced. His whole philosophy is based on doctrine of pantheism. Ethics is monumental work of Spinoza. He writes "By God (Deus) I understand a being absolutely infinite, that is, a substance constituting of infinite attributes, each of which expresses eternal and infinite essence. By Attribute, I understand that which the intellect perceives of substance by constituting its essence. By mode—I understand the modifications of a substance; as that which is in something else through which it is also conceived."

Spinoza's concept of God is analogous to the theistic concept of personal God. He was one of the most misunderstood philosophers of his time. He was born as a Jew but he was excommunicated by Jews brotherhood. In spite of Spinoza's firm faith in God and divinity the orthodox Christians accused him of atheism. Spinoza's concept of God is closer to Hindu concept of Brahman. According to Spinoza everything is manifestation of God's inscrutable nature. He believes in absolute logical necessity. God being the absolute and real there is no possibility of any negation. This has created a great debate among the philosophers and the religious thinkers.

David Hume is one of the most original British thinkers. His *Treatise of Human Nature* is a great work of philosophical originality. In this book the philosophical question that David Hume raised are still unanswered. Here lies the greatness of Hume. The empirical philosophy of Locke-ami-Berkeley was culminated in Hume's scepticism and solipsism. There is great similarity between the Buddhist and Hume's concept of self. I know that I exist. The existence of I that he finds that is based on the many particular impressions and ideas. Hume argues that no specific impression or idea of self-corresponds to the 'I' that have any independent and permanent existence. My feeling or idea of what I am is nothing but totality of isolated impressions and particular ideas. Hume employed the same argument which Berkeley has used against Locke's theory of physical world. So there is no permanent mental substance which is considered wrongly as self. Buddhism makes comparison of the concept of self with the burning of a candle which happens in such quick succession that creates illusion of identity. The basic property of the burning of the candle is change and flux.

I find that there is a deeper understanding of Hume scepticism and his rejection of principle of inductions in Heisenberg's and Schrodinger's doctrine of quantum mechanics. Hume postulated that all, "our reasoning's concerning causes and effects derived from nothing but customs: and that belief is more properly an act of sensation, than of the causative part of our natures."

This is the basis of Hume's scepticism. Hume has raised both philosophical and scientific issues which have kept all the subsequent philosophers and scientists baffled with no finality. Immanuel Kant (1724-1804), is the founder of German idealism. He is one of the greatest and the most original thinker that Germany has produced. It is said that Kant was awakened by Hume's dogmatic slumbers. The *Critique of Pure Reason* is the metaphysical treatise of Kant. He dealt in this book the problem of *analytic* and *synthetic* propositions. The analytic proposition is in which predicate is part of the subject. On the other hand synthetic proposition is not analytic. The source of synthetic proposition is experienced. Analytical proposition is considered as universal and necessary. However, analytical proposition does not throw any new information. It lacks newness whereas synthetic propositions based on experience provide some new information. The basis of empirical proposition is sense perception.

There has been great controversy regarding Kant's doctrine of "things in themselves". Bertrand Russell says, "The thing-in-itself" was an awkward element in Kant's philosophy. I do not agree with Russell's criticism that the doctrine of *thing in itself* of Kant is an awkward element in Kant's philosophy. I think Kant was aware like Wittgenstein that the thought and language have limitation, there are certain truth like "things in themselves", which are beyond the reach of mind and senses. I find Kant's doctrine of things in themselves as the kernel of Kant's metaphysics. If we remove the Kant's doctrine of things in themselves then his whole metaphysical system would become irrelevant, irrational and insipid. I find great similarity between the Kant's doctrines of *thing in itself* with Buddhist concept of *suchness (tathata).*

Hegel is one of the most original and difficult philosopher. He is the last who is considered as philosophical system builder. According to him the reality is the Absolute. The Absolute is spiritual. He doesn't agree with Spinoza's doctrine that substance has attribute of extension and thought. Apart from this distinction the metaphysical system of Hegel has great similarity with Spinoza. Hegel draws the doctrine of absolute from the concept of reality which does not admit any self-contradictions. He doesn't accept anything real except the whole. The whole is the absolute of Hegel but he doesn't accept the views of Parmenides and Spinoza who believed in simple substance. Hegel's whole is like an organism. It is a complex system.

The Hegelian concept of God is different from the Plato and Spinoza. Bertrand Russell writes about Hegel, "His life contained few events of importance. In youth he was much attracted to mysticism, and his later views may be regarded, to some extent, as an intellectualizing of what had first appeared to him as mystic insight."[5]

I am in agreement with Russell's view that Hegel retained a belief in the unreality of separateness and his whole philosophy is based on mysticism.

Ludwig Wittgenstein is considered as most original and one of the greatest thinkers that Europe has produced. He has made a great impact on contemporary Western philosophical movements. His two books *Tractatus Logico-Philosophicus* and *Philosophical Investigation exercised* great influence on the recent philosophical movements especially of Europe and America. I shall confine myself mainly to the impact of mysticism on Wittgenstein's earlier philosophy as formulated in Tractatus. Wittgenstein by making a difference between sayable and unsayable created a theory of Solipsism. His theory of meaning which is the fundamental of the Tractatus is known as the picture theory. He says that *"Aproposition is a picture of reality for if I understand a proposition I know the situation that it represents. And I represent the proposition without having had its sense explained to me."*[6]

Language is a picture of reality. Reality stands here as a fact. Fact means state of affairs. There is a structural similarity between the world of language and the world of facts. The ultimate unit of language is elementary proposition and the ultimate unit of world is atomic facts. Wittgenstein's atomic fact is like *potentia.* According to Aristotle matter is not reality it is logical possibility (*potentia*). This is known as isomorphic relations.

He considers that limit of thought is the limit of language.

"We cannot think what we cannot think; so what we cannot think, we cannot say either."[7]

This remark provides the key to the problem, how much truth there is in Solipsism. For what the solipsist means is quite correct, only it cannot be said but makes itself manifest. The world is my world: this is manifest in the fact that the limits of language (of that language which alone I understand) mean the limits of my world.[8]

According to Wittgenstein proposition does not actually contain it sense but does contain the possibility of expressing it. Proposition contains its form but not the content of its sense. Wittgenstein accepts like Upanishadic seer that truth and reality cannot be expressed in words because it is indescribable. In place of Upanishadic dictum *'indescribable'* and Buddhist *'unspeakable'* (*avachya*). Wittgenstein uses *unsayable.* He accepts that, "There are indeed, things that cannot be put into words. They make themselves manifest. They are what is mystical. It is not how things are in the world that is mystical but that it exists."[9]

It is very evident from Tractatus that it does not deny the existence of the mystical reality and accept that it is beyond the reach of our thought and language. Wittgenstein's concludes in formulating the seventh and the last proposition in Tractatus "Whereof we cannot sayeth thereof we must consign to silence". Wittgenstein's makes a bold declaration that concept of language cannot be defined. After analysis and close examination of the structure of thought and language both Kant and Wittgenstein's draw a line between sayable and not sayable.

Lao Tzu and Confucius are two greatest personages in Chinese history. Confucius is an ethical teacher. Lao Tzu is a philosopher. There is a great controversy regarding the life and the teachings of Lao Tzu. There are some historian's beliefs that Lao Tzu was not a historical personage. However, after the examination of different views on the historicity of Lao Tzu, I have come to conclusion that he was a historical figure who was a curator during the Chou dynasty. After witnessing the decadence of Chou Dynasty he left for some unknown place towards West. On the way he met the keeper of Han-ku Pass named Yin Hsi (Kuanyin), who requested Lao Tzu to write about his philosophical thoughts and leave it for the benefit of the people. The philosophical thoughts that have been handed over by Lao Tzu is known as *Tao Te Ching.* This is the canonical literature of Taoism. This work has been interpreted by different thinkers and historians in a different way. This book has been written in twilight language, like the canonical literatures of Hindu and Buddhist Tantra and works of Zen Buddhism. This probably was the practise to communicate the incommunicable ideas and thoughts through parables, myths and allegories. This is why *Tao Te Ching* has been explained in various recensions.

Another great work of Taoism is known as *Chuang Tzu* written or compiled by Chuang Chou. With the passage of time the Taoism has undergone great change. Taoism is spirituality and not a religion. The whole philosophy of Taoism is based on mysticism. There is another important event in the life of Lao Tzu. His meeting with Confucius to me is an historical event which speaks of the Lao Tzu sublimity and profundity of his mystical thoughts. This meeting has been recorded by the first historian named Ssu-ma Ch'ien of China round about 100 B.C. The work of Ssu-ma Ch'ien is called *The Shih Chi* (historical Memoirs). In this memoir the meeting of Lao Tzu and Confucius has been recorded in following words: "When Confucius went to Chou, he asked Lao Tzu to instruct him in the rites. Lao Tzu replied, "Even the bones of those you mention have fallen into dust; there only remains are their words.

Furthermore, when a gentleman lives in favourable times, he hastens to court in a carriage; but when he lives in unfavourable times, he drifts with the wind. I have heard it said that a good merchant hides his wealth and gives the appearance of want; if endowed with a rich supply of true person.

Inward virtue, the superior man has the outward appearance of a fool. Get rid of that arrogance of yours, all those desires, that self-sufficient air, that overweening zeal; all that is of no use to your "That is all I can say to you." Confucius withdrew and told his disciplines, "I know a bird can fly; I know a fish can swim; I know animals can run, Creatures that run can be caught in nets; those that swim can be caught in wicker traps; those that can fly can be hit by arrows. But the dragon is beyond my knowledge; it ascends into heaven on the clouds and the wind. Today I have seen Lao Tzu, and he is like the dragon!"

Geoffrey Red Mound rightly observes, "It has become a cliche that the West developed the objective aspects of thought while Asia developed subjectivity."

Taoism is a metaphysical treatise based on monism and ontological mysticism. Lao Tzu and Chuang Tzu and their followers have taken metaphors and symbols to express the inexpressible. According to Taoism the Tao is unsubjectivated, transcendentality just as light and heat coexist in fire in the same way Tao and Te coexist in the absolute. The absolute of the Tao is beyond the limitation of time, space and causality. It is unchanging, eternal, infinite, one and uncaused. It is the supreme reality. It is beyond the categories of existence and non-existence. It is of the nature of light, bliss, beatitude and consciousness. For the layman who is not conversant with the inner meaning of the metaphors and the symbols used by Taoism for them they are nonsensical and full of contradictions. Geoffrey Red Mound writes, "It must be said at once that these contradictions are often only apparent: Taoist minds and Western minds (perhaps we should say modern minds) categorize their thoughts quite differently. Yet synthetic, 'organicist' thinking of the ancient Chinese is providing worthier of interest as our knowledge of it increases. Thus it is true for the history of science as for the history of ideas: the very mysticism of the fathers of Taoism contained some elements that could have favoured the rise of a scientific movement."[10]

Present civilization is foreboding waves of materialism and consumerism. The spirituality and ontological mysticism of Taoism is hope and promise for better world. It could be the salvation of the crisis-ridden present global society.

The crisis in the present world has become a cliche. T.S. Eliot has rightly summarized the crisis of the present civilization as how we have lost the path in the search of the truth and the meaning of existence.

The Buddha is a greatest philosopher that the world has produced till this date. Historically speaking he is the only person in the annals of human history, who has founded a School of Philosophy and a World Religious Order. The Buddha after the attainment of enlightenment (*nirvana*) under Bodhi tree at Bodh Gaya reflected on the nature and significance of *nirvana* which resulted into the birth of new school of philosophy and a new religious order, known as Buddhism. Buddhism is a sublime and profound form of spirituality. It is monotheistic and it represents the highest form of monism. According to Buddhism, *Advaya* represents the eternal co-existence of *Prajna* and *Upaya* which constitutes the infinite unity and transcendent reality (*Bodhicitta*). The most profound ontological doctrine is considered to be the Madhyamika which claims *Sunyata* to be intrinsic in nature, to be the ultimate mode of existence. *Vijnanavada* (*Yogacara*) and *Sunyavada* (*Madhyamika*) deal with soteriological and speculative metaphysics. Buddhism believes in two truths or reality—a conventional or nominal and an ultimate truth.

The *Mulamadhyamakakarika* (literally Fundamental Verses on The Middle Way) of Nagarjuna, the founder of the *Madhyamika*—the middle path schools of Mahayana Buddhism deals with the metaphysical and epistemological problems. This treatise is the foundation of *Madhyamika School* in which dialectical analytic arguments have been employed to establish the basic principles of metaphysical and epistemological issues; the central concept of this text is *Sunyata* (Emptiness). The Emptiness is the essence of all things and at the same time Emptiness itself is empty. All other Buddhist metaphysical, soteriological concepts and the principles are based on this root concept of Emptiness.

Jay L. Garfield writes, "Most bizarre of all, however, at first glance is the doctrine that all phenomena, including self and its objects, are empty. For indeed Nagarjuna and his followers do argue that the entire everyday world is, from the ultimate standpoint, non-existent. And that does appear to stand just a bit deeper into philosophical left field than even Berkeley dares to play. But, if the interpretation I will urge is adopted, the real central thrust of Madhyamika is the demystification of this apparently mystical conclusion."[11] Buddhism denies the permanent reality as advocated by other schools of Indian philosophical systems except Carvaka. According to Vedanta Self is identical with Brahman. The Buddha refutes the very existence of permanent self on the argument that if we accept the permanent soul, the *karma* loses its signification and importance. Acceptance of permanent self would destroy the very spiritual life of a man because the belief in self is the source of our all desires. And these desires are the root cause of our sufferings.

> "If prior to desire
> And without desire there were a desirous one,
> Desire would depend upon him.
> Desire would exist when there is a desirous one."[12]

The concept of non-self is the root concept of Buddhism. I do not agree with the observation of Prof. Radhakrishnan and Mrs. Rhys Davids that Buddha believed in the permanent self. This would amount to the rejection of the soteriological and metaphysical foundation of Buddhism. There is another misunderstanding about the teachings of the Buddha. In the *Cula Malunkya Sutta,* Buddha compared the metaphysician with a man wounded by an arrow, and he argues that we would discuss the metal and structure of the arrow instead of treating the wounded man with removal of the arrow. People have concluded from this philosophical enquiry that Buddha was not aware of the metaphysics or he considered philosophy as unnecessary pursuits of knowledge. The Buddha was aware of the antinomical character of the reason and this is why he kept mum on some metaphysical enquiries and issues but this does not mean that Buddha was not aware of profound philosophical truth and its knowledge.

According to Nagarjuna the absolute is beyond the four categories of *Bhava* (existence), *Abhava* (non-existence), *Ubhay* (nor both existence and non-existence), No *bhaya* neither *Bhava* nor *Abhava* (neither existence nor non-existence). All the views have been rejected because of the inherent defects. The Buddha's dialectics is used as *reduction and absurdum.* Dialectic used by Buddha stands for the inability of reason to comprehend the absolute. The absolute is transcendent. It is *Sunya,* free from any kind of differentiations, change and metamorphosis. There is a great similarity between the philosophy of Madhyamika and the Kant. Kant also considered criticism is itself a philosophy. Madhyamika is a profound philosophical system. *Prajnaparamita* (perfection) is mystic experience of the truth and reality. It is *Nirvana.* It is called *Nirvana.* T.R.V. Murti writes, "Metaphysics or true philosophy (*Prajna*) is non-dual knowledge—Intuition of the real. The possibility of intellectual intuition is not only accepted but is taken to be the very heart of reality. It is the Truth. In intuition, Knowledge and the Real coincide; essence and existence are identical."[13]

Hinduism is most profound school of philosophy. Hinduism is a protean. Hinduism is monastic. Hinduism is non-dual (*Advaita*) and accepts all forms of philosophical concepts as an aspect of one truth and reality. Indian culture and civilization have had an extremely long and complex development. It is the longest history of continuous growth than any other living cultural tradition of the world. The historical perspective of cultural tradition and philosophical analysis are very useful in understanding the basic and the fundamental cultural spiritual spirit of Hinduism.

It is a very difficult and complex task to present a chronological sequence of the philosophical evolution of Hinduism. In the broad outline the philosophical history of Hinduism can be studied in four sub-titles: (1) Kashmir Saivism, (2) Vedanta, (3) Tantra and (4) Yoga. I have selected these four topics of Hinduism because they are all based on metaphysical and ontological mysticism. Hinduism is basically and essentially spirituality. Spirituality and science are rooted in ontological mysticism. Ontological mysticism is the common ground of both spirituality and science. On the analysis and evaluation of these different metaphysical and the mystical concept of Hinduism, I come to the conclusion that it is rooted in Indus Valley Civilization. The excavation at Mohenjo-Daro and Harappa revolutionized the concept of Indian history and civilization. The Indus Valley Civilization goes back to the Neolithic period (7000-6000 B.C.). This was very organised and developed urban culture. Mohenjo-Daro and Harappa are separated by some forty miles, were two of the world civilizations most important cities where the inhabitants enjoyed high standards of living.

The antecedents of this culture can be traced to the site of the Mergarh (150 miles north of Mohenjo-Daro in Baluchistan) cultural community that existed before 6000 B.C. and has established an unbroken cultural continuity from that early date to the period of the Indus Valley Civilization. Saivism and Saktism represent the beginning of Indian culture and metaphysical traditions. Saivism and Saktism were the two official religions of the non-Aryan of the Indus Valley Civilization.

According to Hindu Metaphysics estrangement of man is known as bondage. The state of oneness is called *Nirvana*. This is a state of spiritual sublimity and self-consciousness where the distinction between 'me' and 'the world' breaks down. It is a state of mystic realization in which the plurality is fused into unified undifferentiable whole, i.e. reality. Fritjof Capra observes, "The picture of an interconnected cosmic whole emerged from modern atomic physics has been used extensively in the East to convey the mystical experience of nature. For Hindus, the Brahman is the unifying thread in the cosmic wall, the ultimate ground of all being."[14]

The Kashmir Saivism, Advaita Vedanta, Buddhism and Taoism are based on metaphysical non-dual ontological mysticism. Ontological mysticism is the foundation of the non-dual systems of metaphysics and the modern science. Gaudapada is the founding father of non-dual system of Vedanta. *Mandukya Karika* is a treatise of non-dual system of Vedanta and it could be considered as the source of modern scientific thinking. There has been harmonious and happy blending of Buddhism, Taoism and non-dual Vedantic systems. Professor S.N. Das Gupta in his celebrated work '*A History of Indian Philosophy*' has made observation regarding Gaudapada, "Gaudapada thus flourished after all great Buddhist teachers—Asvaghosa, Nagarjuna, Asanga and Vasubandhu and I believe that there is sufficient evidence in his Karikas for thinking that he was possibly himself a Buddhist and considered that the teachings of the Upanishads tallied with those of Buddha."

Knowledge is a dialectical process. Hence, it is natural that a system of thoughts incorporates some of the basic ideas and thoughts of previous metaphysical systems and those ideas are assimilated in a systematic way which gives birth to a new thought in form of a new synthesis. Thus it is no wonder that the great Buddhist truth of indefinable and unspeakable *Vijnana* and *Sunyata* have been assimilated in Gaudapada's *Mandukya Karika* and it has been equated with *Ataman* or *Brahman* of Upanishad. This could be the new synthesis of Vedantic thoughts in form of Buddhist tradition and thinking. Prof. Das Gupta has tried to prove that Gaudapada might have been a Buddhist and his whole philosophical thought has been borrowed from the teachings of Buddha. I would not agree with Prof. Das Gupta that Gaudapada was a Buddhist but I do agree with Das Gupta that Gaudapada had incorporated some of the thoughts and ideas of the *Vijnanavada* and *Sunyavada* in his *Mandukya Karika*. There is a great similarity between Nagarjuna's doctrine of *No origination* and Gaudapada's theory of *Ajativada*.

Mandukya Karika says, "There is no dissolution, no birth, none in bondage, none aspiring for wisdom, no seeker of liberation and none liberated. This is the absolute truth."[15]

According Gaudapada Brahman appears as the phenomenal world without losing its essential nature and transcendentality. It is like rope appearing as a snake. Gaudapada being an ardent believer in non-dual system of thought and propagator of *Ajativada* according to which the *Brahman* has never become the universe. And he outrightly rejects the causality of causation in the fourth chapter of *Mandukya Karika*. According to Gaudapada as *Atman* is the only reality and it is always in the state of transcendentality. He just rejects any form of worship and practice of meditation or the attainment of *nirvana*. Gaudapada says, "The Jiva betaking itself to devotion (*upasana*) thinks itself to be related to the *Brahman* that is supposed to have manifested Himself. He is said to be of narrow intellect because he thinks that before creation all was of the nature of the unborn (Reality)."[16] According to Gaudapada, it would be futile exercise to indulge in any kind of devotional practices to attain liberation. In the second chapter Gaudapada has dealt in detail about the concept of illusion, according to which the whole theory of dualism that includes the object and the act of worshipping and meditating is illusory because only the attributeless non-dual *Brahman* is ultimate reality. It would be wrong on the part of the individual self or devotee to think that by practicing meditation and other rituals he would regain his lost glory and spiritual sublimity of *Brahman*. Only the fools and the narrow-minded intellect indulge in such kind of devotional practices and thinking that he or she would regain the real nature of *Brahman* which he was before the birth. The *Kena Upanishad* also supports this kind of stand. According to *Talavakara* (*Kena*), "That which is not uttered by speech, that by which speech is revealed, know that alone to be Brahman, and not what people worship as an object."[17] The *Avadhuta Gita* which is also considered a text of school of Vedanta representing the real form of Advaita and non-dualism is in full agreement with Gaudapada and it observes, "The wise, my child, give up all meditations; they give up all good and evil deeds and drink the nectar of renunciation. I am free from disease—my form has been extinguished."[18] Further *Avadhuta Gita* states, "In thy mind there is neither the meditation, nor the object of meditation. Thou hast no *samadhi*. There is no region outside thee, nor is there any substance or time. I am the nectar of Knowledge, homogeneous Existence, like the Sky (formless)."[19]

The reality is neither void (*sunya*) nor is non-void (*asunya*). The reality is a cosmic consciousness. It is neither a pure nor of impure nature, neither form nor formless. Reality is of the form of its own nature. The purity and impurity, the virtue and the sin, bad and good are all rooted in dualistic nature of things and beings. But the cosmic consciousness which constitutes ultimate reality is beyond any kind of dualism, subject or object, virtue or vice etc. It is beyond also transcendental and relative states. The reality does not come within the purview or domain of our knowledge and hence there could not be versification. The cosmic consciousness lives and has its being in the consciousness of homogeneous being. The philosophers and the rationalist only prattle about the Truth and Reality. And hence there is no need of any kind of religious prostration, worship, performance of rituals or the attainment of enlightenment and liberation because self is ever luminous, pure cosmic consciousness and state of liberation (*turya*). *Avadhuta Gita* rejects all kinds of religious practices and performance of rituals in a strongest possible condemnation. It says, "By making pilgrimage to Thee Thy all pervasiveness has been destroyed by me. With my meditation Thy transcendence of the mind has been destroyed by me. Thy transcendence of speech has been destroyed by me by my singing Thy praise. Ever forgive me these three sins."[20]

This is a pure form of non-dual metaphysical school. In the state of ultimate reality (cosmic consciousness) there is no difference between cause and effect. Reality is one indivisible and all comprehensive absolute.

We cannot make any differentiation between self and non-self, the world and the God, *Purusa* and *Prakriti*. According to this system of thought there has been no creation. The world is not a modification of the *Brahman*.

The *Mandukya Karika* says that, "The immortal cannot become mortal, nor can the mortal ever become immortal. For it is never possible for a thing to change its nature."[21] *Mandukya Karika* further says, "The unreal cannot be born either really or through *Maya*. For the son of a barren woman is neither in reality nor in illusion."[22]

From the Gaudapada's metaphysical perspective the introduction of the concept of *Maya* does not explain the existence of the phenomenal world rather it creates confusion and contradiction in propagating the teachings of Vedanta as system of *Advaita*. It loses its purity and fervour of non-dual system of Vedanta.

Mandukya Karika and *Avadhuta Gita* have enunciated the non-dual school of thought from the transcendental point of view, but when we discuss the nature and reality from empirical point of view the world is a relative truth. It is a modification of Spinoza's Substance, the Vedantic *Brahman*, the Buddhist's *Sunyata* (emptiness) and Taoist's *Tao*. There is a creation. The Buddhism and Vedanta have discussed the truth from transcendental and empirical point of view. The whole metaphysical and the scientific formulation are based on ontological mysticism. From one perspective there is a *Brahman* and from the other there is a world. Both the scientific and the spiritual perspectives are required for understanding the truth and the nature. The question of Who am I? This is not a heuristic hypothesis. Reality, existence, being, *Brahman* or God are not empty words. These are pregnant with deep metaphysical and scientific import. Schrodinger writes, "Hence this life of yours which you are living is not merely a piece of the entire existence, but is in a certain sense the whole; only this whole is not so constituted that it can be surveyed in one single glance. This, as we know, is what the Brahmins express in that sacred, mystic formula which is yet really so simple and so clear: *Tat tvam asi,* this is you. Or, again, in such words as 'I am in the east and in the west, I am below and above, I am this whole world'."[23] I am in complete agreement with the observation of Schrodinger, "Briefly stated, it is the view that all of us living beings belong together in as much as we are all in reality sides or aspects of one single being which may perhaps in Western terminology be called God while in the Upanishads its name is *Brahman*."

A comparison used in Hinduism is of the many almost identical images which a many-faceted diamond makes of some *one* object such as the sun. We have already conceded that we are here dealing not with something logically deducible but with mystical metaphysics—just like the acceptance of a real object-world (usually called an external world, but it includes one's own body)."[24]

For proper understanding and comprehension of Eastern metaphysics one will have to equip himself with proper frame of mind, cultivated by mystical and moral discipline of non-attachment discrimination and the longing for the realisation of truth in its wholeness. Without proper understanding and study of philosophy and science in a dilettante fashion will land him in confusion and contradiction. The path of spirituality and ontological mysticism is like walking on the razor's edge. The Upanishadic seers have rightly stated "Arise, awake, and learn by approaching the excellent ones. The wise ones describe that path to be impassable as a razor's edge, which when sharpened, is difficult to tread on."[25]

Ontological mysticism is the happy and harmonious blending of the Eastern metaphysics and Western metaphysics and science and spirituality. Nature has not set any limit to the realization of human hopes and aspirations. Spirituality is a path of truth, virtue and *nirvana.*

Science gives us knowledge, spirituality brings wisdom. In the state of spiritual sublimity we are face to face with truth and reality. Integrating and mediating between two planes of ratiocination and reflections given by science and spirituality would be greatest intellectual and moral adventure and most rewarding achievement of today.

The modern sciences have succeeded in revealing some of the mysteries of the nature and in course of their penetration deeper into the knowledge of natural harmony they have got a glimpse of awareness that there is harmony and order which rules the universe. And this harmony and order are beyond the realm of scientific ratiocination and experiments. This natural harmony and order is the result of the activation of some hidden reality which I consider as cosmic consciousness. However, scientists do accept the existence of an *ontological order* which is beyond the reach. Prince Louis De Broglie considers that the truth is that humanity has been able to adapt itself to live in this world in which there is some isomorphic relation with our mind. If there would not have been so, perhaps humanity would not have been able to survive. He writes, "How remarkable is the harmony between the resources of which our mind disposes and the profound realities which conceal themselves behind natural appearances. To bring this harmony more completely into the light, to glimpse yet more the ontological order of which Duhem spoke—such appears to be the true mission of pure science. Removed from all utilitarian preoccupation, solely devoted to the search for truth, it appears to us as one of the noblest activities of which we are capable. By the wholly ideal nature of the goal it pursues, by the intensity and the disinterested character of the efforts that it demands, it possesses a moral value which cannot be denied."[26]

Recent scientific development especially the Quantum Mechanics has paved the path for the convergence of science and spirituality and Eastern and Western metaphysics. From the metaphysical perspective ultimate reality is one and homogenous being and existence. It is cosmic consciousness. There is only one consciousness. The world and the reality are constituted of this cosmic consciousness. It is beyond the reach of both philosophy and science. Neither exact science is really possible nor can any philosophical knowledge comprehends the nature of reality. It is mystical and metaphysical.

Notes

1. *The Critical History of Greek Philosophy*. pp. 284-285.
2. Friedrich Nietzsche. *Thus Spoke Zarathustra*, Translated by Walter Kaufmann. The Viking Press, New York, 1954, p. 12.
3. Rene Descartes. *Replies to the penultimate counter-objections. Meditations and other Metaphysical Writings* Penguin Books. London, 1998. p. 177.
4. Rene Descartes. *Meditation and Other Metaphysical Writings*, The Complete Essays, Penguin Books. London, 1998, p. 669
5. *The History of Western Philosophy*, p. 730.
6. *Tractatus* 4.021.
7. *Ibid.*, 5.61.
8. *Ibid.*, 5.62.
9. *Ibid.*, 6.522.
10. *Science and Spiritual Traditions.*, p. 144.
11. *The Fundamental Wisdom of the Middle Way. Nagarjuna's Mulamadhyamakakarika, Translation and Commentary* by Jay L. Garfield. New York, Oxford University Press, 1995. p. 94.
12. *Ibid.*, p. 16.
13. T.R.V. Murti. *The Central Philosophy of Buddhism*, George Allen and Unwin Ltd. 1960. London, p. 214.
14. *The Tao of Physics*.
15. *Mandukya Karika*, Chapter II, Verse 32.
16. *Mandukya Karika*, Chapter III, Advaita Parakaranas. Verse 1.
17. *Kena Upanisad*, Chapter I, Verse 5.
18. *Avadhuta Gita*, Chapter IV, Verse 24.
19. *Ibid.*, Chapter III, Verse 41.
20. *Ibid.*, Chapter VIII, Verse 1.
21. *Mandukya Karika*, Chapter IV, *Alatasanti*. Verse 7.
22. *Ibid.*, Chapter III, *Advaita Parakaranas*. Verse 28.
23. Erwin Schrodinger, *My View of the World*, pp. 21-22.
24. *Ibid.*, p. 95.
25. *Katha Upanisad* I. iii. 15, Verse 14.
26. *Quantum Questions, Mystical writings of the World's Greatest Physicists*, p. 123.

12
Anand Math and the Rise of Nationalism

T.S. Eliot says in his essay 'Tradition and Individual Talent', that every writer while writing, writes his age. Bankim Chandra Chattopadhyay is not an exception of this dictum. Shri Chattopadhyay wrote *Anand Math* in 1883, which was one of the darkest period in Indian history. *Anand Math* is one of the greatest works of Bengali literature which captivated the imagination and aspiration of youth of Bengal. It portrays the sufferings of the people of Bengal and their aspiration to rid the country of slavery and sufferings.

Anand Math gives a vivid description of the poverty and the sufferings of Bengal. *Anand Math* starts with following descriptions of a village known as Padsin. While describing the sufferings and the famine of the village Padsin. Mr. Chattopadhyay writes in detail.

There were many houses in the village but there were no inhabitants. There were lines of shops, hundreds of mud houses—some small and big mansons, but today there was a complete silence. Shops were closed. Nobody knew where the shopkeepers have gone. Today was the day of village market but the market didn't take place. It was the day of begging but no beggar was seen begging. The weavers were weeping after closing down their weaving machines. The workers were weeping with their children in their laps. The benefactors have stopped giving alms. Teachers closed down their village school. Children didn't have the courage to weep. Nobody was seen on the footpaths.

Bathing place was empty. Nobody were at the doors of the houses. No bird was seen on the trees. Cows were not at the cowshed. The only dogs and jackals were at the burning places. One high palace was visible. Its high pillars could be seen from the distance. The door was closed.

There was no trace of human beings. There was complete silence. Even there was no space for the wind to blow. Inside the room, there was a complete darkness at the room, and in that darkness of night one couple was sitting and was contemplating on the famine which was haunting before them.

The famine was so severe that out of starvation people started selling everything even their children and wives but there were no takers. People started deserting their homes. People started eating leaves, cats and dogs. People started dying out of starvation. There were outbreak of cholera, T.B. and smallpox. Mahendra Singh was the Zamindar of Padsin. He was the richest man of the village but in this state of famine and starvation, rich and poor became equals. Mahendra Singh and his wife Kalyani started debating about their future. They had small baby girl. Ultimately they decided to leave the village. Kalyani kept poison with her, which may help her in the hour of crisis. On their way at one place Mahendra Singh went out in search of some milk for the baby leaving behind Kalyani and child in a haunted house. When Kalyani was alone few figures of men were seen approaching her. They abducted Kalyani and her child and took them in a nearby forest. The robbers started fighting among themselves over the distribution of booties. They had hot exchange of words with their leader and ultimately over the distribution of booty they killed the *sardar*. They now decided to eat the flesh of their *sardar* and started roasting. When the robbers were fighting amongst themselves, Kalyani took the advantage and escaped from their clutches with her daughter. In the hours of crisis and suffering, some time man becomes a beast. Kalyani was a devoted Hindu woman. She had strong faith in God.

With the divine grace Kalyani saw that there was a Math in the thick of the forest. This Math was Buddhist Vihar. Shri Chattopadhyay has given beautiful description of the forest and the moonlight night when Kalyani was wading through the jungle. She became senseless and ultimately she met a Swamijee. Swamijee was the head of the Ananda Math. His name was Satyanand. Satyanand took Kalyani and her daughter to the Ashram. Swami Satyanand and his followers have started Anand Math to liberate Bengal from the shackles of Muslim and British rule. When Mahendra Singh did not find his wife and daughter he started in their search. On his way he met same constable who thought Mahendra was a robber. Bhavanand was chasing the British forces and he was in look for the opportune moment to overpower them and took away all the revenue collection which they were carrying to Calcutta.

Bhavanand was in a ordinary dress and when the opportune moment came he came out in his real form and lead the entire campaign successfully. Bhavanand started singing the song of freedom—*Vande Mataram*:

वन्दे मातरम्
सुजलां सुफलां
मलयज शीतलां
शस्य श्यामलां
मातरम्।
शुभ्र-ज्योत्सनां-पुलकित-यामिनीम्
फुल्लकुसुमित-द्रुमदल शोभिनीम्
सुहासिनीं सुमधुर भाषिणीम्
सुखदां वरदां मातरम्
वन्दे मातरम्
सुजलां सुफलां
मलयज शीतलां
शस्य श्यामलां
मातरम्।
शुभ्र ज्योत्स्ना पुलकित यामिनीम्
फुल्ल कुसुमित द्रुमदल शोभिनीम्
सुहासिनीं सुमधुर भाषिणीम्
सुखदां वरदां मातरम्।
सप्तकोटि कंठ कलकल निनाद कराले,
द्वि सप्तकोटि भुजैर्धृतखर कर वाले
अबला केनो माँ एतो बले।
बहुबलधारिणीं
नमामि तारिणीं
रिपुदलपरिणीं
मातरम्।
तुमि विद्या तुमि धर्म
तुमि हृदि तुमि मर्म
त्वंहि प्राणा: शरीरे।
वाहुते तुमि माँ शक्ति
हृदय तुमि मा भक्ति
तो मारह प्रतिमा गड़ि
मंदिरे मंदिरे
त्वंहि दुर्गा दशप्रहरणधारिणी
कमला कमल दल विहारिणी

वाणी विद्यादायिनी
नामि त्वां
नमामि कमलात्
अमलां अतुलाम्
सुजलां सुफलां
मातरम्।
वन्दे मातरम्।

There is a powerful dialogue in the book between Bhavanand and Mahendra. Mahendra enquired that this was the image of our nation. Where is mother? Bhavanand replied that he did not recognise anybody except motherland as his mother. जननी जन्म भूमिश्च स्वर्गादपि —Motherland is greater than heaven.

The story of *Anand Math* takes a dramatic turn. Swami Satyanand and Mahendra were taken to prison. News of Satynand taken away as a prisoner by Muslim ruler spread like wildfire. All his followers who were called *Santan* (sons) gathered and attacked the prison, killed the guards and liberated Satyanand and Mahendra. They started dancing in jubilation. They burnt the houses of Muslim. When they came to know that British forces were coming with canons they thought that they could not face the canon with sticks and spears as such they fled away. The first chapter completes here.

Anand Math, with its socio-religious historical background of Nineteenth century Bengal, is a conceptual construct. It is both religious and literary discourse. As we are aware that the articulating a discourse is a dialectical act. Anand Math played an important role in the rise of nationalism in India. It captivated the young minds of Bengal in particular and India in general and awakened the dormant soul of India. It did create national ambience and motivated the young mind to fight against slavery and sufferings. Sri Aurobindo Ghose, Sri Subhas Chandra Bose, Shri Surindernath Banerjee, Sri Chitranjan Das, Khudiram and Swami Vivekanand and others were the creation of Anand Math in some and other form. To understand the impact of Anand Math we must study the text in its structural constitution of syntactic and paradigmatic formation. Its architectonic structure is constituted the conceptual domain, which is domain of thought in praxis par excellence.

Second chapter of the *Anand Math* begins with the story of Shanti and Javanand. Shanti was a Brahmin girl who became helpless and homeless after the death of her father who was a teacher. Mr. Chattopadhyay gives a vivid description of human feelings and emotions. When Shanti started learning Sanskrit from a pandit, Pandit started getting out of control emotionally in the face of the budding youth of Shanti. Pandit had forgotten the vow of *Sanyasin.* Shanti had the courage and determination to guard herself from every immorality of the society. Shanti was the wife of Jivanand but Jivanand had taken a vow not to lead a household life unless he got his motherland liberated from the Muslim rule and British imperialism. Novelist portrays the feelings and emotions of Shanti and Jivanand in very natural and aesthetic forms. In the meantime Satyanand informs Mahendra that his wife and daughter were alive. However, he motivated him to get initiated in *Sanatan Dharma.*

Shanti christened herself as a Navinananda and put on the dress of male *Sanyasi* and entered into the room of Jivanand. Jivanand did recognise her but she refused to get away with normal emotions and feelings. Shanti had also got initiated in *Sanatan Dharma* in her male dress. The central objective of this literary discourse here is to take a man and woman for the mundane existence to supermundane existence of suffering and sacrifice for the motherland.

Anand Math presents a socio-religious construct, which is upheld by the traditional values of Hinduism and which was threatened by various Islamic assertions and British intrigues.

Matthew Arnold says that a writer is a Zeitgeist. In the literary discourse historical sense is depicted. In fact a literature is an awareness of tradition and contemporaneity of experience. Writer weaves out the historical sense and traditional awareness in and through different characters and situations. The colour and contours of different characters and situations speak out the historical and cultural form of life.

Bankim Chandra Chattopadhyay in his immortal work *Anand Math* articulates the most rigorously realised nationalism. He tries to arouse the sense of nationalism and total commitment to the motherland. In this text the social, religious and political is in perpetual dialectical interaction with its anti-structure. The literary discourse and its structuration and de-structuration are dialectical and reciprocal.

The third and fourth chapters of the novel highlight the strength and the weakness of the Hindu nationalism. *Anand Math* expounds clearly and very strongly Hindu nationalism. Accordingly to it, Hinduism is nationalism and nationalism is Hinduism.

The chapter third starts with the story of Warren Hastings and his military campaign against Anand Math. Anand Math became very strong both in its military and manpower. Warren Hastings was the

Governor General of India at that time. Anand Math became so powerful that Warren Hastings could not control the situation. Under the leadership of Satyanand, his followers started burning the houses of Muslims. Captain Thomas was made incharge to quell the revolt. The company had many established warehouses for silk with palatial residences. There was one such *kothi* in Shivagrama. Doniworth was the head of the *Kothi.* There was good security arrangement for that *Kothi* because of which Doniworth could save his life. He sent his children to Calcutta for safety. However, he was greatly tortured by the followers of Anand Math. Even the scavengers and vagabonds started looting the supply of the Captain. There were carriages full of supply of rice, chickens, butters which were attacked by the scavengers and hoodlum. But they could not face onslaught of guns and as such fled away. Captain Thomas sent the message to Calcutta that with 157 constables he quelled the revolt of 14700 persons. Seven persons had been captured. In this message only the last part was true. Captain had the illusion that he had won the second battle of Welham. He became overconfident and started pontification to Doniworth. Doniworth asked him to stay for ten days so that by that time situation would become normal. There were enough eatables at the house of Doniworth. The new cook was another Draupadi.

On the other hand Bhavanand was becoming restive and he was in a look for the oportune moment to kill Captain Thomas. The followers of Anand Math could not realise that Britishers had come for the welfare of India. Even the Britishers were not aware of this fact. At that time only god was aware of this truth. Bhavanand was contemplating on the ways and means to demoralise the descendents of demons. Captain Thomas was fond of hunting. He went to the forest in search of wild animals. There was no road. Horse could not wade in the forest. Captain left the horse and started moving in the forest on foot in search of tiger. He couldn't see any tiger. He was enamoured to see woman sitting beneath a tree in the forest. A new *Sanyasin.* The whole forest was glowing with the beauty of that woman. Divine beauty of that woman had filled the flowers with rare fragrance. Captain Thomas was first surprised and then became very angry. He knew the native language.

He asked: Who are you?
SANYASIN replied: I am a *Sanyasin.*
CAPTAIN enquired: Are you a rebel?
SANYASIN: So what!

CAPTAIN: I shall shoot you dead.

SANYASIN: Kill me.

Captain started debating with himself whether he should kill her or not. In the mean time she pounced upon him with a lightening speed and snatched away the gun from him. Sanyasin took of her leather cover and throw away her false hair, dresses and wigs. Captain Thomas saw that a most beautiful woman was standing before him. She said with a smile that she was a woman and didn't attack anybody. She would like to know from him that why the Britishers had come between Hindus and Muslims. The war was going between Hindus and Muslims.

SAHAB: Who are you?

SHANTI: You see that I am a Sanyasin. I am one of them against whom you are fighting.

SAHAB: Will you live with me?

SHANTI: What! As a concubine?

SAHAB: You will be like a wife but without marriage.

SHANTI: I would also like to enquire from you one thing. I had one monkey in my house. Now he is dead. His cage is empty. I shall chain you. Will you stay there? There are enough bananas in my orchard.

SAHAB: You are a very spirited woman. I am very happy with your courage. You come to my house. Your husband has died in the battle. What will happen to you?

SHANTI: Let us make a pact between me and you. If you will win I shall become your concubine and if I shall win you will remain in cage and eat banana.

SHANTI: Take this gun. Who would converse with such an uncultured person. And after throwing the gun she left with a smile in her face.

Shanti went into the thick forest and entered into a cottage. Jivanand was playing with *Saranga.* He enquired from Shanti if there had been a tide in her life? He told her that he had broken the vow of *Sanatan Dharma* and hence he would have to lead down his life. Shanti did not allow her to talk about death. She said that she was his wife. She also came out in the jungle to help him in his mission. She said she was his wife. She is co-religious follower. The marriage is not only for this life. You have taken now not to live with woman until the motherland is liberated. You have not lived with me. Where is the question of atonement. You are a brave man. How can I teach you the *Veer Dharma.* You just love me. I love you. I don't want more than this. Let us sing *Vande Mataram.*

Bhavananda went to a town. He met Gauri Didi. Kalyani was there. She was very beautiful. Bhavananda had fallen in love with Kalyani but Kalyani was still in. love with her husband, Mahendra.

BHAVANANDA: Once who plants a tree and waters it everyday one feels happy to see the growth of the tree. I had planted a new life in you. It is blossoming now.

KALYANI: Poison tree never die.

BHAVANANDA: Is life a poison?

KALYANI: If it would not have been the case I would not have tried to kill it by pouring nectar (*Amrit*).

BHAVANANDA: I wanted to enquire from you. Who had made your life miserable?

KALYANI: Nobody has made my life miserable. Life itself is miserable.

BHAVANANDA: My life has also become miserable.

KALYANI: No.... When a learned man like you becomes sinner, learning becomes useless. How is my husband, Lord.

BHAVANANDA: Why you always enquire about your husband? He is already dead for you.

KALYANI: With death, the relation does not die. How is he?

BHAVANANDA: He is well.

KALYANI: Where is he! Is he in Padsin?

BHAVANANDA: Yes? He is there.

KALYANI: What is he doing?

BHAVANANDA: He is making fort and weapons. All the *Sanatans* are equipped with weapon manufactured by him.

Now we don't have the dirth of gun powder, cannons and guns. He is great amongst the *Sanatans*. He is doing great work for us. He is our right hand man.....

BHAVANANDA: You have rebirth. You can remarry again.

KALYANI: Bring my daughter.

BHAVANANDA: I shall bring her. Will you marry again?

KALYANI: With you!

BHAVANANDA: Will you marry?

KALYANI: To you!

BHAVANANDA: Suppose this is the case?

KALYANI: What will happen to your vow?

BHAVANANDA: It would be drowned in the ocean.

KALYANI: And this great vow? And this name Bhavananda.

BHAVANANDA: Drowned in the fathomless ocean.

KALYANI: For whom will you drowned everything in the fathomless ocean.

BHAVANANDA: For you. Listen whether one is a seer or a common man, a devil or deity, mind is not in the control of anybody. There is no doubt that *Sanatan Dharma* is my life but you have become life of my life, whole of my existence and being. For last four years I have been burning with love-sting. Now it is becoming unbearable. I can't live without you. Will you become mine!

KALYANI: I have learnt from you that who breaks the vow, for him death is the only atonement.

BHAVANANDA: Yes.

KALYANI: Then your atonement is death.

BHAVANANDA: Yes! Death is my only atonement.

KALYANI: If I fulfil your desire, you will die.

BHAVANANDA: Yes.

KALYANI: If I won't, then?

BHAVANANDA: Even then I shall die as my mind is under the control of sense organs.

KALYANI: I won't fulfil your desire. When you will die?

BHAVANANDA: In the coming battle.

KALYANI: Then you go. Please send my daughter. Bhavananda with tears in his eyes promised to send her daughter. He enquired: would she remember him after his death.

KALYANI: Replied. She would remember as man who had fallen from his path.
Bhavananda left Kalayani started reading books.

There is a vivid description of the battle between the followers of Anand Math and British army. Satyanand was the supreme commander. Under his command, the followers of Satyanand attacked and killed the British army. The news of arrival of Satyanand spread like a wildfire. The followers started assembly in the moonlit night. Satyanand had to give some special message. People had no knowledge where Satyanand had gone. People believed that he had gone to Himalayas to do penance for the success. People started guessing about the new course. They started planning to build temple after demolishing Masjid. Satyanand blessed everybody. He said that there was one Thomas who had killed many of our followers. He directed them to wage a war and establish Hindu Raj.

Cannons started booming. There had been a long battle. They started killing Muslims. Some Muslims started calling themselves Hindu.

The fusion of religion with nationalism was the hallmark of Nineteenth century Indian thought and movement. The Arya Samaj in Northern and Western India, various forms of Kali worship in Bengal, Ganesh worship in Maharashtra symbolised this fusion which had a deep and profound impact on the psyche of youth in this country. It was not uncommon even in the later day revolutionary moving towards gallows with the hymns of *Geeta* and *Gurugranth* on their lips. The failure of Sepoy Mutiny of 1857 did left great impact in the history of national movement in India.

In the fourth chapter which is also the last chapter of the novel, Shri Chatttopadhyay summarises the whole literary discourse. Warrren Hastings sent army under the command of Major Edward. Edward was a very able army officer. He made a plan to capture Padsin which was the headquarters of *Sanatan* army. Fullmoon of month of Magh was approaching. On this very day there used to be a big gathering at the bank of river to take holy dip in the water.

Shanti entered into the enemy camp and she could know the whole strategy of Major Edward. The *Sanatan* army took a strategic position and attacked the British army. There was a fierce battle. Most of the *Sanatan* army were killed. In the dead of night Shanti started the search of her husband's body. She met a Mahatma. Mahatma helped her in finding the body of Jivananda. Jivananda was almost dead. There was no sign of any life. With the divine touch of Mahatma Jivanand came to life.

However, in this battle British army suffered a humiliating defeat. There was none left to send a message to Mr. Warren Hastings.

Swami Satyanand went to Anand Math and started meditating. All of a sudden physician Mahatma appeared before him. He greeted him. Satyanand wanted to know about the mystery. When he won the battle and established the supremacy of *Sanatan Dharam* why he was asked to quiet.

He stated that your mission had been fulfilled. Muslim rule had been vanquished. Now there is no work for you. Satyanand enquired that Muslim rule has been vanquished but Hindu rule was not established. Britishers were still ruling at Calcutta.

Mahatma said that Hindu rule would never be established.

Satyanand was in great pain and agony after knowing this and he asked Lord! If Hindu rule would not be established then who would rule India. If the Muslims would again establish their rule here?

Mahatma said No. Britishers would be the rulers. Mahatma gave a long discourse on the historical necessity of British rule. The worship of thirty three crore of deities is not *Sanatan Dharma.* The real knowledge is both mundane and superamundane. The superamundane knowledge is the real *Sanatan Dharma*. However, without the mundane knowledge supermundane would not grow and blossom. To awaken the real supermundane knowledge one will have to first cultivate mundane knowledge. This knowledge is not available now in this country. There is nobody now who can impart this knowledge. And hence we will have to impart this knowledge from foreign land. Britishers are well-versed in this knowledge. The English education would be of great help to us and it would help in the growth and develcpment of divine knowledge. And hence we would make Britishers as our rulers. Hindu would become strong and educated under British rule. Satyanand enquired that if the British rule were beneficial for us then why we had so much of killings. Mahatma replied that Britishers were traders. Their only aim was to make money. Now after the revolt of Anand Math, they would take the responsibility of administration. Britishers are friends. Nobody has any power to defeat the Britishers.

Mahatma took the hand of Satyanand in the forest of the statue of Lord Vishnu. Knowledge embraced Devotion. *Dharma* embraced Action. Kalyani embraced Shanti. The literary discourse ends here.

The literary discourse is a specific articulation of a specific perception of a specific existential situation. Claude Levi-Strauss developed the methodology of semio-anthropological analysis. According to him the literacy discourse is a linear progression. Anand Math as a literary discourse does contain a historical consciousness and a religious message but it is a neither a history nor a religious treatise. It is primarily an articulation of specific perception of a specific conceptual construct. In the act of writing and reflection, Shri Chattopadhyay presents the socio-cultural complexities in their sublimation and profundities without ignoring the paradoxes of human existence. Shri Bamkim Chandra Chattopadhyay in his work *Anand Math* tried to explain and elucidate the contradictions and conflicts due to social and existential tension which existed in the Nineteenth century cultural milieu of Bengal. However, *Vande Mataram* heralded a new era of nationalism, revolution and renaissance in India.

13

Hinduism

Retrospect and Prospect

Hinduism is a protean. Hinduism is pluralistic and accepts all forms of religious practices and philosophical concepts as aspects of one truth. Hinduism stands for religion, philosophy, cult, culture, civilization, race, jurisprudence, ritualism, esotericism, emphacism and 'something more'. This 'something more' gives a special identity to Hinduism.

Indian culture and civilization have had an extremely long and complex development. It has the longest history of continuous growth than any other living cultural tradition of the world. The historical perspective of cultural tradition and philosophical analysis are immensely useful in studying and understanding the basic and the subterranean cultural spirit of Hinduism. However, it is a very difficult and complex task to present a chronological sequence of the cultural evolution of Hinduism. In a broad outline, the cultural history of Hinduism can be divided into two major periods of development — (i) Tantric, and (ii) Vedic.

If we examine and analyze the different philosophical, religious and the mystic concepts of Hinduism, we come to the conclusion that the roots of Hinduism lie in the Indus Valley Civilization and Vedic culture of early Indian Hindu society. The excavation at Mohenjo-Daro and Harappa revolutionized the concepts of Indian history and civilization.

The Indus Valley Civilization goes back to the Neolithic period (7000 to 6000 BC) that faded away by 1500 BC. This was a very organized and developed urban culture. Mohenjo-Daro and Harappa, separated by some forty miles, were two of the civilization's most important cities where the inhabitants enjoyed high standards of living. The cities had a developed culture and technology and most of the houses had a drainage system etc. The antecedents of this culture can be traced to the site of the Mergarh (150 miles north of Mohenjo-Daro in Baluchistan) cultural community that exited before 6000 BC and has established an unbroken cultural continuity from that early date to the period of the Indus Valley Civilization. The excavation of the Indus Valley has firmly established that it is one of the oldest living civilizations of world. The indigenous inhabitants of India were highly developed, both intellectually and spiritually. There is no evidence to prove that there was any affinity between the Indus Valley Civilization and the Middle-East. The cities were built by the people who inhabited the Indus Valley itself for several centuries. It was the inner conservatism and the spiritual humanism of Harappan culture that kept them alive and vibrant. For the survival and the development of any culture and civilization, some conservatism is essential. The growth and the birth of a civilization cannot be explained either in terms of race and environments or in terms of challenge and response as has been conceived by Arnold Toynbee. He says, What is it that brings a civilization to birth? I do this by examining a number of test cases, and I find that, although a strong stimulus is needed to bring a civilization into existence the challenge must not be so severe as to stifle creativity." (Toynbee, 1972).

If we examine the above findings of Toynbee then we find that his challenge and response theory does not give a satisfactory explanation to the birth of civilization. To my mind, it is the quest for one's own identity and destiny that gives birth to civilization. The inhabitants of the Harappan civilization, who have been wrongly painted as pagan and uncivilized in the process of reflection and insight on the real nature of their own beings and existences, discovered the divine effulgence of self. This gave birth to Tantras and a great civilization.

The only male God of the Harappan culture is Lord Siva. He is characterized by a horned head-dress, the symbol of great occult power. A seal showing Siva seated on a raised throne in the posture of *yoga* has been discovered at Mohenjo-Daro. In this, he is shown as three-faced that means he knows of the past, present and future, (*trikaladarsi*). He is in the *urdhuamedhra* (*penis eructus*) form that is a proper yogic posture for meditation. Four animals are shown near Siva, a rhinoceros and a buffalo on his right, and an elephant and a tiger on his left. Below the throne are two radiant deers with their horns turned inside towards the centre. This symbolizes the great spiritual power of Siva, in whose presence a tiger and an elephant behave like pet animals. Sir John

Marshall says, 'The figure represents a prototype of the historic Siva'. (Sir John Marshall, 1931). The people belonging to the non-Aryan culture used to worship Mother Goddess apart from Lord Siva. Dr. R.C. Majumdar believes that "some fundamental ideas of Hinduism as well as some beliefs and observances still current in India may be traced as far back as the third millennium BC" and that "the worship of Siva and Sakti may be regarded as the oldest form of the Indian theistic religion". The Vedic Samhitas imbibe some of the mystic forms of non-Aryan religion that brought modification and change in the content of Vedic hymns. The harmonious blending of the two traditions blossomed into a great and profound Indian culture that is known as Hinduism. The quest for identity and destiny became the characteristic of Hindu mind. Referring to the Indians, Deussen has remarked "...no people on earth took religion so seriously, none toiled on the way to salvation as they did." (P. Deussen, 1972). Another Western scholar, Cramb, has remarked about India that, "In religion it is the earth's central shrine. India is religion." (Dr. Bhagvan Das).

Hinduism is *dharma* and not a religion. The word *dharma* is derived from the root that means 'to grasp'. It connotes the property of anything and being. As, for example, what is the *dharma* of fire. To burn is the *dharma* of fire. Now the question arises, what is the *dharma* of man? To understand the real and deeper meaning of *dharma*, a philosophical investigation on the longings and aspirations of man is warranted. Human longing is infinite bliss (*ananda*). This quest of infinite bliss has been instrumental in discovering the transcendental nature of man's being and existence. Man is not just another creature. He is a hibernated cosmic being. If man does not have this longing for the infinite, he would not have discovered the Brahman and he would not have established his identity with him. This is the most profound and greatest discovery of Hinduism. Ayamatma (1 am self) *aham brahma asmi* (I am Brahman), *tatvamasi* (That Thou art), *soham* (I am That) are known as *Mahavakyas* in the Upanishadic lore. The *Mahavakyas* are not just philosophical truths experienced by seers (*rishis*) and saints, *yogis* and *munis* of Hindu tradition in their state of spiritual sublimity that is known as enlightenment (*nirvana*), but are living realities. Gavin Flood rightly observes that, "The term *dharma* is untranslatable in the sense it has no ditect semantic equivalents in any western languages which convey the resonance of associations expressed by them." (Gavin Flood, 1998).

Hinduism is called *sanatana dharma* because it takes man beyond the world of dualism of subject and object, matter and mind to the world of oneness and transcendental truth (*sanatana satya). Brihadaranya Upanishad* says: "Where there is duality, as it were, there one sees another; there one feels another; there one tastes another. But where everything has become just one's own self, then whereby and when would one see? Then whereby and whom would one smell? Then whereby and whom would one taste?"

The state of *nirvana* is a state of self-consciousness where the distinction between 'me' and 'the world' breaks down completely. It is fused into a unified undifferentiable whole that is *Brahman* or *atman*. Fritjof Capra observes, "The picture of an inter-connected cosmic whole which emerged from modern atomic physics has been used extensively in the East to convey the mystical experience of nature. For Hindus, the Brahman is the unifying thread in the cosmic wall, the ultimate ground of all being." (The *Tao of Physics*).

The basic oneness of the universe is the root concept of Hinduism. In our ordinary life, we are not aware of this basic unity. To believe in the world of separate objects and events that are mental constructs of our discriminating and categorizing intellect is called illusion (*avidya*). The central objective of Hindu meditation is to maintain a dynamic balance and mental equilibrium, because in this state of mental equilibrium alone, one would become conscious of the absolute oneness of the universe. Modern science, specially quantum mechanics and theory of relativity, express in different ways that there is a basic unity in the universe. The so-called separate objects and events, the different constituents of matter and the phenomena are all inter-connected, interrelated and interdependent though we understand them as isolated and separate entities. To consider these abstract concepts of separate things and beings as natural realities is what is called in Hinduism as *maya*. This estrangement of man has been viewed by Hinduism in the form of bondage. According to the *Saṁkhya* and the *Vedanta* systems, the erroneous identification of man with non-self is nesience or *avidya*. The Upanishad says:

> 'Man' is *brahman* but due to the *avidya* he is estranged with himself. The Upanishadic seers have been in the quest of liberation from this estrangement. 'Know thyself' is the *dharma* of man. It is sacramental and sacerdotal. It is sotereological commitment to value and the goal. Man is a unit of value and the quest for his own identity and destiny is the *dharma* of man.

Man is both rationalist and divine, an empiricist and transcendentalist. He has the unique power of living simultaneously in the present and the future. This uniqueness makes him the most superior creature in the world and provides him the spiritual power of transcendence. According to Hinduism: '*Dharmasya Tattavam Nihitim Guhayam*'.

The *dharma* resides in the innermost recesses of one's being and existence. This is the quintessence of Hinduism. *Dharma* is the root concept of Hinduism. Different concepts and religio-philosophical systems of Hinduism are corollaries of this root concept. The concepts of *karma*, rebirth, *atman* or *brahman* and *moksha* are different dimensions of *dharma*. However, Kashmir *Saivism* and Vedanta have gone deeper into the philosophical and mystical inquiry. *Siva Sutra* begins with *Chaitanya-atma,* conscious self, which has absolute freedom of all knowledge and activity is the self or nature of Reality. In the meditative insight and philosophical investigation, Hinduism discovered the path of liberation and christened it as *moksha*. *Moksha* or *nirvana* is nothing but the realisation of one's own being. In the realization of one's own identity with the Brahman, lies the solution of man's estrangement and freedom. Thus, Hinduism is a socio-spiritual discipline that aims at the realization of the supreme goal of life, not by renunciation but by enriching the social system. According to Hinduism, human society is one and indivisible, because there is only one *dharma* of man. This is the basic thrust of Hinduism. Hinduism works against the destruction of spiritual values that bind man with himself and with society. The scientific and technological advancement is getting out of balance with our moral, spiritual and social performances. Instead of having control over the biosphere, we must exercise control over ourselves. Hinduism does provide various disciplines and spiritual techniques to exercise control over ourselves and make life fuller and richer.

Science and the social system are organic and integral. In the socio-economic system, this organic relation manifests in linear cumulative and quantitative forms. In this process of growth and differentialism, man is becoming more and more independent of nature. According to Hinduism, only man possesses the scientific knowledge, power and spiritual vision to create a society of his own imagination and requirement. Yet, man does not enjoy absolute freedom. He is constrained by the axial facts that each social system has a different rhythm of change. All social changes are not compatible with one another. Our analysis and examination of social change from pre-historic to modern times have revealed that our perceptions of time, space and causation have undergone a great change. The power that we possess today to transform nature and the extent and the range of man's socio-political life are on a scale that our ancestors would have been unable to comprehend. Our social and moral structures have undergone tremendous changes and transformation through scientific and technological advancement. However, under technological society, man is becoming bereft of a self-identity. This process of dehumanization is a bad omen. The genetic engineering, eugenics and test tube babies have dehumanized our social system. The unholy alliance of science and technology is leading man towards a technological society that would unleash courses of history that would be self-destructive. Hinduism is aware that in the concept, of technological society lies the very seed of human destruction.

If we summerize the discussion on Hinduism, we come to the conclusion that the grandeur and glory of intrinsic genius of Hinduism, would be stifled if it accepts the survival of the old as a sufficient substitute for new and creative departures. Any attempt to nationalize Hinduism, would lead to its dehumanization. The practise of ethical, rational and mystical religion which is the essence of Hinduism, would transform Hindu society into a global society and Hinduism would become the hope and the promise of the new millennium.

Human society today is unified both in terms of space and time. To annul the dangerous fissures of the social order we have to learn to live together in harmony in spite of differences of civilization, culture, religion, race, languages and nationality. The situation is both delicate and dangerous. Toynbee is right in his observation, "We are now waking up to the truth that we have unintentionally put ourselves in a new position in which mankind may have to choose between two extreme alternatives of committing genocide and learning to live hence forward as a single family.... Historical forces can be more explosive than an atom bomb." (*The Study of History*). The very survival of mankind is in doubt. It is human nature that threatens its total annihilation. The question of survival is related to human nature. The very existence of mankind depends on the cultivation of such motives that would annihilate the very animality in man and lead to the harnessing of the real being which is divine. Man is essentially a divine being. The experience of divinity has given birth to religion. Hinduism, with its mystic technique and spiritual humanism has the vision and power to lead the bewildered humanity, to the Vedantic truth 'all is *Brahman*', and I am *atman'* where *atman* and *Brahman* become one and lead to the vision of one world and one humanity (*Vasudhaiva kutumbakam*). The choice before mankind is plain and simple 'One World or none'. Hinduism is universalism. It has a historical role to play in fostering the feelings of non-violence and truth, love and compassion and, thereby, to negate the forces of self-extinction. Hinduism, Buddhism and Sufism could herald an era of new renaissance. According to Hinduism, pursuits of *dharma* mean pursuits of survival. All human history is relevant to present and the future society, so long mankind pursues the path of *dharma*.

14
Integral Humanism: An Analysis and Reflections

Before I dwell upon integral humanism, it is important to know about humanism. Humanism is a homo-centric philosophy and to understand it better, we need to have an insight in the nature and evolution of *Homo sapiens*, which is the Latin expression for human species. The study of humanism tries to resolve all philosophical issues, keeping in mind the Man at its centre. The Western view about humanism is dualistic and doctrinaire, while the Eastern view perceives it as monastic and mystical. Man, according to Western view, is a measure of everything but in the Eastern philosophy, divinity is considered the measure of everything and Man, only as a hibernated cosmic being. Deen Dayal Upadhyaya, the political thinker treats Man as integral to Indian Culture and Civilization and calls this 'integral humanism'. I will try to analyze and evaluate this subject from both scientific and philosophical perspectives.

The Vedas have defined humanism in a wider and universal sense. A verse in the Upanishada describes the semantic and signification of humanism tellingly. One can notice this verse inscribed on the arch of Central Hall of Indian Parliament. It reads: "The narrow-minded people think that this is mine, and that is your but for the men of truth and value, the whole world is one family."[1]This is the quintessential teaching of the Vedas. No wonder, the Indian culture believes in one world and one humanity, as Indian humanism draws its strength from spirituality. I call this Spiritual Humanism.

There is no need to be obsessed with western thought and ideology. But that does not mean, everything about western thoughts are either irrational or wrong. A happy and harmonious blend of Indian spirituality with scientific temper of the west is what we should desire for. This concept of spiritual universalism is ingrained in India which is not just a geographical boundary or merely a political entity. India is not just even a sovereign nation-state. It is actually a state of mind and consciousness, a myth, a metaphor, a history, a renaissance, a culture, a civilization and spirituality, all rolled into one entity. Simply put, India is Dharma.

Swami Vivekanand and Mahatma Gandhi had a proper understanding and awareness of Indian ethos and culture. Vivekanand awakened the dormant divinity and spirit of India. Gandhi, on the other hand, spiritualized politics under the guidance of Gokhale and lit the social and political soul of India. Both Swami Vivekanand and Mahatma Gandhi laid down the social, moral and spiritual foundation of New India, based on liberal notions of equality, freedom and democracy. They also guided the coming generations to evaluate integral humanism from the prism of universal acceptance and pragmatism.

Upadhyaya defines integral humanism broadly on the same lines. He writes: "It needs to be realized that not all thoughts and principles that have sprung up elsewhere are necessarily local in space and time. The response of human beings varies depending upon the place, time and social surroundings in which they are placed. They often react differently to different situations. Therefore, to ignore the progress and developments achieved by other societies in the past or present, will be unwise. All the positives in these developments must be taken note of and accepted. However, while absorbing the wisdom of other societies, it is only proper that we avoid their mistakes and perversities and adapt only their wisdom that suits our situation and circumstances. In brief, we must not hesitate in imbibing the knowledge and gains of the entire humanity as far as ethical principles and truths are concerned. The ideas and achievements that keep flooding in as we move with time, should also be reworked in accordance with changing times and conditions. At the same time, we must also absorb truths that we import from other societies."[2]

Humanism accepts the subject and object and the individual and society as a unit. Different thinkers in different periods of history have evaluated it in a broader and universal sense. Tagore and Gandhi insisted that humanism must harmonize with Indian spiritual ethos. Upadhyaya was once asked, why in India, where Gandhi professed "Ram Rajya" and "Gram Rajya", capitalism and socialism were allowed to dominate the political and economic systems. He replied that after Independence, India should indeed have walked on the path showed by Gandhiji but unfortunately, he was ignored, and Indians began following the western ideologies. He averred that the Gandhian thought was holistic and fitted well within the Indian school of thought which does not divide "individual" and "society" nor it recognizes individual only as a material being."[3] Besides, Gandhi was a great humanist who used *dharma* as a powerful instrument to serve humanity and which forms the core of Gandhian philosophy. Gandhi, he said, spoke for the entire mankind. His humanism was holistic, inclusive and universal and his faith in human race which was endowed with spiritual and moral potentials, was abiding. These attributes, according to Gandhi, had helped human beings to perfect themselves. Upadhyaya thought that Gandhi was an incorrigible optimist and he had immense trust in the future of mankind.

During the European renaissance, it was argued that education could transform Man into a fully evolved being and nature could help him harness his immense potentiality to bring joy and happiness in his life. Renaissance thinkers found no contradiction between earthly happiness and spiritual pursuits to attain bliss and beatitude in all walks of life. A few others observed that enrichment of humanity should alone be the end and means of politics. However, if we analyze the European renaissance art, we will notice that though it is essentially human-centered, it is not exclusively based on worldly experiences nor it negates the essence of human spirituality.

The *Encyclopedia Britannica* has summarized humanism in these words: "Whatever might be its weakness and inner conflicts, the humanistic movement was heroic in its breadth and energy and remarkable in its aspirations. For human development in all fields, it created a context of seldom-equllued fertility. Its characteristic modalities of thought, speech and image lent themselves to the promptings of genius and became the medium for enduring achievement. Its moral program formed the basis for lives that are remembered with admiration."[4]

Humanism is also the philosophy of art of living and peaceful co-existence. Socrates provided moral imperative for it. Others have defined it differently. Hence, we have different schools of humanism such as scientific humanism, secular humanism, naturalistic humanism, democratic humanism, socialist humanism, radical humanism and spiritual humanism. Integral humanism tries to reconcile the differing stream of thoughts from rational, spiritual and scientific perspective so that it remains relevant in the present global order. With the advancement of technology, the world has become a global village. Any ideology or view of humanism which is not universal in character and is not inclusive in contents and forms, cannot propel human history to march towards attaining the goal of peaceful co-existence and a just social order.

Merleau-Ponty, a noted thinker and pioneer of socialist humanism, argues that humanism is not a choice between violence and non-violence. It is a choice only between two mores of violence, prevalent in the capitalistic and socialist systems. In the Russian Federation and China, violence and deceptions are officially accepted as instruments to sustain the socialist system. In a democratic system, the situation, however, is better as its governing principles draw their strength not only from deception and violence but also from human values and divine aspirations. The two systems have been at loggerheads to get acceptance in the global power politics. Integral Humanism seeks to bring down their differences by providing an alternative order of governance.

Herbert Marcuse while evaluating the claims of two humanistic systems writes, I quote- "Socialism appears again as an abstract idea; loyalty to its idea excludes the fostering of illusions. However, its new abstractness does not signify falsification. The proletariat which was to validate the equation of socialism and humanism pertained to an era when society was developing industrially. Socialistic theory, no matter how valid, can neither prescribe nor predict the future agents of a historical transformation. In fact, it disrupts the established societies more than ever before. It mirrors the image of a vital need, develops and protects the consciousness of this need and thus lays the groundwork for the dissolution of the false unity in defense of the *status quo*."[5]

Integrated Humanism accepts the possibility that if we adhere to the moral and spiritual chores, then it is possible to create an egalitarian society. It may not be so in materialistic humanism. It is true that the enormous advancement in science and technology will accelerate economic productivity, paving way for a better life for the large section of population. People will not have to work for hours for earning their bread and other necessities. They will have adequate reasons to live in a world in which slaves will be non-existence. But they will also be required to work very hard to sustain themselves, without cutting down their leisure. Let us not forget that *leisure is essential to a healthy and enduring growth of civilization*. Man is not a dependent variable and there cannot be a greater tragedy than Man subjecting himself to the will of others.

Upadhayaya's support to individual's right to freedom and dignity is unflinching. He observes that Indian tradition considers human being as an "integral entity" which means that he cannot be divided. In other words, he is an indivisible, 'integrated' unit. Similarly, society and individual cannot be separated as they are interwind. Every human being is thus an integral part of the society, he emphasizes."[6]

This integrated view of man was not prevalent in France prior to the French Revolution. The individual had been completely alienated by the society. In due course, this alienation provoked Rousseau to propound his thesis of the social contract which played a key role in bringing about the French Revolution in 1789. He wrote that, "Man is born free; and everywhere he is in chains. One thinks himself the master of others, but he still remains a greater slave than they."[7]

Humanism, as we know, originated with the advent of *Homo sapiens*. Hence it acknowledges the sovereignty of Man. Sovereignty and humanism are inalienable and non-transferable. Without sovereignty, Man is less than a Man. Without humanism, society is less than a society. Humanism and sovereignty define Man as a unit of value. Taking a dig at Marx, Bertrand Russell writes, "In the new creed which controls the government of Russia, while there is much that is very different from the traditional teaching of the West, there are a few things that have remained unchanged. The attitude of the governing classes and especially of those who conduct educational propaganda on the subject of dignity of labour is almost the same, which the governing classes of the world have always preached to the 'honest poor'. In the Marxist dispensation, commitment and willingness to work for long hours for distant advantages and even submissiveness to authority are frequently on display. The authority represents the will of the Ruler which is termed as "Dialectical Materialism".[8]

Upadhyaya rejects dialectical materialism on the ground, that it is against the very being of human life and its existence. He says that Man is essentially a spiritual being. Other humanists also believe in Man's near perfectibility, meaning that he can achieve his perfection, with or without the grace of God. The history of human civilization has by and large not accepted the semitic culture of exclusiveness. The stamp of semitic traditions, however, is quite invisible in the thinking of Spinoza and Goethe who were devoid of spiritual orientation and mystical salvation. Not surprisingly, Spinoza unites the body and mind in one substance which he calls God.

Upadhyaya agrees with this perception. He underlines that

spirituality is the substance of humanism and humanism is semantic of spirituality. In other words, humanism is spirituality and spirituality is humanism. Bertrand Russell, in "Analysis of Mind" also suggest that mental state is constituted from the same kind of elements as body. His view finds a fuller explanation in Vedanta philosophy which points out that life that we are living is not only a part of the entire existence, but it is the whole existence. It has been similarly expressed in *Mahavakya Tattvamasi* (Thou Art That) which clarifies that there is only one consciousness, one truth and one reality and that there is no dualism.

According to Schrodinger, the explanation of one and the many can be found in the teachings of Upanishad. He says that "the external world and consciousness are one and the same thing, as both are constituted by the same primitive elements. We have no other formula that can guide us in defining the essential components of these elements in individuals and that there is only one external world and that there is only one consciousness."[9]

M.N. Roy who propounded Radical Humanism looks at the problem of Man and his existence in the society from historical, economic, political and philosophical perspective. According to him, human history is not merely a narration of economic forces. The destiny of Man has been majorly shaped by the dialectic of development and the longing for freedom. He writes: "We should regard Man as the archetype of society; the potentiality of evolving the entire social pattern is inherent in every human being. His place in society need not be that of a mere cog in the wheel of a gigantic machine. He can discharge his social responsibility without surrendering his individual liberty; a free community can be composed only of free men, otherwise freedom is a fiction and a fraud. "[10]

M.N. Roy was a friend of Lenin and was one of the architects of Comintern. But he became disillusioned when he saw the functioning of the communist government of the USSR which had robbed freedom from Man and used him as a tool to exploit the masses. In the communist society, Man became a soulless creature, Roy thought.

Karl Marx did dream of weathering away of the state but not at the cost of individual's freedom. The communist governments deviated from his fundamental doctrine and treated man just as the cog. Radical Humanists abhorred this development. They recognized Man as a unit of value and underlined that Man without freedom and moral entity could not create a sound egalitarian society. M.N. Roy insisted that moral values in public life was of supreme importance and could not be sidestepped. He wrote: "The disconcerting experiences of the contemporary world compel thoughtful people to re-examine the fundamental principles of social philosophies from which different political theories of the right and left, conservative and liberal, reactionary and revolutionary have emerged. The experience is that in practice there is little difference among them because, capture of power irrespective of the diversity of means advocated for the purpose, is the common postulate of all political theories."[11]

There is no denying fact that there can be no sound political philosophy if it is not based on ethical values. But there is a fundamental shortcoming in Roy's thesis. Morality is only one aspect of spirituality. It is only a stepping stone towards leading a spiritual life in the attainment of enlightenment. According to the Vedantic teachings, man is Brahman i.e. spiritually evolved. But Roy does not accept the paramount importance of spirituality in the making of Man.

According to Upadhyaya, an exponent of Integral Humanism, Man has an inalienable right to pursue liberty, truth and salvation. No discrimination against any people or nation is acceptable to him. Going a step further, he accepts the doctrine of one world and one humanity. He writes: "The ideal of the Indian State has been Dharma Rajya. Tolerance of and respect for all faiths and creeds is an essential feature of the Indian State. Freedom of worship and conscience is guaranteed to all and the state does not discriminate against anyone on grounds of religion either in the formulation of policy or in its implementation. India is a non-sectarian state and not a theocracy."[12] Pluralism is the strength of India.

Elaborating his concept further, Upadhyaya says that the creative and religious dimensions of Man distinguish him from other creatures. By developing and imbibing the spiritual values he acquires a unique ability to work for a peaceful and harmonious co-existence in the comity of nations. Man, according to him, is essentially a divine being. By invoking divinity which is *sine qua non* of the Indian culture, he fosters unity between different races and civilizations. The fundamental duty of the members of society is to shun differences and live in peace and prosperity. An ideal civil society has to be the one that is based on acceptance of all human beings as equal and in which, Man and society show benevolence towards each other and readiness to live in mutual friendship.

This can be possible only if individual is accepted as sovereign. Concentration of power in one man or in one state is dangerous for democracy and individual freedom. A man is less than a man without freedom. Upadhyaya is against such concentration of power. He writes: "Concentration of power is repugnant to democracy and human freedom. Decentralization is highly congenial to the all-round development of a man's personality. Small scale mechanized industries, small trades and farms that can be run and managed by an individual, family or by cooperative ownership should be the basis of our economy. Setting up of large units should be rare."[13] Integral Humanism as defined by him is against capitalism and the communist system. He argues that in such systems, economic and political power get concentrated in the state or corporation and man is neglected. This situation can be avoided only if economic power is decentralized and individuals occupy pivotal position in socio-political regimes. He emphasizes the importance of spirituality without which no system can effectively serve humanity. In his words: "If you deny spiritualism then human behavior and the relationship between man and the Universe cannot be explained."[14]

In a Marxist system, as mentioned before, individual loses his individuality. It goes against the cardinal principles of human existence. As Chandi Das says: "Humanity is the highest truth. There is nothing beyond mankind."[15]

We can call it the quintessential essence of the Indian Culture and Indian civilization. India has been able to survive centuries of assault on its rich cultural, social and philosophical heritage and plunder of its glorious past because of its sound spiritual and moral foundation, laid down by saints and seers since antiquity.

The concept of nation-state which is an ugly reality of modern times, has led to conflicts and confrontations. The most illustrative examples of this are the first and second world wars in which nation states fought bitterly against each other, ending with the nuclear bombing of Hiroshima and Nagasaki on 6th and 8th August, 1945, that brought horrific devastation upon innocent people. Echoing this pain, Upadhyaya writes: "Nationalism leads to conflict between nations which leads in turn to global conflicts."

Another issue that troubles our times is that many regard *status quo* as synonymous with world peace. If we persist with this impression and accept it universally, aspirations of small nations to be independent will remain unfulfilled. It is a dilemma and will remain so, because world unity and nationalism inherently conflict with each other. There are some who advocate suppression of nationalism for world unity, whereas others regard world unity as utopian and say that national interest should be the foremost objective.[16] If we talk of absolute peace and harmony, then it cannot be established on the foundation of nation-states. It is desirable that people of all nation-states should work for cooperative and peaceful co-existence and betterment of humanity. A nation that craves for material prosperity and dominance over others cannot create an inclusive, egalitarian, socio-political system. Nuclear bombs may serve a nation's strategic interests, but they also irreparably destroy the creative soul of human beings. Unless man and his socio-political system overcome the poison of exclusive nationalism, human beings have no hopes for living in peaceful co-existence in any civilization.

Rabindra Nath Tagore's analysis of nationalism reflects similar sentiments. He says, and I quote, "Peace or unity cannot be manufactured by organizations, they can only well out of the mind of man, a mind which is blessed with generosity and goodwill towards all." Peace, in his view, can be achieved only by those "who are gifted with the moral power of love and vision of spiritual unity; who have the least feeling of enmity against aliens, and who can solve problems of their times with the help of higher nature."[17]

Humanism is thus a philosophy of being in sublime existence. Sixth Century BC is known in human history as an era of renaissance and regeneration of mankind. Lao Tse and Confucius of China, Buddha and Mahavir of India, Pythagoras, Parmenides and Zeno of Greece kindled the spiritual, moral and rational consciousness of human beings. Considered as founding fathers of spiritual humanism and makers of harmonious and enlightened civilizations, these visionaries have propounded the philosophy of art of living and laid down a sound philosophical foundation for human civilization to be based on the doctrine of peaceful co-existence.

However, the contemporary humanism took a new shape during the Italian or western renaissance in sixteenth century. During this period, Man was considered as a measure of everything and reason was considered as the essence of human existence. Hegel explained that real was rational and rational was real. But Indian renaissance perceived humanism differently. It stipulated that divinity was the measure of everything. Man was divine and a cosmic being and took the spirituality of Man as his defining nature. According to thinkers of Indian renaissance, the *summum bonum*, an Italian expression of the highest good, of man was attainment of Moksha. They also recognized *dharma* (virtue), *artha* (wealth), and *Kama* (enjoyment) as integral to human existence.

Upadhyaya has clarified this concept further. To quote him: "The four Purusharthas of Dharma, Artha, Kama and Moksha have been conceived as means for the achievement of the twin objective of individual advancement and social welfare. Dharma, Artha and Kama sustain one another and are complementary. To accept any one of them as the sole inspirer of human activity and to evaluate actions by that measure alone, will be taking a lop-sided view of things. However, Dharma being the means for realizing Artha and Kama, is of prime importance".[18]

Man's importance can hardly be overstated. He discovered philosophy and religion in his quest for identity and destiny and laid down the foundation of culture and civilization. He realized truth and reality which became the *summum bonum* of his life. He also sought truth as metaphysical and mystical experiences while analyzing the ultimate nature of his being and his existence. Indian seers and saints found the real nature of Man and described it as Upanishadic truth or *Tattvamasi*.

Mahatma Gandhi's thoughts about Man ran close to this truth. In this regard, Pandit Jawaharlal Nehru, in his historical speech, "Tryst with Destiny", quoted Gandhi's quintessential message, which reads like this: "Wipe Every Tear from Every Eye." Gandhi, the harbinger of a New Renaissance, laid dawn the foundation of ethical norms in the form of purity of both means and ends. He succinctly summarized philosophy of humanism in these words: "I will give you a *talisman*. Whenever you are in doubt, or when the self becomes too much with you, apply the following test. Recall the face of the poorest and the weakest man whom you may have seen and ask yourself if the step you contemplate is going to be of any use to him. Will he gain anything by it? Will it restore to him the control over his own life and destiny? In other words, will it lead to Swaraj for the hungry and spiritually striving millions? Then you will find your doubts and yourself melting away".

Upadhyaya also focusses on the importance of Man living in harmony with nature, wherein, he thinks, lies the future of mankind. According to him: "Man is not only integrated in society, he is also an integral part of this world and nature. If he misbehaves with nature, he will come to grief. Indian tradition worships nature as 'Mother.' To pollute nature is a sin. This universe does not constitute of only human beings and society; Man should learn to behave with nature. "[19]

The modern quantum mechanics agrees with the basic concept of Integral Humanism. Bohr and Heisenberg, the founding fathers of quantum mechanics, say that there is unavoidable mutual interaction between the observer and the world of nature. Heisenberg writes: "Our Scientific work in physics consists in asking questions about nature in the language that we possess and in trying to get an answer from experiment by the means that are at our disposal. In this way, quantum theory reminds us, as Bohr puts it, of the old wisdom that when searching for harmony in life, one must never forget that in the drama of existence, we are ourselves both players and spectators."[20]

Upadhyaya also advocates the historical necessity of coordinated cooperation between the individual and society. He writes, "Man does not exist merely as an individual. The Individual comprising body, mind, intellect and soul is not limited to a singular 'I' but is inseparably related to plural 'We' Therefore, we must also think of the group or the society."[21] He goes on to say that the highest ethical objective of humanism is to live in peace and harmony with each other based on reason, love and compassion.

In fact, the modern science is coming closer to Vedantic concept of truth and reality. Erwin Schrodinger opines that consciousness is singular and not plural. The cosmic consciousness is the only reality that exists. Schrodinger in his series of lectures delivered on Science and Humanism deals with the *spiritual bearing of science in life.* He writes: "I do not think I am prejudiced against the importance that science has, from purely human point of view. I have expressed in the original title of these lectures and explained in the introductory passages that I consider science an integrating part of our endeavour to answer the one great philosophical question which embraces all others, the one that Plotinus expressed in his brief: *who are we?* And more than that: I consider this not only of the tasks, but the task of science—the only one that really counts."[22] This is affirmation of Upadhyaya's thesis of Integral Humanism.

For Upadhyaya, history of Man is narration of his struggle against himself. Unless a Man conquers his own self and adopts moral values and norms, he cannot lead the society towards humanistic goal of peaceful co-existence. Upadhyaya's understanding of humanism is quite relevant but when he declares it as a manifesto of Jan Sangh, he contradicts his own doctrine of universalism which is the essence of humanism. Despite this shortcoming, his Integral Humanism is a commendable work and it does contribute to knowing about the concept of truth and values, and their importance for human beings.

With the advent of globalization there has been an erosion in the idea of nation-states. Twenty first century is often termed as an era of multilateralism, but multilateralism can survive only if spiritual or integral humanism becomes the charter of multilateralism. A spiritually evolved community of human beings will alone help in the emergence of a harmonious world order of lasting peace and prosperity. It will also save the world from untold sufferings including those from nuclear holocausts. Rabindranath Tagore in his poem *he mor chitto* (Oh! my soul) brings out his innate belief that India can take the lead in creating one world and one humanity in the following lines:

> "We shall give and take
> We shall bring peoples together and embrace them
> We shall not shut our doors
> This is the identity of India in the vast ocean of great humanity."[23]

Notes

1. अयं निज: परो वेति गणना लघुचेतसाम् ।उदारचरितानां तु वसुधैव कुटुम्बकम् ।। …….. The Vedas.
2. *Integral Humanism: An Analysis of Some Basic Elements*, pp. 80-81 Deendayal Upadhyaya. Prabhat Paperbacks, 4/19, Asaf Ali Road, New Delhi-110002.
3. *Integral Humanism: An Analysis of Some Basic Elements*, pp. 64–65 Deendayal Upadhyaya.
4. *Encyclopedia Britannica*, p. 676.
5. *Socialist Humanism*, Erich Fromm (Ed.) Allen Lane, The Penguin Press London 1967, p. 106.
6. *Integral Humanism*, Deendayal Upadhyaya, p. 65.
7. Rousseau, *The Social Contract*, Book 1, Chpt. 1.
8. *Socialist Humanism*, pp. 231–232, Allen Lane, The Penguin Press, London, 1967.
9. *My View of the World*, Erwin Schrodinger, p. 37, OX Bow Press, Woodbridge, Connecticut, 1964.
10. *Radical Humanism*, M.N. Roy, p. 4, Eastern Economist Pamphlets. Eastern Economist Pamphlets 14, General Editor E.P.W. da COSTA P. 08.
11. *Radical Humanism*, M.N. Roy.
12. *Integral Humanism*, Deendayal Upadhyaya, p. 49.
13. *Integral Humanism*, Deendayal Upadhyaya, p. 55.
14. *Integral Humanism*, Deendayal Upadhyaya, p. 56.

15. सवार उपरे मानुष सत्य। तहार उपरे नाय, Chandi Das.
16. *Integral Humanism*, Deendayal Upadhyaya, p. 81.
17. *Rabindranath Tagore and Universal Humanism*, p. 36, By Soumyendranath Tagore, Rabindranath Tagore Centenary Year.
18. *Integral Humanism*, Deendayal Upadhyaya, p. 47.
19. *Integral Humanism*, Deendayal Upadhyaya, pp. 65–66.
20. *Physics and Philosophy*, Werner Heisenberg, p. 32, Harper perennial Modern Thought, 2007.
21. *Integral Humanism*, Deendayal Upadhyaya, p. 94.
22. *Nature and the Greeks and Science and Humanism*, Erwin Schrodinger, p. 155, Cambridge University Press.
23. दीवे आर नीवे
    मिलावे आर मिलिवे
    जावे ना फिरे
    अयि भारतेर महामानवेर सागरतीरे
    —गीताञ्जलि, विश्व भारती ग्रन्थालय, कलकत्ता, 1954 (1910).

15
Philosophy of S. Radhakrishnan

S. Radhakrishnan is a seminal figure in the history of contemporary philosophy. He is an exponent of Vedanta philosphhy. According to him nothing is inevitable in life except *Nirvana*. Essence of life is creativity. Real life is a genuine becoming. The higher knowledge is *Para-jñāna*. This knowledge is not a-logical but super-logical.

Radhakrishnan in his autobiography writes: "I was born on September 5, 1888, at a small place, Tirutani, forty miles to the north-west of Madras, in South India, the second child of Hindu parents, who were conventional in their religious outlook. I have not had any advantage of birth or of wealth."[1] He was born in an orthodox Brahmin family but was educated in Christian Missionary Schools and College. The philosophical and religious tradition, where great Vedant schools were originated and still guide and weave the life of common people, provided proper spiritual ambience to the young Radhakrishnan to dwell deep into the innermost being and discover the pearls of wisdom. He says: "Electrons and protons do not clear up the mystery of reality. Besides, God and soul cannot be treated as mathematical equations. Life is not a geometrical pattern. It is a living creation of something new, not a dead connection of cause and effect."[2] Life moves on not by nullifying the past but by accepting it and in which the past takes a new birth in the form of a future. Confucius says: "He who by reanimating the old can gain knowledge of the new is fit to be a teacher."[3]

Philosophy as conceptual knowledge is a preparation for meditative insight. The great truths of philosophy are not proved but experienced. This integral experience is a vivid and vibrant realization of ultimate reality. Radhakrishnan writes: "At an impressionable period of my life, I became familiar not only with the teaching of the *New Testament*, but with the criticism levelled by Christian missionaries on Hindu beliefs and practices. My pride as Hindu roused by the eloquence of Swami Vivekananda was deeply hurt by the treatment accorded to Hinduism in missionary institutions. It was difficult for me to concede that Hindu ascetics and teachers who preserved for our world a living contact with the classical culture of India, which is at the root of much that we know and almost all that we practice, were not truly realigious."[4] He took the study of Vedanta in order to be able to give "a reply to the charge that the Vedanta system had no room for ethics."[5] In the partial fulfilment of the M.A. degree of the University of Madras, he submitted a thesis on the *'Ethics of the Vedanta'* which was highly commended by his teacher, Professor A.G. Hogg of the Madras Christian College. In the College he had been taught only Western philosophy, but his interest was aroused becáuse of the fact that it was criticised by Christian teachers who had no grounding in Indian philosophy. This early work praised and recognised as a work of scholarship, encouraged Radhakrishnan to pursue the study of Hindu philosophy with vigour and faith.

He strongly defends the importance and significance of ethics as the stepping stone to salvation. However, he is fully aware of the philosophical implication of ethical values and he took stand that ethical norms and values are not ultimate. However, the transcendence of ethics, should not be misconstrued as nullification of the importance of ethics, as it speaks of its intrinsic embodiment in the very existence of being.

According to Radhakrishnan one who has attained *nirvana* or enlightenment is no longer bound by ethical norms and values. The enlightened being is vitally interested in the welfare of the world. He writes: "....the normal mystic has a burning passion for social righteousness."[6]

Radhakrishnan is very clear in his thought that *mokṣa* or *nirvāṇa* cannot be achieved by treading ethical path, as enlightenment is an altogether different dimension of reality and being. However, he does not deny the signification of ethics. Charles A. Moore rightly observes: "It is in this sense that ethics in spite of all the absolutism of the idealism of Śaṁkara and Radhakrishnan is indispensable and truly significant, though ultimately transcended."[7] The doctrine of transcendence is integral to the philosophy of Radhakrishnan. The experience of Brahman, the ultimate reality, is the spiritual destiny of man. It is something more than moral goodness. Transcendence is not an extension of the ethical.[8] "To realise the ideal we must pass beyond the moral life and rise to the spiritual realization in which the life of finite struggle and endeavour is transcended ..... *Karma* cannot lead to *mokṣa.*"[8]

Like all other great Indian thinkers the basic concern and philosophical postulation of Radhakrishnan is rooted in the concept of *Salvation*. The philosophy of Radhakrishnan and all Hinduism, is in a sense a lonely pilgrimage of spirit and in other sense a function of life. Civilization is an expression of cosmic spirit. All life is sacramental. Indian culture is an effort to embody philosophical wisdom in social life. All truth about God has its source in God. True knowledge is to know one's own ignorance. Law of *Karma* affirms the implicit presence of the past in the present.

There is a very close relationship of metaphysics and ethics in the philosophy of Radhakrishnan. There is an indispensable relationship between Brahman and man. Radhakrishnan says: "Any ethical theory must be grounded in metaphysics, in a philosophical conception of the relation between human conduct and ultimate reality. As we think ultimate reality to be, so we behave. Vision and action go together."[9] The philosophy of Radhakrishnan raises many metaphysical and ethical questions. The authority of ethical norms and values would be philosophically vindicated if and only if the structure of cosmic process is spiritual. We cannot worship and pray an object if it is to be a mere mental fiction. One would adhere to ideals in face of all adversaries only of one is sure that they are rooted in the universal nature of things. Moral consciousness must include an intrinsic faith in the spiritual nature of existence and being. Radhakrishnan, while dispelling the above doubts and metaphysical issue, says: "Our moral life tells us that God is not only the good but the spring and sustainer of moral effort."[10] "If the indwelling of God in man is the highest truth, conduct which translates it into practice is ideal conduct. The several virtues are forms of the truth."[11] Philosophy according to Radhakrishnan, is to realise the "ideal possibility"[12] and spiritual endeavour to divinise the life of man because man is essentially Brahman.

The philosophy of Radhakrishnan is based on the teachings of Upaniṣad, *Brahmasūtra* and *Bhagavata Gītā*, which are known as *Prasthāna-Trayi*. Teachings of *Prasthāna-Trayi* are so profound and sublime that the philosophical import of it have been interpreted by different *acharyas* differently at different period of history out of which grew the different schools of Vedanta. Different schools of *Vedanta* are the high water-marks of Indian philosophy. Radhakrishnan takes an Absolutistic stand and he tries to weave the different schools of Vedantic thoughts into monism. He expounds and interprets Śaṅkara with special warmth and vigour. The basic philosophical preference of

Radhakrishnan is for Absolutism and Mysticism. When we start contemplating on the philosophy of Radhakrishnan, we are sometimes led to theism and belief in personal God (*Saguṇa Brahman*). But when we analyse and elucidate Radhakrishnan's concept of reality, we are led to absolutism. The way he interprets the teachings of the Upaniṣad and quotes F.H. Bradley then it is evident that his thought is driven to a system of absolute idealism. The reality is the One of Platinus which is experienced in the flight of the alone to the alone. In his celebrated book, *The Reign of Religion in Contemporary Philosophy* it is very clear that religion does not reign over philosophy. Clement C.J. Webb while examining theism and Absolutism in Radhakrishnan's philosophy, writes: "...that the reign of religion has been deleterious, because the religion which has reigned has been theistic, and theism leads (as we have seen) to finite God and thence to pessimism and despair. This seems to commit him to non-dualistic absolutism."[12]

There is enough evident that Radhakrishnan was greatly influenced by Western philosophy also. The influence of Hegel's absolute idealism is very much pronounced in his philosophy. There is evident similarity with Vedanta.

'The Philosophy of Rabindranath Tagore' was the first attempt of Radhakrishnan to weave the whole Indian philosophical and religious thoughts and practices into a systematic order. He says: "we do not know whether it is Rabindranath's own heart or the heart of India that is beating here."[13] *An Idealist View of Life* and *Eastern Religions and Western Thought* are two important works of Radhakrishnan during this period. The former is the collection of Radhakrishnan's Hibert lectures delivered at the universities of London and Manchester in 1929. Later is the outcome of his lectures delivered at Oxford in 1936-38, where he was appointed as Spalding Professor of Eastern Religions and Ethics. These two works of Radhakrishnan embody his original philosophical thoughts.

In *An Idealistic View of Life,* Radhakrishnan expounds his Absolutistic Idealism and he traces the idealistic ideas and currents pervading both in Indian and Greek classical traditions. The essence of all idealism and all philosophy, in the words of Hegel, is spirit. The basic comcept of Absolute, self, God, matter, life, intuition and salvation have been integrated in such an organic *whole* that Radhakrishnan's philosophy becomes original and profound. The study of his works create an impression that Hegel, Bergson, Śaṅkar, Nāgārjuna and Plato—all have been fused in the grand philosophical system of

Absolutism. Radhakrishnan from an interpreter of Indian philosophy, becomes a wholy original thinker. Here lies the greatness and originality of Radhakrishnan as a philosopher. In Radhakrishnan's philosophy, 'Absolute' transcends the finite but the doctrine of *maya* does not relegate the phenomenal world to the status of illusion and "insignificance. Radhakrishnan writes: "When Kierkegaard tells us that truth is identical with subjectivity, he means that if it is objectified, it becomes relative. He does not mean that the truth is peculiar to and private to the individual. He makes out that we must go deep down into the subject to attain the experience of Universal Spirit."[14] This universal spirit is what is known in *Upaniṣad* as *Sākṣhi cetā* (Supreme Subjectivity) and *Jñātṛitvanibandhana,* Radhakrishnan's philosophy is an exposition of his belief in the universal spirit that manifests in the form of empirical world and guides the destiny of being and existence of all being. He says: "History is in this sense the epic of the divine will, a revelation of God, the Divine works and shines through the earthly medium."[15] Further he says: "There is such a thing as spiritual gravitation."[16]

In *'Eastern Religions and Western Thought'* Radhakrishnan tries to synthesise the eastern spirituality with Western rationalism. Spirituality is not hostile to reason nor reason is against spirituality. The happy and harmonious blending of spirituality and reason, East and West, would alone herald a new era of human understanding and renaissance. Radhakrishnan, steeped as he had been in the great spiritual tradition of India, he was also aware of the fact that God does not say: "God is Tradition" he says, "God is Truth". This truth is Universal Spirit and Brahman. All through his life, Radhakrishnan's persistent endeavour has been to assimilate Western rationalism and humanism into the Eastern inner spirituality which inculcates and fosters a life of love and compassion, peace and non-violence. He says: "May we not strive for a philosophy which will combine the best of European humanism and Asiatic religion, a philosophy more profound and more living than either, endowed with greater spiritual and ethical force, which will conquer the hearts of men and compel peoples to acknowledge its sway."[17] This is why while paying tributes to Radhakrishnan for his great contribution in synthesising reason and intuition, West and East to elicit this common core into the explicitness, Muirhead says that Radhakrishnan is "a philosophical bilinguist" upon the "spiritual wisdom of the world."[18]

The concept of intuition occupies an important position in

Radhakrishnan's philosophy. For the better understanding and appreciation of Radhakrishnan's philosophy, the elucidation, analysis and examination of the concept of 'intuition' is *sine qua non.* As a cognitive faculty it has been used in many senses. It refers to faculties, capacities, products, processes, sources and realization. It is said that intuition is non-conceptual, non-discursive and trans-rational. Intuitive experience is different from logical and rational knowledge. It is also different from sensory experience and it should not be confused with instinct. Radhkrishnan himself admits that there are three kinds of cognition. "While all varieties of cognitive experience result in a knowledge of the real," he writes, "it is produced in three ways which are sense experience, discursive reasoning and intuitive apprehension."[19] This marks the three stages of mental evolution, sense, reason and intuition. Sense experience and rational cognition are unable to apprehend the real. Plato, Bergson and Bradley are of the same view. Intuitive knowledge is a fusion of mind with reality. It is a choiceless awareness of truth of things by identity. We become one with the reality. It is a mystic experience of Universal Spirit—which is *Brahman.* It is vivid, integral, direct, non-dual in which knowledge, knower and known became one.

Robert W. Browning has presented a critical analysis of Radhakrishnan's concept of intutive in a brilliant paper entitled Reason and Types of Intuition.[20]

Browning put intuition into five categories[21]:

(1) Sensory intuition
(2) Rational intuition
(3) Descrying of complex structures
(4) Valuational intuition
(5) Integral experience

Radhakrishnan's intuition comes under the fifth category, namely integral experience. It is what is called in Upanisad *Parājñāna* and in Buddhism, *Bodhi.* He propounded the doctrine of *Nirguṇa Brahman,* of the Absolute *qua* Absolute. *Brahman* of Radhakrishnan transcends both finite and infinite expressions as it is an expression of the freedom of the Absolute. For Radhakrishnan, philosophy is not a purely cerebral activity but a way of life. Radhakrishnan says: "The destiny of the human soul is to realise its oneness with the Supreme. There is a difference between the substantial immanence and the conscious union which demands voluntary identification. If the substantial reality of the human soul abides in that quality which we call spirit, growth or spiritual life means conscious realization of the fundamental truth."[22]

Notes

1. *My Search for Truth*, p.l, Shivalal Agraval & Co., Agra. Second Edition, 1956.
2. *Ibid.,* pp. 28-29.
3. Analeeits, 11.10, Arthur Waley's English Translation.
4. My Search for Truth, p. 5.
5. *Ibid.,* p. 9.
6. Eastern Religions and Western thought, p. 109. London, Humphrey Milford, Oxford University Press, 1939.
7. Philosophy of Sarvepalli Radhakrishnan, p. 290. Ed. P.A. Schilpp. Motilal Banarsidass Publishers, Delhi, 1992.
8. *Indian Philosophy*, Vol. II, p. 626. George Allen & Unwin, London, 1931.
9. *Eastern Religious and Western Thought*, p. 80.
10. *The Idealist view of Life*, p. 333. Goerge Allen & Unwin, London, 1932.
11. *The Heart of Hindusthan*, p. 25. G.A. Natesan & Co., Madras.
12. *Philosophy of S. Radhakrishnan*, p. 397.
13. *The Philosophy of Rabindranath Tagore* (1918), p. vii. MacMillan & Co., London, 1918.
14. *Philosophy of S. Radhakrishnan*, p. 70.
15. *My Search for Truth*, p. 31.
16. *Ibid.,* p. 48.
17. *Eastern Religious and Western Thought*, p. 259.
18. *Hibbert Journal*, xxxi: 149 (October 1932).
19. *The Idealist View of Live*, p. 134.
20. *Philosophy of S. Radhakrishnan*, pp. 175-277.
21. *Ibid.,*pp. 180-1.
22. Eastern Religions and Western Thoughts, p. 96.

16

Translation of Buddhist and Christian Scriptures in Chinese

An Examination of Theories and Praxis from Hermeneutical Perspective

Before we start hermeneutical understanding of the translation of Buddhist and the Chinese Christian Scriptures in language we must examine the structural features of Sanskrit, Chinese and English languages. Sanskrit language is based on the sound. Panini is considered as the greatest grammarian of the world. According to Panini, Sanskrit alphabet is known as Varnamala (the garland of letters). Its fifty letters from *a* to *ksa,* are the fifty basic vibrations of the Cosmos. Each letter is *bija-mantra* to fifty human instincts. Here *bija-mantra* means the acoustic root of different psychic expressions. It is said that the divine nectar that secretes from the pineal gland *(Sahasrara)* takes different forms of letters in six different *cakras* or *Padmas*. These six *cakras* are: *Muladhara, Svadhisthana, Manipura, Anahata, Visudha* and *Ajna*. They are called *Padmas* (Lotuses) because they are in the form of a lotus with a distinct colour and petals. The different petals of the respective *cakras* represent the different basic human longings and instincts. *Varnamala* is known as *matrikavarna* (mother of colours). The world is composed of waves and vibrations and these innumerable waves and vibrations are controlled by fifty sounds. These fifty sounds are represented by fifty Sanskrit alphabets from *a* to *ksa* which are the resultant sounds. *A* of Sanskrit, *a* of Latin, *alpha* of Greek and *aliph* of Persian are the first letter of their respective alphabets because they represent the creative manifestation. The fifty letters of Sanskrit are embodiment of fifty basic sounds.

The other striking feature of Sanskrit language is the

vowel-consonant pronunciation of the Sanskrit language. The consonant becomes a syllabic unit only when it is compounded with vowel. The sixteen vowels are the basic voice pattern of the sounds and the thirty six consonants are the form of the basic voice pattern of the basic fifty sounds. This is the unique feature of Sanskrit language. Another unique feature of the Sanskrit word is its formation. In Sanskrit the root words are called *dhatu* and one can create any number of words by adding a proper prefix and suffix.

Language occupies unique position in both Chinese and Indian culture and civilization. The Chinese language is logographic. The language represents words in a non-phonetic way. Chinese language is quite different from the Western languages in its structural features. It is not alphabetic. Chinese characters are ideographic symbols. The monosyllabic structures, the voice pattern and the open vocabulary nature, the flexible wording structure with sounds and the elasticity in word ordering are an example of structural uniqueness of Chinese language. It means that Chinese language represents sounds and not words. There is a very close relation with ancient Sanskrit language. The whole grammar of Panini is based on the concept of sound. Both Sanskrit and the Chinese languages are based on Ontological Mysticism.

According to modern thinking language is a mental construct and it is believed that word is not referred to any objective reality. Word is a conceptual construct in the mind and it is hypostatic as an external object. It creates some problem in communication. If we accept that meaning is the sole possession of the subject how could it be communicated to other? The subjective concept is not the concept of another which one like to communicate, so what would be the basis of the communication between two persons when the ideas are not communicable and amenable to perceptions by different persons. Even we accept that the two persons are having the possession of same concept, it does not provide the basis of communications, as there is no ground of knowing the mental concept of one is possessed by another.

Satkari Mookherjee writes, "Santaraksita replies that the difficulty would have been actually insurmountable if the conceptual image was confined within its limits and had not extra-subjective reference. Though in reality the speaker and the hearer are conversant with what is their private possession, both of them think they understand the objective reality, and the cause of illusion being similar in both, there is no difficulty in inter-communication, just as two persons suffering from ophthalmia, see two moons and when one communicates his experience to the other, his word is believed to refer to an actual fact. Language is, therefore, a convenient instrument for communication of concepts, which, however, are fictitious representatives of reality."[1]

The hermeneutic is a study of basic principles of religious scriptural interpretation. The exegetical methods employed in interpretation of truth and values of the religious scriptures. There are four basic schools of hermeneutic interpretations such as literal, moral, allegorical and anagogical. Hermeneutics is employed in understanding and interpretations of linguistic and non-linguistic expression. As exegetical method employed in interpretation has a long tradition since the ancient Greek philosophy. In the beginning, particularly Middle Age and since the time of Reformation and Renaissance, hermeneutics became a major branch of Christian scriptural interpretation. In course of time Hermeneutics was employed in the study of ancient and classic cultures.

The historical, critical, existential and structural interpretations hermeneutics employed into a broader academic and philosophical tradition during the Eighteenth century. Its horizon has broadened and gone beyond the methodological or didactic methods and started philosophising the problem of communication as such. The question how do we communicate? has become the main hermeneutical problem of interpretations. Wilhelm Dilthey, Martin Heidegger, and Hans-Georg Gadamer have transformed the hermeneutics from the symbolic communication to examine the more fundamental problems to understand human life and existence as such. If we look back to the change in the structural interpretations of hermeneutics Benedict de Spinoza, employed hermeneutics in the study of history as an indispensable tool in the process of unlocking hermeneutic meaning and the language of Holy Scriptures. Spinoza believes that the Holy Scriptures could be properly understood in keeping the fact that historical and cultural context in which these Holy Scriptures were written. He considers that understanding the parts of the scriptures depends on understanding of the larger whole. Larger whole could be understood only by understanding its part and this forms the *hermeneutics circle* and this became the hermeneutic theme which put emphasis on the interpretations and understanding of scriptures by means of philological work.

In the Twenty first century, Martin Heidegger considers hermeneutics is ontology. It deals with the philosophical problem of man in the world. Gadamer thinks we are a part of tradition in which we stand and the historical texts have an importance that precedes our own. The scriptural texts are kept alive to the extent that it is considered alike and important for the present. We do understand the authority of texts by becoming engaged with its textual explication and interpretations by entering into dialogical relationship into the past. Gadamer calls it the *fusion of horizons.* It is not easy to understand the meaning and the signification of the texts in our first glance. It is a very complex dialogical interplay between past and present. Understanding of tradition and knowing ourselves are both interminable processes. The Gadamer's humanistic ontology is based on understanding ourselves which is conditioned by past.

In the background of linguistic structure of Sanskrit, Chinese and the English and the changing views on hermeneutics as the principles of religious scriptural interpretation we now examine the theory and praxis of Buddhist and the Christian scriptures. According to Ludwig Wittgenstein language depicts the cultural form of life. The concept of language cannot be defined. The meaning of word depends on its use and it could be determined in its cultural context. Hence, it is but natural the problem of translation and its hermeneutical interpretations of early Buddhist and Christian scriptures in Chinese because of the different cultural milieu in which the Buddhist and the Christian scriptures were written and developed. There is no common factor present in all the languages on the basis of which the scriptural texts of one language could be translated into another language. According to Wittgenstein there may be a family resemblance between some languages.

There is a controversy whether Buddhist missionary reached China by sea route or through Silk Route. However, there is a common belief that Buddhism came to China through Silk Route based on existing historical evidence and the archaeological iconographic evidence.

There has been happy and harmonious blending of Buddhism, Taoism and Confucianism. There are lot of legends related with introduction of Buddhism into China.

According to the most popular one, Emperor Ming (28-75 CE) precipitated the introduction of Buddhist teachings into China. The (early 3rd to early 5th century) *Mouzi Lihuolun* first records this legend, "In olden days emperor Ming saw in a dream a god whose body had the brilliance of the sun and who flew before his palace; and he rejoiced exceedingly at this. The next day he asked his officials: "What god is this?" the scholar Fu Yi said: "Your subject has heard it said that in India there is somebody who has attained the *Dao* and who is called Buddha; he flies in the air, his body had the brilliance of the sun; this must be that god."[2]

There is some controversy regarding the first documented translation of Buddhist scriptures into Chinese. According to one theory the first translation of Buddhist scriptures into Chinese language started in 488 CE by Parthian prince, who became a monk named An Shigao. Credit goes to him to establish first Buddhist monastery in Luoyang. He not only started translating the Buddhist scriptures into Chinese but he organised a group of translators who started working with translation work of Buddhist texts with An Shigao in coordinated cooperation. The Chinese minds were captivated by the profundity and sublimity of Buddhism. Buddhism was popularised and propagated in China by other Kushan monk Lokakṣema (164-186 CE), who came from the ancient Buddhist kingdom of Gandhāra.

The Buddha is the first historical person in the annals of human history who has founded school of philosophy and a world religious order. The school of philosophy is constituted of metaphysics, epistemology, logic, aesthetics and ethics. The Buddha after getting enlightenment under Bodhi tree at Bodhgaya started reflecting on the nature and significance of Nirvana which resulted into the birth of a new school of philosophy and a new religious order known as Buddhism. Buddhism is a sublime and profound form of spirituality. It is monotheistic and represents the highest form of monism (*Advaita*). According to Mahayana Buddhism *Advaita* represents the eternal co-existence of *Prina* and Upaya which constitute the infinite unity and transcendent reality (*Bodhicitta*). The most profound ontology considered to be *Madhyamika* and *Yogacara* system of Mahayana Buddhism. *Yogacara* (*Vijnanavada*) and *Madhyamika* (*Sunyavada*) deal with soteriological and speculative metaphysics.

Buddhism believes in two truths or reality—a conventional or nominal and an ultimate truth. The *Mulamadhyamakakarika* (literally Fundamental Verses on The Middle Way) of Nagarjuna, the founder of the *Madhyamika* the middle path school of Mahayana Buddhism deals with the metaphysical and epistemological problems. This treatise is the foundation of Madhyamika School in which dialectical analytic arguments have been employed to establish the basic principles of metaphysical and epistemological issues; the central concept of this text is *Sunyata* (emptiness). The emptiness is the essence of all things and at the same time emptiness itself is empty. All other Buddhist soteriological concepts and the principles are based on this root concept of emptiness. Jay L. Garfield writes, "Most bizarre of all, however, at first glance is the doctrine that all phenomena, including self and its objects, are empty. For indeed Nagarjuna and his followers do argue that the entire everyday world is, from the ultimate standpoint, non-existent. And that does appear to stand just a bit deeper into philosophical left field than even Berkeley dares to play. But, if the interpretation I will urge is adopted, the real central thrust of Madhyamika is the demystification of this apparently mystical conclusion."[3] Buddhism denies the permanent reality as advocated by other schools of Indian philosophical systems except Cārvaka. According to Vedanta self is identical with Brahman.

Buddha refutes the very existence of permanent self on the argument that if we accept the permanent soul, the *karma* loses its signification and importance. Acceptance of permanent self would destroy the very spiritual life of a man because the belief in self is the source of our all desires. And these desires are the root cause of our sufferings.

> "If prior to desire
> And without desire were a desirous one,
> Desire would depend upon him.
> Desire would exist when there is a desirous one."[4]

There is some controversy regarding Buddha's denial of self. There are even some believe that Buddhism being a profound philosophical system and world religion could not be dominated by the negative concepts of non-self, suffering and impermanence. Mrs. Rhys David's who has been a great exponent of Buddhism believes that these concepts of *Anitya* (impermanence), *Anatma* (non-self), *Dukha* (suffering) have been interpolated by the latter pseudo Buddhist thinkers and followers. According to Mrs. Rhys Davids Buddha did not deny the soul. S. Radhakrishnan writes, "The fundamental difference between the Buddhism and Upanishads seems to be about the metaphysical reality of an immutable substance, which is the true self of a man as well. We have to decide whether it is the idea of the Buddha to look upon the universal order as coming out of nothing and going back to nothing. It is true that Buddha finds no centre of reality or principle of permanence in the flux of life and the whirl of the world, but it does not follow that there is nothing real in the world at all except the agitation of forces."[5]

Kumarajiva is considered as a great scholar and a prolific translator of Buddhist scriptures from Sanskrit to Chinese. Kumarayana was the father of Kumarajiva who belonged to Kashmir and his mother was a

Kuṣāṇ princess who had great influence on the early life of Kumarajiva. There was a tradition of mendicant in Kumarajiva family. His father became a monk in search of his own real identity and destiny. He crossed the Pamir Mountains, reached Kucha and became a royal priest. The sister of king Jiva also known as Jivaka married him and they gave birth to Kumarajiva. Jivaka became a nun and settled in monastery (nunnery) and deserted him when he was just seven years old. Kumarajiva was a man of destiny and he had a prolific memory. It is said that even at the age of seven he memorised some of the difficult scriptures and *Sutras*. At the age of nine he came to Kashmir in search of higher studies and during his three years sojourn at Kashmir he studied Buddhist scriptures. At Kashgar he met an enlightened Buddhist monk belonging to Theravada tradition who predicted that he would be a great Buddhist patriarch. He also studied Vedas and other Hindu sacred scriptures.

Kumarajiva left Kashgar at the age of twelve with his mother Jivaka and came to Turpan, the North Eastern limit of the Kucha. It is stated that there were ten thousand monks living in different monasteries. He came in contact with a great scholar of Mahayana Buddhism, Suryasoma. Kumarajiva's mind was captivated by the profundity and sublimity of teachings of Mahayana Buddhism. And he started working on the other works of Nagarjuna. King Po-Shui of Kucha came to Turpan to make a request to Kumarajiva to return to Kucha city. Kumarajiva came to Kucha on the request of King and became the teacher of princess A-kie-ye-mo-ti. The princess after understanding Avatamsaka Sutra was overwhelmed with the spirituality and became *bikkhuni.* At the age of 20 Kumarajiva became a monk and started living in a new monastery built by the courtesy of King Po-Shun. He started studying other Mahayana texts such as *Prajnaparamita Sutra*. Kumarajiva's name and fame enamoured the Chinese Buddhist monk named Seng who visited Kucha in 379 CE. Emperor Fu-Jian of the former Qin Dynasty made efforts to bring Kumarajiva the Qin capital of Chang'an. The emperor deputed a general Lu Guang to conqueror Kucha and bring Kumarajiva. But the imperial army was defeated and the general Lu Guang deserted the emperor and declared his own independent state and became a warlord in 386 CE and Kumarajiva was imprisoned for many years.

This imprisonment came as a blessing in disguise and he studied and became very proficient in Chinese language. Kumarajiva was also forced to marry Kutcha King's daughter. After the former emperor of Qin Dynasty was overthrown Yao Xing became the new emperor who persuaded warlord Lu family to free Kumarajiva. When Lu family didn't agree to free Kumarajiva the emperor Yao Xing sent his army to defeat the warlords of the Lu and finally, emperor Yao succeeded in freeing Kumarajiva from the hostage and brought back to the capital Chang'an in 401 CE. Kumarajiva revolutionised the Chinese Buddhism by introducing the Taoist and Confucian concepts and terminologies for better understanding of Buddhist scriptural thoughts. As we have already discussed that literal translation of scriptural texts is not possible hence Kumarajiva employed the moral, allegorical and anagogical hermeneutic methods for proper understanding of the complexities and profundity of early Buddhist scriptural teachings. His translation of some canonical and seminal Mahayana scriptural texts occupied a very important place in the history of Chinese Buddhism. The Kumarajiva rendering of the Mahayana texts exercised great influence on Xuanzang and Sengrui and other Chinese Buddhist scholars. Kumarajiva work has some basic structural uniqueness. Some of the rendering of Sanskrit Buddhist texts in Chinese is shorter than the original Sanskrit texts. This speaks of the originality of Kumarajiva's understanding of Hermeneutics. His work speaks of the inner spirituality in the Sanskrit Mahayana texts and he employed allegorical and anagogical (spiritual) tools of hermeneutical interpretations.

Mahayana Buddhism captivated the mystic and the metaphysical Chinese mind. Mahayana Buddhism is based on ontological mysticism like Taoism. Hence, Mahayana Buddhism became almost a native religion of China. Mahayana Buddhism was propagated and popularised in China by Kushan monk Lokaksema (164-186 CE). It is stated that he got initiated in Buddhism at the ancient Buddhist kingdom of Gandhar and he rendered some of the canonical scriptures of Mahayana Buddhism like *Prajnaparamita Sutra* and others into Chinese. Wikipedia states, "Paul Harrison has worked on some of the texts that are arguably the earliest versions we have of the Mahāyāna sutras, those translated into Chinese in the last half of the second century CE by the Indo-Scythian translator Lokaksema. Harrison points to the enthusiasm in the Lokaksema sutra corpus for the extra ascetic practices, for dwelling in the forest, and above all for states of meditative absorption *(samādha)*. Meditation and meditative states seem to have occupied a central place in early Mahāyāna, certainly because of their spiritual efficacy but also because they may have given access to fresh revelations and inspiration.

Another School of Buddhism known as Zen Buddhism became very popular in China. Zen Buddhism is an ontological mysticism and intuitional science. It is based on the canonical literatures entitled *Lankavatara Sutra, Prajna Paramita Sutra, Bajra Chedikam Sutra* and *Avatanaska Sutra.* This is a branch of Mahayana Buddhism. According to Zen Buddhism all beings possess the Buddha nature *(Bodhi Citta).* Buddha nature is called Sunya or Tathatta. The realization of which is the central objective of Zen Buddhism. There are two views regarding the founder of Zen Buddhism. According one school Sakyamuni is the founding father of Zen Buddhism. He transmitted this mystic experience and teachings to Mahakashyapa. According to this school the Buddha himself has declared that he has transmitted his mystic power and knowledge of inner spirituality and esoteric mysticism to Mahakashyapa. According to this tradition there are twenty eight patriarchs from Lord Buddha to Bodhi Dharma who are considered as the founding fathers of Zen Buddhism. The names of the patriarchs are as follows:

> 1. Sakyamuni, 2. Mahakashyapa, 3. Ananda, 4. Savansa, 5. Upagupta, 6. Dhritaka, 7. Mischaka, 8. Buddhanandi, 9. Bodhamitra, 10. Bhikkhu Parsva, 11. Punyayasgas, 12. Asvaghosa, 13. Bhikkhu Kapimale, 14. Nagarjuna, 15. Kanadeva, 16. Arya Rahulata, 17. Sanaghanandi, 18. Sanghayashas, 19. Kumarata, 20. Jayata, 21. Vasubandhu, 22. Manura, 23. Haklenayasas, 24. Bhikkhu Simba, 25. Vasasita, 26. Punyamitra, 27. Prajnatara, and 28. Bodhidharma.

According to other school Bodhidharma is the founder of Zen Buddhism. He came to China in 520 A.D. After crossing the Yangtzi he came to the famous Shaolin monastery situated at the Song Shan mountain range. He became famous and revered because of his nine long years practising meditation while facing the wall of the cliff that was visible from his monastery and he was called *Biguan*, the wall gauging monks. According to this school there are six patriarchs: 1. Bodhidharma, 2. Hui-ko, 3. Seng-Ts'an, 4. Shing-Hsimming, 5. Houng-Zen, 6. Hui-Neng. Hui-Neng is called the second Bodhidharma. He is considered as the greatest Zen masters who provided the philosophical and spiritual background for this new school of Zen Buddhism during the T'ang dynasty of China. Hui-Neng died at the age of seventy-six in 712 A.D. and he was honoured with the robe of Bodhidharma by his teachers Houng-Zen. There is another controversy regarding the sixth patriarch. According to this school there were only five patriarchs and after the demise of fifth patriarch the Zen Buddhism was split into two sects known as northern school founded by Shen-Shui and southern school founder by Hui-Neng.[6] Later on Zen Buddhism was divided and split into several sects which still exist in China and Japan.

Spiritual enlightenment or *nirvana* is known as *satori* in Zen Buddhism. It is a state of experience of the whole truth and consciousness. It is a spiritual realization of one's own being and existence in totality. D.T. Suzuki says, "The knowledge contains in *Satori* is concerned with something universal and at the same time with the individual aspect of existence."[7]

Buddhism is a philosophy of mind *(Citta Darshan).* Theravada Buddhism reduces the mind into a set of thoughts and feelings and seeks enlightenment from nescience through detachment. Mahayana Buddhism considers mind as the seed of enlightenment *(Bodhi Citta).* According to Mahayana meditation is to transform mind into ẽternal emptiness. This eternal emptiness is called *Bodhi Citta. Bodhi Citta* is bereft of all existence. The *Bodhi Citta* remains unpolluted and pure in spite of defilements and cravings. This *Bodhi Citta* is pure consciousness and infinite bliss (*Maha Sukha*). Lalan Prasad Singh writes, "According to Buddhism, reality is in eternal flux. Our experience is only the point instant. Reality is in the state of flux. Existence is contingent. There is no logical foundation for the theoretical basis of natural science. The natural world is known in relation to our modes of experience. The mind is the only instrument through which we know mind and consciousness. Consciousness is a continuum flow. The duality of the physical and the mental does not exist in the state of the pure continuum. This continuum is known as emptiness."[8] Reification in science and philosophy is greatest impediment in understanding the nature of being and reality in totality. The reality exists in relation to our theoretical framework of language and consciousness. The basic question whether world exists the way it appears or whether its mode of existence is different from its mode of appearance. The physical reality does not define in terms of scientific realism. There is truth in Schrodinger's observation that world is nothing but conglomeration of a "construct of our sensations, perceptions and memories."[9]

The Chinese and the Persians are famous in converting simple legends and myths into profound spiritual narration. The story of a Sufi Saint Mullah Nasreddin has been portrayed as a wise fool and his story telling is a narration of profound spiritual and moral significance. The

Chan Buddhism (Zen) is a narration of profound mystic and the metaphysical truth in the form of *Koan* and *Mondo*.

Albert Low, Director and Teacher at Montreal Zen Centre writes in the foreword of the book *Zen Masters of China*, "However, it is with the koan that the true value of the story is revealed. Everyone has surely heard of the sound of One Hand. The full koan reads, You know the sound of two hands clapping. What is the sound of one hand clapping?" A number of collections of koans have been made; among the most popular are *The Mumonkan*, *The Hekiganroku* and *the Book of Serenity*. Many koans are indeed simply mondo and tthat have been stripped down to the essential. Comments are added to the koan to help the student gain an entry into it. Each koan, therefore, is a miniature drama. To "work" with the koan—that is, to plumb its meaning—one must inhabit the koan. We must understand the conflict, twist, or incongruity described and dwell with the contradiction and so allow the higher mind to awaken."[10]

Zen Buddhism has incorporated the elements of naturalistic mysticism of Taoism and down to earth philosophy of Confucianism. The Buddha nature and the Tao stand for same truth and reality but speak in different languages. Zen Buddhism was also very much embraced the Taoist concept of nature. However, it is development of the root concepts of Buddhism propounded by its founder the Buddha, Fritjof Capra observes, "Zen Buddhism is thus a unique blend of the philosophies and idiosyncrasies of three different cultures. It is a way of life which is typically Japanese, and yet it reflects the mysticism of India, the Taoist' love of naturalness and spontaneity and the thorough pragmatism of the Confucian mind."[11]

Xuanzang became very famous Buddhist monk during Tang dynasty. He has done a service to Buddhism by translating the Buddhist scriptures into Chinese (602-664 CE). He was born in Henan province. He had a very inquisitive mind from his early boyhood days and started reading Chinese classics and the biography of ancient sages. He was first initiated as a novice monk at the age of thirteen and at Chendu in Sichuan, he became a Buddhist monk (*Bikkhu*) at the age of twenty. He enjoyed the patronage of emperor Taizong of Tang dynasty and expressed his desire to make a pilgrimage to India the place of origin of Buddhism like Faxian. He spent nearly seventeen years journey to China which speaks of his scholarship, courage and devotion to Indian culture especially of Buddhism as recorded in the Chinese Classic *Great Tang Records on the Western Regions*. The great Chinese novelist Wu

Cheng'en was inspired that reflects in his novel *Journey to the West.* He visited almost all the famous Buddhist monasteries. He visited Takshila, where with his great excitement he found with the discovery of 100 monasteries and 5000 Buddhist monks. He visited Kashmir in 631 and met a great Buddhist monk Samghayasas. He devoted much of his time in understanding the deeper meaning and significance of Buddhism between 632-633 CE with famous monks Vinitaprabha and Candravarman. He visited Shravasti and from there he went to Kapilavastu, where Buddha's father was a king and from Kapilavastu he went to Lumbini, where Buddha was born. From Lumbini he went to Kusinagar where Buddha passed away. He visited Sarnath where Buddha delivered his first sermon after his enlightenment. He also visited Varanasi, Vaisali, Patliputra and Bodhgaya where Buddha attained *nirvana*. And from Bodhgaya he went to Nalanda which was famous for its learning centre. He started studying Buddhist logic, grammar and Sanskrit and Vijnanavada (*Yogacara*). At Nalanda University he came in contact with famous Buddhist monk and teacher Silabhadra who was the director of the university. Silabhadra was an enlightened Buddhist monk and he had the dream of Xuanzang's visit to Nalanda. Silabhadra was attracted with the razor sharp mind of Xuanzang and he became confident that he would become a great teacher and would make Buddhism popular and popularize in China.

Grousset writes: "The Chinese pilgrim had finally found the omniscient master, the incomparable metaphysician who was to make known to him the ultimate secrets of the idealist systems....The founders of Mahayana idealism, Asanga and Vasubandhu... Dignaga... Dharmapala had in turn trained Silabhadra. Silabhadra was thus in a position to make available to the Sino-Japanese world the entire heritage of Buddhist idealism, and the *Siddhi* Xuanzang's great philosophical treatise.... is none other than the *Summa* of this doctrine, the fruit of seven centuries of Indian [Buddhist] thought."[12]

During his stay at Nalanda he got initiated into Yogacara school of Buddhism (*Vijnanavada*) which was founded by Asanga and his younger brother Vasuvandu the teacher of Dignaga. This is the idealist school of Buddhism. It is called Yogacara because it believes enlightenment can be attained only by the practice of *yoga*. This school rejects the phenomenal world. According to this school only consciousness exists.

Consciousness, it constitutes the whole phenomenal world. Vijnana is the only truth. The Vijnana as consciousness is the universal subject and not the empirical self. The illusion of self arises out of commingling of consciousness (*Vijnana*) with ignorance (*Avidya*). M. Poussin writes, "All the Buddhist philosophers, maintainers of the doctrine of *karma*, had to admit that thoughts. Although momentary do not perish altogether, but originate new thoughts, sometimes after a long interval of time. As long as they believed in the existence of matter and considered man as a physico-psychical complex, it was not difficult for them to explain the interdependence of thoughts."[13]

Milinda Panha, the dialogue between the Buddhist scholar Nagasen and the Greek king Menander is also considered as canonical literature of Buddhism. Nagasen rejected the existence of permanent soul. There is a great similarity between Vijnanavada school of Buddhism and the subjective idealism of Berkley. According to Berkley, existence lies in its being perceived. According to him, only the mental event exists. *Esse est percipi.* David Hume in his famous philosophical work, *Treatise of Human Nature,* writes, "What we call mind's nothing but a heap of bundle of different perceptions united together by certain relations, and "supposed though falsely, to be endowed with a certain simplicity and identity."[14]

The philosophical problem that has been raised by Vijnanavada and Hume that pure experience is not sufficient ground for the basis of science. If we accept all our knowledge is based on experience then the induction as an independent logical principle loses it validity and without which the science becomes impossibility. The philosophical question raised by Vijnanavada and Hume is still unanswered.

Radhakrishnan while summarizing the Vijnanavada writes, "While the *Yogacara* theory did a great service to the science of logic, by pointing out the necessity of thought for all reality, it betrayed its weakness by its frequent denial of all non-mental reality and experience. The use of the term *alayavijnana* is too indefinite. It is sometimes considered a synonym for *Tathata*, when it is identified with *vastumatra*, the mere abstraction of being, the pure existentiality, the Hegelian Seyn, the ultimate which remains when we abstract from every fact and form of existence. Again, it is considered to be a phenomenon of the mind including other phenomena in its scope. It is also cosmic mind with the principle of negativity in it. Sometimes, it is equated with the stream of consciousness within the individual. The indefiniteness of the theory on such a central issue has exposed it to a good deal of legitimate criticism."[15]

According to Radhakrishnan, *Alayavijnana* which has been

considered as a synonym for *Tathata* speaks of the Advaita nature of both the schools of Vijnanavada and Sunyavada. Radhakrishnan identifies *Alayavijnana* with cosmic mind. If, we examine the metaphysical status of *Vijnanavada* and *Sunyavada* we come to a conclusion that reality could be known only by enlightened person and it is beyond the reach of mind and senses. The ultimate reality is cosmic consciousness. This cosmic consciousness has been used as *Tathata* (suchness) or *Sunyata* (thatness), *alayavijnana* in Buddhism, Brahman in Vedanta and Tao in Taoism. Taoism had used heaven Tao Te Ching sense of ultimate reality like Brahman.

Xuanzang returned from India to China in 645 A.D. He was greeted with honour. However, he did not accept any position of power offered by the emperor Tai zong of Tang dynasty. He established a committee of Buddhist monks, well-versed in Sanskrit and Chinese to translate over 600 Mahayana and Hinayana scriptures which he brought with him from India. Xuanzang's disciple Quiji became the first patriarch of Faxinang school of Buddhism. Xuanzang has done great service to Buddhism by translating the Buddhist scriptures into Chinese some of which have been lost in India particularly with the burning of the Nalanda University Library by Muslim invaders. Some of the famous Buddhist scriptures have been re-translated from Chinese to Sanskrit and other Indian languages and thereby the philosophical, the lost glory of the great Buddhism over time have been restored.

Xuanzang's version of Heart Sutra has become the basis for the commentary on Sutra in China and Korea. Many biographies of Xuanzang have been written and the most famous is by Buddhist monk Huli. Xuanzang's work, the *Great Tang Records on the Western Regions,* and Hull's biography of Xuanzang was rendered into English by Samuel Beal, in 1884 and 1911 respectively. The English translation with valuable notes and comments by Thomas Watters was edited by the Great Buddhist authors, T.W. Rhys Davids and S.W. Bushell, published in 1905 in London.

It is said that Christianity was introduced in China during Tang dynasty. However, Christianity could not occupy the prestige and the recognition that Buddhism was accorded in China. Chinese mind is mystical and metaphysical like Indians. The theism of Christianity though a very important concept it could not make inroad in Chinese culture though some of the great leaders of China were Christians. The leader of Taiping Rebellion, Hong Xiuquan was a Christian. The Taiping Rebellion was the culmination of the series of peasant revolution during

1940s and it goes down in history as world's bloodiest and a largest civil war in the annals of human history. Sun Yat-sen who became the first president of Republic of China on 10th March, 1912 after the fall of the last Chinese Quin dynasty was a Christian and his successor Chiang Kai-shek, the head of Kuomintang was also a Christian. According to Wikipedia the first early translation of the *Bible* was in the Nineteenth century. *Bible* which is the canonical literature of Christianity did not play any important role in introducing Christianity in sixteenth century. The Jesuit missionary in Beijing were granted permission in 1615 to conduct mass in vernacular and got permission to translate the sacred text into Chinese. The Jesuit missionaries started the translation of the Ten Commandments, the Sermon on the Mount and the biography of Christ. The Chinese were not acquainted with the biblical narration of the religious teachings of Christianity. It is stated that the first translation was not started until the Eighteenth century. The first translation in Chinese by Robert Morrison is available with British Museum. The first Catholic Chinese Bible was translated by Gabriele Allegra. He started translating *Old Testament* from the original Hebrew and Aramaic language in 1935. Due to the long march led by Mao, stadium biblicum were shifted from Beijing to Hong Kong. The first translation of *Old Testament* in Chinese was published in 1954. The New and the *Old Testaments* were published in one Volume in 1968.

John C.H. Wu, a Catholic convert, who served as the Republic of China's minister to the Vatican, also made a translation of the *New Testament* and the Psalms into Classical Chinese in 1946. The translations were not direct and often noted to be florid, and his translations of the Psalms were paraphrases.

The Orthodox translation of *New Testament* in Chinese was made by Archimandrite Gury (Karpov), head of the 14th Russian Ecclesiastical Mission in Beijing (1858-1864).

Another important version of the translation is known as *Taiping Bible. Taiping Bible* had a political and religious impact. It has been depicted that a deity who awards punishment to the nation, who indulges in evil and rewards blessing who are engaged in the pursuits of virtue and good. This narration and depiction of deity has a close relation with cultural practices such as music and marriage customs. It became popular amongst the poor and the downtrodden section of society.

It would not be out of place to mention here that the treaty of Nanking which is known as unequal treaties imposed upon the King by Western powers after the defeat which is known as Opium War. The

Western powers were given permission to propagate Christianity in 1842. During the Cultural Revolution which was started from 16th May, 1966 and ended with the death of Mao in September 1976 much of the scriptures related to Confucianism and Taoism and others were destroyed. However, the PRC in 1980 gave recognition to Taoism, Confucianism, Buddhism, Islam and Christianity.

In summarizing the hermeneutic understanding of translation of early Buddhist and Christian scriptures: theories and Praxis, we face some problems in the translation of the holy books of Buddhism and Christianity because of the different cultural context from the Chinese culture. Sanskrit has been originated from mystic and the metaphysical culture and tradition. According to this every entity has a characteristic vibration. This vibration is a serial name or a *mantra*. *Sabda* (word) is used in three senses— (i) *sabda* (word) is a symbol or a sign, (ii) *sabda* (word) is a concept or a construct, and (iii) *sabda* (word) is an expression of vibrational creating energy. It is opposed to modern philosophical or linguistic conception for view about *sabda* (word). Words are esoteric names. Berkley has stated that things are nothing but meaning in the cosmic mind. The Chinese language is quite different from Western languages. Chinese characters are ideographic symbols. Both the Sanskrit and the Chinese languages are rooted in mysticism. Hence, we find some similarity between the Buddhism and Taoism, because the Buddhism and Taoism are monastic, mystical and metaphysical. However, the translation of Buddhist and Christian scriptures in Chinese language have enriched the Chinese life and culture. Religious civilization of Buddhism and Christianity enriched the modern Chinese culture which is based on religious pluralism. This could be the basis of philosophical inter-religious dialogue in the emerging new global order. Though literal translation of Buddhist and the Christian scriptures pose great difficulty but the moral, allegorical and anagogical hermeneutical interpretations is a religious, cultural and historical necessity for understanding the fundamental truth and values of Buddhism and Christianity in emerging pluralistic global order. Both the Buddhist and the Christian scriptures have deeper spiritual meaning and the proper understanding of which would become the semantic of the modern pluralistic world.

Notes

1. Satkari Mookherjee. *The Buddhist Philosophy of Universal Flux*, Motilal Banarsidass Publishers, 2006. p. 139.
2. Henri Maspero, *Taoism and Chinese Religion,* tr. by Frank A. Kierman Jr., University of Massachusetts Press, 1981, p. 402.
3. *The Fundamental Wisdom of the Middle Way*. Nagarjuna's Mulamadhyamakakarika, Translation and Commentary by Jay L. Garfield. New York, Oxford University Press, 1995, p. 94.
4. *Ibid*., p. 16.
5. S. Radhakrishnan, *Indian Philosophy*, Volume 1, Oxford University Press, 1999, p. 375.
6. *Encyclopaedia Britannica*, p. 386.
7. *Essays in Zen Buddhism*, Vol. II, p. 39.
8. Lalan Prasad Singh, *Buddhist Tantra, A Philosophical Reflection and Religious Investigation*. p. 140.
9. Erwin Schrodinger. *Mind and Matter*, Cambridge: Cambridge University Press, 1958, p. 1.
10. Richard Bryan McDaniel, *Zen Masters of China, The First Step East*, Tuttle Publishing, Tokyo, p. 13.
11. Fritjof Capra, *The Tao of Physics*, p. 108.
12. Rene Grousset, *In the Footsteps of the Buddha*. J.A. Underwood (trans.), Orion Press. New York. 1971, p. 161.
13. *Indian Philosophy*, p. 637.
14. *Hume's Works*, Vol. I., pp. 3 ff.
15. *Indian Philosophy*, p. 637

17
Philosophy and Life World
The Zen Buddhist Perspective

In the Western philosophical tradition life world is understood as universe that is self-evident or given the world that is being experienced by the subject. According to Husserl, "The life world is the fundamental of all epistemological enquiries." This concept has its root in biology. The concept of the life world is referred and used both in philosophy and social sciences like sociology and anthropology. The concept of life world which is called in German *Lebenswelt* has been further developed by Martin, Heidegger and Mauric Merleau-Ponty. The life world is a dynamic concept. It refers to the life we live. It is an experience of "lives with us". There is a lot of debate and discussions of life world in Husserl's phenomenology and Max Weber's sociology. Marxist concepts of *alienation* and Habermas perspective present a general phenomenal life world colonisation.

To my mind the Western concept of philosophy and life world does not represent the proper understanding and meaning of life world. Life world comes within the purview of ontology which is the study of existence and being. Philosophy is a quest for truth, reality and one's own identity. In the quest of identity and destiny man discovered philosophy and enlightenment.

Sixth century B.C. is known to the world history as an era of Renaissance. History has never before and after witnessed the presence of galaxy of great thinkers who have changed the course of history by regenerating mankind spiritually, morally and intellectually. The wheel of change was set in motion in history by the Buddha of India, the Lao Tzu and Confucius of China, Parmenides and Heraclitus and Zeno of Greece. The whole philosophy of the world is elaboration, evaluation and examination of the issues and the principles that has been formulated by these thinkers. Ascetism is considered as *sine qua non* for mystical experience and spiritual enlightenment. This has been the hallmark of the Indian sages, Greek thinkers and Taoists and Confucians of China. They all considered continuity of life, immortality of self, cycle of birth and death as kernel of philosophy and life.

The Buddha, the Lao Tzu and Confucius are the greatest philosophers that the world has produced till this date. Lao Tzu is a philosopher and Confucius is an ethical teacher.

To my mind Chinese philosophy has exercised great influence in making life richer and fuller. We have to examine Taoism and Confucianism in the modern context. The term *Tao* has been interpreted by different thinkers at different period of history in a different way. *Tao* is sometimes translated as a path or way. It is sometimes translated as absolute reality. It is considered as totality of all things and beings. *Tao* is sometimes equated with order or the principle of order and harmony and unity. In the *Tao Te Ching* this word *Tao* has been used seventy six times with different meanings and connotations. According to Wittgenstein, a meaning of word is determined in a cultural context and to understand the word *Tao* we have to know in which cultural context this word has been used. Sometimes, it is used as a doctrine or as a natural law. However, *Tao* is not used in the sense of name, name is a personal and it connotes individual. *Tao* has been used in the sense of mother also without any kind of anthromorphic relations. In *Tao Te Ching, Tao* has been used as a mysterious female or mother.[1]

Confucius', wisdom and knowledge captivated the both ruling elites and the masses of Chinese minds, and his teachings created a political upheaval in late second and third century A.D. The intense intellectual activity and its resultant political awakening forced Chinese mind to accept Confucianism as other official ideology. The whole Chinese political and statecraft derived the moral and ethical ideas from him which regulated the behaviours and the social conduct of the ruler and the ruled. However, in the beginning of the third century Confucianism started waning and lost much of its glory and political appeal because it could not save the empire from schism and disintegration. The Chinese intellectual and the ruling elites became disenchanted with Confucianism for some time and started searching new political and moral grounds for the revival of both Chinese empire and social system. In search of new ideals and goals they started revising legalism with its insistence upon measure to re-establish law and order system. These intellectuals started reinterpreting Taoism. However, this intellectual awakening and movement neither re-established Taoism nor rejected Confucianism. In this dialectical movement of thought and ideas Confucianism lost its metaphysical basis and Taoism supplied the philosophical and speculatic philosophy to sustain the Chinese philosophical provenance. This intellectual awakening and movement gave birth to the system which dominated the intellectual and cultural life of China. One of these two system put emphasis on the importance of social duties, rituals and the practical affairs of the government in maintaining cohesion and progress of both individual and society. This system was the outcome of the cultural metamorphosis of Confucianism and legalism and it assumed a new name called "Ming-Chiao" (The doctrine of names). The other system pronounced the importance of ontological and metaphysical commitment. It considered the quest for permanent behind substratum. Permanent substratum behind the phenomena of change and flux. According to this philosophical tradition there is an impersonal principle which is unlimited, unchanging, and indescribable behind all temporality. This movement imbibed the basic ideas and support both from Taoism and Confucianism and gave birth to a new school of thought known as Hsuan Hsuch ("Dark learning").

If we examine the social and cultural life of China we find that Confucianism and Taoism have played most dominant role in creating systems of value both political and moral which kept Chinese people together. Confucianism imparted knowledge on social and moral values to define individual's place in society. It helped both individual and the state in maintaining the cooperate life by providing the value system and social reality which bind man with society, husband with wife, state with subjects, ruler with the ruled.

Chinese society is one of the most ancient one and it is but natural that there have been innumerable systems of rituals and customs even before the advent of Lao Tze and Confucius. It is evident from all available historical materials and data that Confucianism, Taoism and Buddhism have influenced the Chinese mind and culture and they have kept Chinese philosophical, political, social and cultural traditions alive. These systems are still influencing the Chinese moral system and social conduct. Buddhism played the part of moderating the moral behaviour of Chiense people. Buddhism with its middle path kept the Chinese mind from going astray. It avoids the life of extreme that is the life of indulgence and the life of renunciation. It says that middle path is the only way to deliverance. We can live in the society only through observing the moral and the social conduct. For the observance of moral conduct both the inner urge and external pressure are required. We cannot enforce any moral conduct to people in absense of inner urge. The inner urge is created by the implicit faith in the system and the pattern of values. This inner urge can be created only by creating a faith in the system. Buddhism with its profound philosophy and doctrines of *Karma,* Re-birth, *Nirvana* and *Paticcasamuppada* created faith in life of goodness. *Karma* they says "as you sow, so you will reap". This doctrine creates an earning for moral life to get deliverance and emancipation from the cycle of birth and death. The Chinese society gets the moral support both from Confucianism and Buddhism to lead a life of filial piety. On the other hand Confucianism with its political philosophy and doctrine provided the system of external pressure to keep the behaviour of individual within the four walls of political value system.

The Confucianism is concerned with the outer manifestation of human conduct and behaviour whereas Buddhism was more concerned with inner purification of human mind and consciousness and in this way one is complementary to the other. Chinese Buddhism is not the true copy of Indian Buddhism. It blossomed under the moral and the spiritual care of Confucianism and Taoism. It was but natural that Chinese Buddhism assimilated some of the moral teachings and the spiritual teachings of Confucianism and Taoism which resulted into a new form of Chinese Buddhism which is called Ch'an Buddhism or Zen Buddhism.

The Zen Buddhism deeply influenced neo-Confucianism. The renaissance of Confucian philosophy in Sung dynasty (960-1279) which is called in Chinese the learning of the Tao was the result of Zen Buddhism's impact on Chinese philosophy and learning. With the wedlock with Zen Buddhism Confucianism acquired a universal dimension and greater acceptance. The confluence of three religions ushered in the era of creativity and renaissance. The three religions "San Chiao" which became very popular movement during the Sang and the Ming dynasty of China created a composite culture with mixing the Confucian ethics with Taoist system of merits and Buddhist concept of reincarnation. The book of goodness, "Shan-Shu" as the Kan ying Pi-ien (Tract on actions and retributions). One of the product of these movements of thought and ideas known as the schools of three religions. In this renaissance movement both the Confucian and Buddhist followers of Taoism welcome the cultural metamorphosis of three religions. In spite of the initial resistance by followers of Confucianism the process of interaction and mutual understanding continued and the Taoist participation widened the horizon of Chinese mind. In this process of interaction Buddhism was undergone a process of "Taoisation" and "Confucianisation" for its adaptation to Chinese conditions. However, the Ch'an Buddhist maintained its philosophical and religious identity because of its profound metaphysical, moral and mystical foundation. Buddhist ideas of purgatory have had a great impact on Chinese religions. The schools of three religions was ultimately culminated into a new synthesis of thought and practice which is known as Zen Buddhism. Thus the Ch'an (Zen) Buddhism sheds the align characters of foreign religions for the Chinese masses and elites and in this way Buddhism was absorbed by the Chinese people without any opposition and resistance. The Confucianism created the background by widening the mental horizon of Chinese mind and emphasising the spiritual and philosophical profundity of Buddhism. Humanistic Confucianism worked as catalectic agent for acceptance and assimilation of Buddhism into Chinese culture and way of life. Buddhism on its part provided the Chinese mind a way of life, a spiritual technique to divinise life and attain *Nirvana*. The concept of *Paticcasappada* and the *Nirvana* bewildered the Chinese creativity and they have been left with no other choice but accept it as a way of life, a way of deliverance, and a way of enlightenment.

Confucius formulated his ideas and philosophy similar to those of Lao Tze but he speaks in a different language. In the opening passage of Chung-Yung one of the four books presenting the Confucian Philosophy described Taoist ideals as living in accordance with one's own nature. This is called self-realization in Confucian sense. The pursuit of self-realization is called maturation. One cannot disown his own nature. If one can disown his own nature, it would mean that, it would not be one's own nature. Therefore, the virtuous man is concerned about his self. According to Confucius the wise man retains his own nature whereas the foolish man does the opposite. The wise man retains his own nature because he is wise and he is wise because he retains his own nature. The foolish man does the opposite because he is a foolish and he is foolish because he fails to appreciate what is good. One's own true nature is self-sufficient but it is very difficult to maintain it for long. Nature's way is to be genuine and authentic is to act sincerely and truly and without effect which would lead automatically and spontaneously to realise one's own nature.

According to Confucius, only such man is wise. However, he

believes that more self-concern is not sufficient for realising the fullness of the life. Man is a social being. He finds his expressions only through his association with others. According to Confucius a man undisturbed by pleasure, anger or grief or joy is living with his true nature. If he is stimulated by such things as pleasure, anger or grief in its appropriate way he is living with one's true social nature. This true nature is the primal source from which springs all social affairs. This true social nature is the means for attaining happiness by humanility. Confucian would greatly emphasise on genuineness. He considers genuineness as self-sufficient. According to him genuineness pervades the whole being of man from beginning to end. Nothing can be attained without genuineness. According to Confucius, genuineness is the chief characteristics of a wise man. Genuineness promotes self-realization. It is the means through which one develops his relation with others. Self-realization involves associating himself with others. Associating with others creates sympathetic insight and abilities in which one realises his own nature. One's whole nature (*Tao*) integrates both external relations (social relation) and internal process. According to Confucius genuineness is full, when both of these abilities are appropriately integrated.

Confucius devoted his whole life in observing the practice of various royal societies and studying the records of previous societies, to discover and formulate the most successful ways of organising human relationship and the attitude required for conducting a better corporate life. He considers these ideals to imitate others, which made him to recognise as a teacher of customary morality. According to him, there are four chief characteristics of a wise man. These are referred to as *Yi, Jen, Li* and *Chih*. (1) *Yi* stands for the things behave when they act in accordance with their own nature and this is the best way of all things to act. No man is wise until he understands. It is a natural way of things behaving. We must keep in mind the basic tenets of Lao Tze that nature and human nature are good. The nature provides each being with a nature that is self-sufficient and self-fulfilling, thus as good as it can be. Trying to change is artificial and making it artificial will bring it to unnatural end. (2) *Jen* means goodwill. It is to do what is best for society as we know acting in accordance with one's own nature is the best for each person, goodwill consists basically acting in accordance to one's own nature. (3) *Li* is propriety or a way of giving overt expressions of inner attitudes. It involves here a basic principle, namely that one's inner nature and one's external behaviour are correlative or should be correlative when man's intensions are sincere. (4) *Chih* is wisdom. No man is wise until he is happy. Wisdom consists in confident living. Living confidently involves consenting to things as they are, i.e. to *Yi*, Jen and *Li* three characteristics of the wise man. Wisdom does not require encyclopaedic knowledge.

The Zen monks were on the other hand students of Confucianism and as staunch Chinese they could not be anything else. The difference between Confucian scholars and the Zen masters was that the Confucian based their philosophy on the native system while Zen Buddhists adhered to the basic teachings of Buddhism as enunciated by Bodhidharma but they started speaking Buddhism in Confucian language. The Zen monks interpreted Confucian texts in Buddhistic way and they commented on Buddhist literature from the Confucian point of view. The Zen Buddhism, Confucianism and Taoism were assimilated into one philosophy which is known as Sung philosophy.

D.T. Suzuki says, "Suffice it to state here that Zen is in fact, the Chinese way of responding to Indian thought and represented by Buddhism and that this being so, Zen, as it developed in the Tang and later flourished in the Sung, could be nothing else but a reflection of Chinese mentality—by which I mean it was eminently practical and ethical. In this respect, there was very probability of Zen's taking on Confucian colouring. But in the beginning of Zen's history its philosophy was Indian, that is, Buddhistic, for there was nothing corresponding to it in the traditional teaching of Confucianism. And this was the element the later Confucian thinkers consciously or unconsciously wished to incorporate into their own system."[2]

In short Zen adopted the practical teachings of Confucian morality and social reality and Confucianism absorbed the abstract speculation of Buddhism which provided metaphysical foundation to the waning teachings of Confucianism. It was a normal practice for the Zen monks to become advocates of Confucianism in addition to preaching Buddhism.[3] We do not agree with D.T. Suzuki's observation that Zen Buddhism does not have philosophy of its own. Dr. Suzuki has made a contradictory statement about Zen Buddhism.

At one place he says, that Zen Buddhism provided a metaphysical foundation to the teachings of Confucians and at the same time he says strictly speaking Zen has no philosophy of its own.[4] Zen Buddhism has a profound metaphysical basis which provided infrastructure for both the Confucianism and Taoism. It is another fact that Zen Buddhists are sometimes Confucianists, sometimes Taoists and sometimes even

Shintoists. This explains the universal philosophical outlook and the mystical basis of Buddhism which can even be adopted and explained by Western religious experience. This form of new Buddhism incorporated in itself the naturalistic mysticism of Taoism and down to earth philosophy of Confucianism. The concept of Buddha-nature and Tao represents the same reality. Taoism has also incorporated Zen technique to find out the truth. In an endeavour to find out the truth on the other hand, Zen Buddhism is greatly influenced by the Taoist emphasis on natural life. However, Zen Buddhism owe its origin and development from Indian Buddhism. The technique of meditation and the concept of Buddha-nature have definitely been borrowed from the original teachings of Lord Buddha making certain conceptual change and development suited to the creative Chinese mind. The Zen Buddhism came to Japan in the Seventh century. The Japanese Zen Buddhism owes its development and progress to two great Zen masters, namely Risai and Dogen. These two Zen masters were men of profound spiritual attainment and they transformed Zen into a living religious reality. These two Zen masters were so great and powerful that they are acclaimed as the founders of the two schools of Zen Buddhism, namely Rinzad and Soto. These Zen masters Risai and Dogen were so much Inspired by Zen that they made a pilgrimage to China in search of the authentic and the real form of Zen Buddhism. They visited many monasteries and met many Zen masters of great spiritual attainments with a purpose of gaining knowledge and testify their own meditational technique and spiritual attainments. Risai after returning from China introduced socio-religious element in his new form of Buddhism which attracted the warrier class of Japan to defend the state against all sorts of invasions and Chism which was considered as religious duty of this new school.

Gradually, it covered the whole gamut of Japanese cultural life. Its impact can be traced in the no play of Japanese poetry *Ikebana* the flower arrangement *cha-no-ya, tea ceremony* etc., all of which emphasise on grace and spontaneity. Dogen, the founder of Soto school visited Tendai monastery of mount Hiei in China in search of truth and meaning of life like his teacher Risai. After his return, he introduces method of meditation known as Zazen. He considered the scriptured knowledge and philosophical disputation as an exercise in futility. *Dhyana* is the core-concept of Zen Buddhism. The *nirvana* or *satori* does not mean to comprehend *Buddha-nature* in an intellectual or objective sense. It means to become one with it and feel the existence of

Tathata in every things and beings. This concept of *Dhyana* has been taken from Mahayana scriptures such as *Prajnaparamita* and *Vimalakirtinirdasa* and *Lankevatara Sutra.*

According to Chinese tradition Bodhidharma's long nine years of meditation at the Shao-Lin-ssu temple on the mount of *Saung-Shan* during which he neither study any scriptures nor performed any rituals and ceremonies but kept himself engaged and engrossed in deep meditation proved the efficacy of meditation as the only means of experiencing *satori.* The spirit of this new form of Buddhism in China introduced the practice of *Zazen* and upheld the importance of sacredness of Chinese family life. Thus, Zen Buddhism integrating the meditational technique of Bodhidharma with down to earth philosophical approach of Chinese creative mind became harbinger of a new religious awakening and renaissance. The characteristics of Zen Buddhism are that it does not give any credence to philosophical abstraction and conceptualization. It lives in facts. The object of meditation is to integrate the part with the whole, the conscious mind with the unconscious mind and in this process of unification and transfiguration *satori* is experienced. This process of unification has been termed as an art of walking with no path, with no walker and with no goal. This non-sensical statement contains great sense and awareness that though the intellect is a brilliant tool to understand the thought and knowledge but there is something which is beyond the reach of this truth of transcendental nature which can best be expressed through the language of silence. All the mystical schools like Sufism, Hindu's Sahajiya cult, and Upanishadic teachings, Chinese Taoism belief that that the supreme reality which forms the basis of all existence and all beings, cannot be put into words. It is to be experienced because it is mystical. Language and reason can lead to a certain point but it cannot take us to the core of reality which is called suchness. Intellect, however, serves its purpose by pointing towards the unknown like an arrow mark. This is why the Zen masters say that if you want to experience *satori* you should get yourself disassociated with the process of conceptualization and abstraction. The process of *Dhyana* is a process of freeing the mind from all kinds of dispositions. In Zen Buddhism it is called emptying yourself. There is a famous saying of a Zen master "Those who know do not speak—those who speak do not know."

The twentieth century world has made many experiments and it has come to the conclusion that neither Consumerism nor Western philosophy, neither Existentialism nor Positivism, neither Depth

Psychology nor Comparative religion could unite the man from himself. To create cohesion and harmony in the society Zen Buddhism with its lofty philosophy and technique of meditation can integrate the fragmented life of man which is necessary to build up a better and just society. Zen goes beyond the conceptual teaching of philosophy. It emphasises in integrating the part with the whole and man with humanity.

This concept of oneness is the essential part of the Buddha's life and teachings. Zen takes life as a whole. It imparts practical technique to transfigure one's own personality and in this process of transfiguration it fills every moment of life with grace, spontaneity and significance.

Thus Zen Buddhism is not an institutionalised religion. It is a way of life. It is a way of transformation and transfiguration of human personality. According to Zen Buddhism in each of us there is a Buddha who wants to get himself awakened. Zen Buddhism is nothing but a meditational technique to get our dormant divinity or the Buddha awakened and realized. This is the way through which we can create one world and one humanity.

To me Zen Buddhism represents the correct and the proper understanding of philosophy and life world. Zen Buddhism was originated in China with Bodhidharma's visit in 520 A.D. Bodhidharma is considered by one tradition as the first patriarch. This new Buddhism incorporates in itself the naturalistic mysticism of Taoism and down to earth philosophy of Confucianism.

The concept of Buddha-nature and Tao represent the same reality. Taoism has also incorporated Zen technique to find out the truth. Zen Buddhism is, however, greatly influenced by Taoist emphasis on life world. According to Zen, *nirvana* or *satori* does not mean to comprehend Buddha-nature (*Bodhicitta*) in an intellectual or objective sense. It means to become one with it or feel the existence of life world in every things and beings.

Zen Buddhism does not believe in philosophical abstraction and conceptualization. It believes in living and experiencing life world. The object of meditation is to integrate the part with the whole. With the life world and in this process of unification and transfiguration *satori* is experienced. This process of unification has been termed as an art of walking with no path, with no walker and with no goal. This non-sensical statement contains great sense and awareness that though the intellect is a brilliant tool to understand the thought and knowledge but there is something which is beyond the reach of this truth of transcendental nature which can best be expressed through the language of silence. Ludwig Wittgenstein rightly observes, "There are indeed, things that cannot be put into words. They make themselves manifest. They are what is mystical."[5] "My propositions serve as elucidations in the following way: anyone who understands me eventually recognizes them as non-sensical, when he has used them as steps to climb up beyond them. (He must, so to speak, throw away the ladder after he has climbed up it).

He must transcend these propositions and then he will see the world alright.[6] "What we cannot speak about we must pass over in silence."[7]

Zen Buddhism is very much rooted in the life world. It always lives in the midst of the nature. It does not propagate the philosophy of keeping oneself away from life world.

For Zen humble blade of grass is also a *Bodhicitta*. The Zen insight and philosophy go deeper into the very source of life and existence. Zen lives and feels the life world as we feel the sensation of our pulses.

According to Zen Buddhism the concept of emptiness (*Sunyata*) or (*Bodhicitta*) is not philosophically speaking a concept, it is an experience which binds man with life world. From this concrete experience originates the philosophy of love and *satori*. After realizing the limitation of thought and language in communicating the experience of life world reflected in *satori* the Chinese Zen masters developed new concept of *Wu* to describe this state of consciousness which is beyond the realm of discrimination and differentiation. The literal meaning of this Chinese term *Wu* is nothingness or no mind. The introduction of *koan* in Zen Buddhism is a technique to throw the mind of its familiar way of logical reasoning and to start the process of emptying it is from all sorts of metapsychosis. The Zen masters do not use any statement to transmit his teachings rather he carefully uses a so called device non-sensical riddles known as *koan*. According to Zen Buddhism life world consists of the whole truth. There is no difference between *nirvana* and *samsara*. *Nirvana* is *samsara* and *samsara* is *nirvana*. The use of *koan* is to solve the riddle of 'I' and the world, *nirvana* and the *samsara*. With the practice of *koan* the mind undergoes complete metamorphosis, it is an act of integration of *nirvana* and *samsara* and it is the total experience of true philosophy and the life world.

Notes

1. *The Essential Tao*, Translated and Presented by Thomas Geary, Harpor San Francisco. 1993. *Tao Te Ching*. p. 11.
2. D.T. Suzuki, *Zen and Japanese Culture*, pp. 43-44.
3. *Ibid.*
4. *Ibid.*
5. *Tractatus Logico-Philosophicus*, 6.522.
6. *Ibid.*, 6.54.
7. *Ibid.*, 7.

18

Status of Women in Buddhism

Analysis and Reflection

Women have been the centre of great controversy and condemnation throughout the annals of history. A new image of woman can be seen through an analysis and examination of their religious portraits. The religious traditions have described women in different ways, which has resulted in a wide variety of attitudes and beliefs towards woman. An objective and in-depth study of Asian culture is required for understanding the status of women in the light of classical religious values and institutions.

The status of women in Buddhism is a study of ideological concept and a social history of women's actual behaviour in Buddhist society. The Buddhist and other religious thinkers were greatly concerned about gender in their time. Normally they did not make distinction between gender and sexuality. The gender roles were rooted in images and ideals of femininity. Men and women were thought to have separate spheres of activity according to their inherent potentialities and abilities. The potentialities accorded to gender roles were considered natural and legitimate rather than ideological.

L.B. Horner has made an in-depth study of women in her celebrated book *The Women Under Primitive Buddhism.* She writes: "In the pre-Buddhist days the status of women in India was on the whole low and without honour. A daughter was nothing but a source of anxiety to her parents; for it was a disgrace to them and inauspicious as well, if they could not marry her; yet, if they could, they were often nearly ruined by their lavish expenditure on the wedding festivities. Nor was she of any ceremonial benefit for her father, for she was powerless to participate in his funeral rites, and in cases where these had not already been insured by the birth of a son, the distress at the birth of a daughter was almost unmitigated."[1]

However, during the Buddhist period, there was a great change in the status and honour of women. Women came to enjoy greater equality and better respect and authority than had ever been accorded to them. The status of women who were earlier confined to internal spheres such as domestic, social and religious, started to improve. The exclusive supremacy of man began to give way to the increasing emancipation of women. The Buddha gave *Dhamma* to both the householders and their wives that heralded a new era of women renaissance. The birth of girl children was no longer to be considered a curse and girls ceased to be despised and looked upon as encumbrances. Homer writes: "Thus, amid many currents, intricate but potent, the tide turned; and in its flow the position of women, as manifested in secular affairs, became which was no longer intolerable and degraded, but one which was honorable and therefore bearable; women were acknowledged at last to be capable of working as a constructive force in the society of the day."[2]

There has been great change in the portraits of women's spiritual achievements in Mahayana Buddhism. There was emphasis on the metaphysical condition which has been dealt with in greater detail in the *Diamond Sūtras, Vimalkīrtinerdes* and the Sūtras of Queen Srimala who had the Lions Roar. The above Sutras do not make any distinction whether one is a man or woman in the context of the "concept of the conditioned". All phenomena are impermanent and insubstantial, there is no self-existence entity. There is no male or female. Philosophically speaking, all such distinctions and characteristics are illusions. *Sunyata* and *Dhamma* envisage that the path is neither male nor female.

According to Buddhism, religious goal is to attain *Nirvāṇa,* liberation from cycle of birth and death which is the definitive religious characteristics of Buddhism. *Nirvāṇa* is considered and defined as transformative realization of the impermanence of all things and beings. To realize the truth of impermanence and the insubstantiality of all things is to liberate oneself from the bondage of one's mistaken identity and illusion. *Nirvāṇa* involves a thorough transformation of human cognitive and emotive faculties. One is no longer at the mercy of unrealistic illusions and expectations. By understanding the absolute pervasiveness of change, one accepts whatever happens as a natural consequence of one's own action and as a result one attains a state of perfect peace and harmony. The life of renunciation is intrinsic to the quest of liberation. The process of attaining liberation itself is considered as the successive renunciation of assumptions, attitudes, motivation and the evaluation that characterize the human condition. In attaining *Nirvāṇa*, one must rid oneself from the emotional and the social motivation of mind that perpetuates one's continuing existence. In the cycle of *Saṁsāra* the transformation of one's consciousness follows the external change.

The *Mahāvagga* gives an authentic account of introduction of the institution of *Bhikkhu Saṁgha* with the ordination *(upasampadā)* of the five ascetics with whom the Buddha had previously performed austerity. Five years later, *Bhikkhuni Saṁgha* was established when the Buddha acceded to his aunt, Mahāpajāpati's request for ordination. According to *Chullavagga,* the Buddha was very reluctant to accept women in the *Saṁgha.* When Mahāpajāpati, his aunt and foster mother, requested ordination, the Buddha refused three times. Mahāpajāpati and a large number of his female relatives cut their hair, doned the yellow robes of renunciation to follow the Buddha to Vesali. Ānanda, Buddha's closest attendant, took up the cause and requested Buddha to ordain Mahāpajāpati. The Buddha refused three times again. It is only after Ānanda changed his approach and asked Buddha if women could attain *Nirvāṇa?* Mahāpajāpati and others were allowed entrance into the *Saṁgha.* The Buddha acknowledged the capacity and inherent possibility to attain *Nirvāṇa* by women. However, the Buddha complained to Ānanda that without women the *Buddha Dhamma* would have lasted 1,000 years but with the entrance of women it would last only 500 years.

There is much debate about the historicity of this account. However, this story appears in the *Vinaya* of every school of Buddhism. The Buddha's initial reluctance and his prediction of the decline of the *Dhamma* and the institutional subordination contained in the eight rules are found among all the *Vinayas* of different schools. This is still a debatable point. In *Therāvāda* countries where the *Bhikkhunī Saṁgha* has almost disappeared, the story continues to be cited by those who oppose women's entry into *Saṁgha.* These important texts indicate that *Saṁgha* was not egalitarian. *Bhikkhunīs* are explicitly discriminated against, and the Buddha, and at least some of the *Bhikkhus,* were ambivalent about their role in the *Saṁgha.* As many scholars have argued, these features of the *Saṁgha* reflect the gender assumptions of the prevalent social milieu. The social world of ancient India was almost certainly patriarchal. Women were expected to marry, bear children (preferably son), and serve and obey men in their families. The life style of renunciation offered women an alternative, but as we have seen, even in the *Saṁgha,* women were institutionally subordinate to men.[3] Some scholars feel that Buddhist misogynistic attitude grew out of the historical fact that the establishment of *Bhikkhunī Saṁgha* was considered as a great threat to the *Dhamma* and the *Vinaya.* The women's presence in the *Saṁgha* is depicted as a grave tragedy. The prototype of women as evil, the equivalent of *Satan,* whore, in Christianity, finds expression in the *Therāvādi* scriptures known as the *Pali* canon.[4] The interpretation of woman as a temptress and seductress represented a story of reservation for the entry of women in the *Saṁgha.* The primary objective of *Saṁgha* was to maintain peace and harmony in the organization while the religious aim was to attain *Nirvāṇa.* Woman was normally thought to be a potential obstacle in actual life of man's spiritual growth. In fact, woman as wife could pose a great threat to the life of monks particularly in the observance of celibacy. Normally woman is considered profane and belonging to *Saṁsāra.* The perceived threat that woman represented to the monastic community led to the rules of discipline emphasizing the avoidance of woman at all cost. According to *Mahāvastu,* the negative inputs of the woman were not only due to the mythological content that Buddhism inherited. It is true that early Buddhist texts such as the *Jātakas,* the tales of the Buddha, incorporated many misogynist remarks from the orthodox traditions of Brahmanic tradition. However, the soteriological path of Buddhism was opened to women. All soteriological paths for both men and women reflect an asexual ideal in which sexuality has been eliminated. Diana Y. Paul says: "The transformation from a fallen state of sexuality to a religious asexual state suggests complete control of one's sexuality. This is the desired result of the soteriological paths in Mahāyana Buddhism. Men are viewed as the ones most likely to control their sexuality, whereas women as well as men may have the capacity to develop fully and to grow religiously as sexually transformed beings."[5]

Masculine and feminine are two categories like spirit and matter on which Buddhism mediates. The notion that feminine is wise, natural, creative and compassionate gives a high status to woman in Buddhism. Sexuality controlled or denied is transcended in the role of a mother, sexuality is usually seen as in a controlled state. Buddhist Tantra portrayed women as creative, compassionate and necessary for the realization of *Nirvāṇa. Prajñā* and *Upāya* like *Śiva* and *Śakti* of Hindu Tantra constitute transcendentality. The mystic union of *Prajñā* and *Upāya* has nothing to do with the gratification of the senses, rather it represents the complete transformation of ordinary desire. The principle behind *Pañcamakāra Sādhanā* is that man must rise with the aid of *Śakti,* which misused, will cause his fall. Man and woman would have to work out his or her own salvation, not by suppressing his or her own biological instincts, but by sublimating and channelizing them into higher forms of spiritual life. When women's sexuality is regarded as an anomalous, potentially destructive force, it limits their power in society. However, Buddhism does regard women as creative, spiritual and thus women have been given a complementary religious status (or nearly equivalent) to men.

From the accounts of *Therigāthā,* it appears that women were greatly animated by the spiritual motives and asnpirations which resulted into renunciation and entering into the *Saṁgha.* Once the *Bhikkhunī Saṁgha* was established woman was free to decide to enter the life of a recluse or not. It was normal practice for the woman to present her wishes to her father or husband or others upon whom she was dependent, to gain their consent.

In *Therigāthā,* there are instances of women who destitute of husband or relations decided to enter the *Saṁgha.* The stories of *Therigāthā* provide enough historical account that the women had the realization that they have the spiritual power and potentialities like men to attain *Nirvāṇa.* As per the practice, the women desirous of receiving *Upsampadā* ordination had to ask for it as has been shown from both the *Saṁghas.* There is only one exception and that is the Buddha who ordained an entrant by saying: "come", calling the entrant by name. The name of the fortunate woman is Bhadda Kundalakesa, the ex-Jain:

> 'Come Bhadda!' the master said!
> Thereby to me was ordination given.[6]

There is enough evidence that husbands were considered much of hindrance to women as women were to men who were leading higher life.[7] This view is pronounced in Buddhism which is shared by Bhaddākapilani and Pippali who are known as *Mahākassapa* and her husband. They both agreed to part company and joined their respective *Saṁgha.* Bhaddākapilani was received with greater warm and respect than the queen Silave.[8] They used to go for alms round with their alms bowl and returning with the food they had collected. We find references to such practices scattered throughout Pali literature.

Buddhism being the universal religion and an egalitarian movement, it tried to provide equal opportunity both for men and women. Buddhism is a religion of compassion and enlightenment and as such it did not bother about the kind of life women or men had led before their application for their Pabajjā ordination. The *Saṁgha* provided an honourable life to all those who wanted to relinquish the life of business they had hitherto pursued. Once the women were admitted into the *Saṁgha,* they were expected to adhere to a strict moral code. There were instructions or ban upon the admission of woman of loose character. In *Therigāthā,* there is a description of pre-renunciation life of an *Addhakāsi*, who referred to her large wage as prostitute.[9] There is also the mental history of Abhaya's mother,[10] a courtesan of king Bimbisara and Ambapāli,[11] a famous courtesan, who was sought by several princes. Abhaya was motivated and converted into Buddhism by her own son who convinced her of the impurity of the body. Ambapāli was also inspired and stimulated by her son to live the life of virtue and *Dhamma* after throwing philosophical light on the impermanence of everything. He told her that her own ageing body which at one time was full of grace and beauty was becoming ugly due to the nature of impermanence.

Therigāthā and *Therāgāthā* were considered as liberation manuals designed to provide paths of success for the *theris* and *theras* who joined the Buddhist *Saṁgha.* The texts are similar to the *Jātakas* or the *Apāddnā.* However, unlike *Apāddnā, Therigāthā* and *Therāgāthā* were not much concerned with the past lives of *theris* and *theras* and their Karmic causes that led to their attainment of *Nirvāṇa.* Addhakāsi prominently figures in *Therigāthā.* The two verse poems in the *Therigāthā* describe her as a renowned prostitute?

> My wages (of prostitution) were as large as the revenue of the country of *Kāśi;* having fixed that price the town's people made me priceless.
> Then I became disgusted with my figure, and being disgusted I was disinterested (in it). May I not run again through the journeying-on from rebirth to rebirth again and again. The three knowledges have been realized. The Buddha's teaching had been done.[12]

In the *Anguttara Nikaya,*[13] the Buddha showered great praise on Khemā and Uppalavanā who were considered as scale and criterion for measuring of the disciples. They were considered a norm by which to gauge others because of their exceptional accomplishment. Of the thirteen who came from a great merchant family, Dhammadma,[14] became the greatest preacher (*Dhammakathikā).* Sukka and Pattacara also became very famous as they were versed in *Vinaya.* They were revered by many women because they had been instrumental in changing their lives by showing the path of *Dhamma.*

The *Therigāthā* mentions the name of Sujatā who attained arhantship while she was a laywoman. She was probably the only one or at most one of the two among the reputed *Theris* who attained *Nirvāṇa.*[15] The study of the *Therigāthās* and an analysis of different terms and phrases of the formalized *gāthā* composition throws great light on the socio-cultural life of contemporary Indian culture. The portrayals of Subha and Sundarasamudda in the *Therigāthās* and the *Therigāthā* confirm the varying tendencies and the conflicts between the life of renunciation and the life of enjoyment.

Subha is on her way to forest to meditate when she meets a rogue who proposes to her to caste off her yellow robe and enjoy sexual interlude with him in the flowering grove. Subha preaches and propagates on the essential impermanence of her body and she compares her body to a corpse putrefying in the cemetery. The rogue is not convinced and persists, locating the source of his desire in her beautiful eyes. Subha finally resorts to extracting her eyes, the source of his desire and offering it to him. The rogue begs her forgiveness. The central metaphor of the poem is that the rogue is the epitome of the blind and ordinary individual, his perception is impaired by his passion whereas Subha is calm *(anāvil),* dispassionate and her desire has been annihilated and her mind is completely unsoiled and she is without *asavas.*

A great number of *theris* came from the Brahmin families. This speaks of the cultural milieu which is the characteristic mark of Hinduism in particular and Indian society in general where toleration and assimilation of new ideas were considered vital for the very survival of mankind. Bhadda of the Kapilas[16] who came from Brahmin family became very famous because of her memories of past lives. She is described as scholarly, wise and famous for her religious discourses. Nanduttara came from Jain background. She became an eminent speaker and great debater. She was converted from Jainism to Buddhism. In Mahamaggallaya, Sakula and Uttama occupied very high position amongst the Buddhist almswomen and they have been portrayed as having a very close relationship with the Buddha. Sona[17] also became very famous because of her capacity of efforts *(araddhaviriyd).* Her caste has not been mentioned. I.B. Homer observes, that not only did the womenfolk come to the Order from different parts of North India and from various walks in life to mingle in the Order heedless of caste distinctions, but also that there was nothing in their station or in their previous existence to hinder them from attaining *arhantship*,[18] as they are all said to have done, nor to prevent them from becoming remarkably proficient in some respect of their calling, as several cases attest.

The salient features of Buddhism as opposed to Brāhmanism, were that its converts were drawn from all castes and religions. The membership was not confined to any caste or religion, and therefore, its appeal was universal. Women played important role in the dissemination of its philosophy making Buddhism as a way of life. Culla Subhaddā, daughter of Anāthapindikā, was married and living at Ugga. She was instrumental in converting her mother-in-law into Buddhism. Subhadda's father-in-law who was a great merchant of Ugga embraced Buddhism. King Udayan embraced Buddhism because of the persistent effort of his queen Samavati. Samavati was converted to Buddhism by her own female slave named Khujjuttara. It is a well known historical fact that the great king Pasenadit of Kausal was converted by Mallikā, one of his queens. Mallikā was converted to Buddhism after having a conversation with the Buddha. There is a well known story about Mallikā enquiring about the reasons why women rich or poor, beautiful or ugly, in possession of great power follow the path of the Buddha. She became a lay adherent. Men and women bestowed great praise on Mallikā for her virtues and their realization that their liberation was due to the intervention of the queen. Viśīkhī was an outstanding laywoman who played an important role in introducing new ideas and the spread of Buddhism. A long talk between the Buddha and Viśīkhī is preserved in the *Anguttara Nikāya*. It is stated that Viśīkhī was sitting at one side of the Buddha where Buddha had given a long address which formed the substance of the conversation on the cleansing of mind. Mahīpajāpati and Viśākhā were considered to be great women having great powers of discretion acquired through the knowledge of *Dhamma*. I.B. Homer writes that religion which allows this amount of independence of judgement to its women members, and does not differentiate between the capacity of the two sexes, is ennobled, for the women rise and justify the faith which is placed in them. The two, Mahāpajāpati and Viśākhā, never wavered in their loyalty, and Viśākhā, by the constant gifts of alms, clothes and dwellings, and also by her criticism, was an unflagging help in the process of binding the alms people together and to the laity.

She may indeed be regarded as the true and faithful follower of the Order. The almsmen regarded her as a trusted friend of the Order. It is reported that some of them used to take their food and eat it in her house or in Anāthupindikā's,[19] for although they had received it at the king's palace, nobody was friendly to them there.

Sound was an embodiment of wisdom and compassion. She was convicted of the inherently equal capacity of the sexes to attain *Nirvāṇa.* She is so much convinced and confident that her verse speaks of a great challenge for the cause of her whole sex. She takes radical stand for other *theris* insofar as her claim is not the comprehension of the *Dhamma* by herself, but for all women. The words, which were uttered twenty-five centuries ago, challenged the notion of women's inherent inferiority and their capacity to attain higher, mental, spiritual stage. She defied and rejected the notion of sexual inequality. She says:

> How should the women's nature hinder us? Whose hearts are firmly set, who ever move with growing knowledge onward in the path? What can that signify to one in whom insight doth truly comprehend the Norm? On every hand the love of pleasure yields, and the thick gloom of ignorance is rent. In twain, Know this. O Evil one avaunt! Here, O destroyer! Shalt thou not prevail.[20]

The close examination of the status of women in ancient India on the basis of the *Ṛgveda,* shows that women enjoyed a honourable place in pre-Buddhistic Indian society. Women had access to the highest spiritual knowledge and participated in all religious discourses, debates and ceremonies. A number of Vedic hymns were composed by women. With the advent of Brāhmaṇism, caste began to dominate the society and as a result, religion lost its grace, spontaneity and spiritual fervour and became a complex system of rites and rituals. At this point, the status of women began to decline and degenerate. Manu deprived women of their religious rights and access to spiritual life. Women were considered as equal to lower castes and were forbidden from taking part in religious ceremony. According to Manu, a woman cannot attain heaven through any merit of her own but only through obedience to her husband. According to *Manusaṁhitā,* woman was supposed to worship her husband as a god even if he was devoid of any human quality.[21] It is a historical fact that *Manusaṁhitā* did adversely influence the status of woman in ancient Indian society. The Buddhist doctrine of Dependent

Origination *(Patitsammutapadā)* and *Nirvāṇa* presupposes the spiritual equality of sexes. This assertion of gender equality enunciated in the texts, exercised great impact on the social structure. Man and woman were considered equal in the religious domain and they were considered alike in attaining liberation by adhering to the prescribed path. Buddhism brought a social revolution by demolishing the priestly class as intermediary in the attainment of *Nirvāṇa.* In the Brāhmanical society, all religious ceremonies were performed jointly by husband and wife. But according to Buddhism, all religious activities, whether meditation or ceremony, are acts of self-discipline, performed by individuals independent of any priest or partner. Lorna Devaraja writes: "It is against this background that we must view the emergence of Buddhism in Northern India in the sixth century B.C.E. There are records of long conversations the Buddha had with his female disciples. The devout benefactress Viśākhā frequented the monastery, decked out in all her finery, accompanied by a maidservant, she attended to the needs of the celibate monks. The Buddha's liberal attitude towards women had great impact on the behaviour of both men and women in Buddhist societies. This is not to suggest that the Buddha inaugurated a campaign for the liberation of womanhood in India, but he did create a minor stir by speaking out against prevailing dogma and superstition. He condemned excessive rituals and sacrifices. Denying the existence of a creator God, he emphasized emancipation through individual effort."[22]

A.S. Altekar[23] is of the opinion that the advent of nunnery in Buddhism and Jainism created a social problem. Some grown up women entered into *Saṁgha* against the will of their parents and husbands and some of them had fallen from high spiritual life which strengthened the view of the marriage of the girl before attaining puberty. With the establishment of the *Bhikkhunī Saṁgha,* the marriageable age of girl was lowered down. The *Bhikkhunī Saṁgha,* has almost disappeared in the *Theravādi* countries which speaks of the apathy towards women. The Buddha's reluctance to allow women into *Saṁgha* was not out of any apathy towards women, but it was because of his conviction that he was ahead of time and clime. Ānanda's trial for favouring women's entrance into the *Saṁgha* in the first Buddhist council which was held just after the *parinirvāṇa* of the Buddha is a proof that the anti-woman thinkers had taken over the *Saṁgha* after the demise of the Buddha.

The ascetic misogynist attitude become pronounced in Buddhism. The *Jātakas* which are post-Buddha compilation is a clear proof that anti-woman attitude became very much pronounced and Bodhisattvas were being frequently called woman-hater *(anitthigandha)*.[24] Some scholars are of the opinion that Buddhism is a patriarchal religion and as such it does not allow women into its hierarchy. On the other hand, the historical facts speak in favour of the rights of women and support their spiritual aspirations. The close examination of the status of women in Buddhism creates three kinds of images: (i) There is an image of woman as temptress, the incarnation of evil and a snare of *Mārā,* the woman is compared with a serpent and the siren. She is considered as the greatest impediment to man's spiritual evolution. (ii) There is an image of a woman as a mother. As a mother, woman is an embodiment of creativity, regeneration, compassion and self-sacrifice. Elizabeth J. Harris writes: "The first image is dangerous, while the second is life-giving. There is also a third category of woman as the mystic, the goddess one who transcends the material and perhaps, the sexual to gain mystical knowledge and wisdom. Here, feminine is linked with ultimate spiritual reality. It becomes part of godhead or, in some religious groups, the truest expression of the Absolute."[25]

If we summarize the whole discussion and issues emerging out of the close examination of the status and the image of woman in Buddhism, the Buddhist canonical literatures maintain patriarchal, andocentric and misogynistic attitude towards woman. However, the *Therigāthā* is a historical proof to ascertain that women had a history of independent thought and action. The establishment of *Bhikkhunī Saṁgha* heralded a new era of woman liberation and moral awakening. It provided a honourable alternative to family life. It speaks of sexual equality and irrelevance of gender. In the practical aspects, the Buddhist soteriology opened the door of salvation for woman. The soteriological path which was opened both for men and women exhibits an asexual ideal in which sexuality is sublimated.

Buddhism does recognize women as spiritual beings. In the maternal role woman receives legitimate power within the religious structure. Hinduism eulogised motherhood and considered woman as procreator and sacred. Buddhism does not accept the sacred image of women. Mothers are ideal in Buddhism so long as they represent the feminine principle of wisdom which gives birth to the Buddhahood. Diana Y. Paul rightly observes: "Perhaps the most explicit and striking examples from Mahāyāna Buddhist Sūtra literature, which magnify the tensions between misogyny and egalitarian ideas, were the depictions of Bodhisattvas with sexual transformations. Interpretations of the accessibility of the Bodhisattva path for women ranged from fulfilment of this path only after rebirth as a male to a symbolic transformation of a woman's mental state from the profane, sensual world to the *Dhamma* world. Texts which described Bodhisattvas without sexual transformations fully acknowledged the accessibility of this soteriological path to sexes."[26]

Dorothy Dinnerstein's[27] post-Freudian feminist psychoanalytic analysis has some relevance in modern Buddhist context. There is some truth in Dinnerstein's postulate that modern culture places women alone in primary responsibility for child care. Women are subconsciously blamed for the frustration and limitation initiated in *saṁsāra.* They are blamed for such motivation and learning that suffering is an inevitable result of the past *Karma.* Some grown up children have great problem in disentangling what their parents did to them that may have been responsible for their dissatisfaction. She argues that men's monopoly of spiritual teachings is as damaging as the female monopoly of child rearing. The prevailing patriarchal ways of constructing, production and reproduction and linking them with gender have already become obsolete and dysfunctional.

The Buddhist literature depicts a laywoman like Viśakhā with very high admiration. Viśakhā would be the ideal model for future regeneration of feminine and the creative image of woman. In the modern world laywomen have to play a dominant role in creating an atmosphere of peace and harmony. Buddhism believes in the accumulation of wisdom through meditation as a central expression of its identity. The spiritual discipline aims at the development of mindfulness and choiceless awareness in which any distinction of sex and gender is irrelevant. *Therigāthā* is a story of women reflecting upon the attitude of resentment and bitterness towards the prevailing social system but it speaks of their triumph also. *Therigāthā* is not a testament of a feminist rebellion against gender discrimination but it does provide women's persistent and positive struggle of liberation by opening an alternate life style that liberated women from the gender expectations of their social structures. Buddhism, specially Tāntric Buddhism, creates a new hope and promise of the better tomorrow for the laywomen. Tāntric Buddhism believes in esoteric commingling of sexuality and the sacred and thus it heralds a new era of emergence of women regeneration and renaissance.

The concept and status of women in Buddhism can be studied as models of the earnest quest for salvation. This postulation opens up new possibilities for the elucidation and analysis of the concept of women in

Buddhism. The poems of *Therigāthā,* which throw sociological, historical and philosophical light on the status of women in Buddhism, function as models of salvation and dwell upon signification and symbols that reveal social values and preoccupations.

Clifford Geertz's classical work *Religion as a Cultural System*[28] throws enough light on the symbols which exercise great impact in the world in which we live. In fact symbols do reflect and shape the world in which we breath. Clifford Geertz is of the opinion that symbols function both as "models of our social and ideological world and as models for what we think that world should be."[29] George Lakoff and Mark Johnson's doctrine that the symbols which we use and language with which we express are intimately associated with our experiences and social realities. Language is a complex symbol. It influences our conceptual understanding of the world. In this complex process of conceptual understanding of the world, we define and delimit our perceptions of 'reality'.[30]

These doctrines of symbolism and linguistic understanding of social reality provide a useful tool of analysis of canonical literature. The analysis of the different images and symbols employed in the portrayal of women in Buddhism in the canonical and non-canonical literatures, do communicate certain religious and social truths. We have tried in the previous pages to reveal the different dimensions of women as depicted in the vast canonical and non-canonical literatures of Buddhism. Language depicts the cultural life of society. The forms, symbols, images, events and situations uncover the motives, attitudes and the social realities. We have analysed and elucidated the different concepts, images and symbols related with women to understand the status of women in Buddhism.

Buddhism heralded a new era of women emancipation by opening soteriological path to them. The path of women's emancipation has passed through the pillage of time and vicissitudes of history. Women of Buddhism had to undergo period of turmoil and sufferings to attain their rightful place in society, which was basically patriarchal and andocentric.

This short paper may be concluded with paraphrasing some of the arguments presented earlier. With Buddhism we enter into a new socio-religious setup which heralds the equality and freedom of woman in every sphere of human activity. There is a veritable epistemological cut in the ancient Indian perception of a subservient householder. Women began to participate in the sacrosanct spiritual life earlier destined only for men. There are numerous examples all along the Buddhist tradition where women could cross the social threshold with all its existential and philosophical implications. At the same time, it cannot be ignored that at several social levels old habits and prejudices continued to play their nefarious role to the detriment of the anthropological progress envisaged by the Buddha. There were several bold and courageous steps but there were also hesitations and hazards. All the same, the Buddha did herald a new era for both men and women, and if the old traditional order survived in India, the Buddhist ideological universe surcharged the vast regions of Asia. The old order gave way to the new but the residues of the past also continued to subvert the revolutionary ideas.

Notes

1. I.B. Homer, *Women Under Primitive Buddhism*, Delhi; Motilal Banarsidass, 1975, p. 1.
2. *Ibid*., p. 2.
3. Kathryn R. Blacksone, *Women in the Footsteps of the Buddha,* Surrey: Curzon Press, 1998, p. 39.
4. Edward. J. Thomas, *The Life of Buddha—As a Legend or a History,* London: Routledge and Kegan Paul, 1927, 3rd revised edition, 1949, p. 273.
5. Diana Y. Paul, *Women in Buddhism,* Berkeley: University of California Press, 1979, p. 77.
6. *Therigāthā* XLVI.
7. *Ibid*., CCLXI.
8. *Jātaka*-539
9. *Therigāthā*-25.
10. *Ibid*., XXVI.
11. *Ibid*., LXVI
12. *Therigāthā,* 25-26.
13. *Anguttara Nikaya* XII, 2 translation *Gunarfatne.*
14. *Therigāthā,* XII.
15. Another was *Khema. Therigāthā Commentary* LII.
16. *Therigāthā,* XXXV1T.
17. *Therigāthā Xi.V.*
18. *Therigāthā,*, CCLIV, Sumedha, *Therigāthā,* LXXIII, "Nibbana for the daughter of a King."
19. *Jātaka Cmy* on 464.
20. C.A.F. Rhys Davids, *The Psalm of the Sisters.* London: Pali Text Society, 1930, XXXVI.
21. *Laws of Manu,* George Buhler (trans.), *Sacred Books of the East,* Vol. 25,

Oxford, 1986, IX. p. 10.
22. Karma Lekshe Tsoma, *Buddhist Woman Across Cultures,* New York, (ed.), 1999, p. 68.
23. A.S. Altekar, *The Position of Women in Hindu Civilization,* 3rd edition, Delhi: Motilial Banarsidass, p. 54.
24. *Jātaka*, IV-18
25. *Buddhist Woman Across Cultures*, p. 50.
26. Diana Y. Paul, p. 247.
27. Dorothy Dinnerstein, *The Mermaid and the Minotaur. Sexual Arrangements and Human Malaise*, New York: Harper and Row, 1963, pp. 28-34.
28. *Religion* as a *Cultural System,* New York: Basic Books Inc., 1973.
29. *Ibid.*, Chapter IV, p. 87.
30. George Lakoff and Mark Johnson, *Metaphor We Live By,* Chicago: University of Chicago Press, 1980.

19

Polyandry in Himachal Pradesh

A Socio-Cultural Analysis and Reflection

Polyandry in Himachal Pradesh is a unique socio-cultural institution. Himachal Pradesh is known as Divine land (*Deva Bhumi*) and the practice of polyandry in this Himalayan State has got some religious significance apart from its anthropological importance. Polyandry in Himachal Pradesh is fraternal. It is in an adelphic form and as per custom it is expected that brothers will share sexual and reproduction interests in a single woman throughout their lives. It is very deeply ingrained. The word 'polyandry' is derived from Greek word 'polyandria' which means a woman having many husbands, i.e. *poly* means many; *andres* means man. Anthropologists have been trying to understand and define this complex socio-cultural institution in terms of evolution and structural-functionalism. Anthropology defines it as a socio-cultural custom by which a woman is permitted to have more than one husband at the same time.

Broadly speeking there are two forms of polyandry, i.e. fraternal and maternal. In fraternal polyandry the woman comes to live with more than one husband whereas in maternal form she remains in her own house and her husband or husbands come to live with her by turn. In fraternal polyandry right of properly passes from father to son or sons while in maternal form of polyandry the wife or her parents inherit the property. However, there are still different kinds of polyandry in India and abroad. In Himalyan States there is fraternal form of polyandry where husbands are brothers but in Indo-China in a Ua-Da-La Society husbands have uncle-nephew kinship. There are still another type of polyandry prevalent in some parts of Tibet which is known as bigenerational polyandry. In Himalayas polyandrous societies are present among the people of Kinnaur, Sirmur, Lahaul and Spiti, Kullu, Shimla and Pangi Valley of Himachal Pradesh, Jaunsar-Bower[1] sub-division of Dehradun District, Tehri areas of Uttar Pradesh and Leh district of Jammu and Kashmir and Bhotia and the Lepchas of Sikkim. In Arunachal Pradesh some kind of polyandry rather cicisbeism is in existence among the Gailong, the Dafla, the Ramo and the Khampa tribes. In the Toda and the Kota tribes of Nilgiri in South India polyandrous marriage is very much in existence. However, I shall limit my analysis and examination of polyandry in Himachal Pradesh. The practice of polyandry in Himachal Pradesh has got great religious significance. The Himachalis have been a religious people and their lives are intertwined with mythological stories of *Pandavas* having a common wife which is considered to be embodiment of chastity and virtue. The people of Himalayan regions considered the practice of polyandry as religious act and have great respect for this institution.

The practice of polyandry which is, of course, a dying institution, has been quite popular in Sirmur, the Shimla District, Lahaul and Spiti, Kinnaur and some other parts of the state. In the District of Sirmur, Shimla and other neighbouring areas Brahmanic influence has not been very much pronounced. Society is divided into the upper and the lower castes. Bhat, Deva Dethi and Kanet belong to upper strata of society, whereas the Koli, Lohar, Bhadi, Bajgi, Chanal, Daki, Turi, and Dumra belong to the backward castes. There was a practice in past that only the Bhat, Deva and Kanet can enter into temple. There has been a practice in the polyandrous tradition of Sirmaur or in Shimla Hill tracts that anyone hardly call himself a Brahman or the Rajput. The usage of word Rajput was confined only to the ruling houses. In these areas the Kanets, Rathis, Rawats, Negis and Thakurs belong to the Rajput castes.

Bhats of the Sirmaur District claim themselves as Brahmins. However, Bhats of Sirmur have accepted widow marriages (*Karewa*). If we make sociological study of the caste system in Himachalis, particularly in the District of Sirmur or Shimla, the Bhat is considered to be a title which offered to the person who had the ability to cure people from the influence of evil spirits and who were adept in practising *Tantra Sadhana* like Kolis and Dhakis, Kanets. The Kolis and Dhakis who were adept in *Tantra Vidya* were also conferred the title of Bhats.

The polyandry is considered to be the outcome of the extreme poverty amongst the people. The practice originated because of the extreme poverty and scarcity of land. The polyandrous marriage has greatly benefited the people living in difficult terrain of mountains where the scarcity of land poses a great problem for maintaining the large population. The prevalence of this custom has great economic benefit as division and the fragmentation of the land holding has been arrested. The other cause of the polyandry is the excess of male over female population. This population imbalance is very much pronounced in Jaunsar-Bawar in the sub-division of Dehradun and other Himalayan regions where polyandry is practised. The woman was in great demand because of her scarcity and utility.

Along with the polyandry the polygyny is very much prevalent in Shimla Hills, Kangra, Sirmur, and other parts of the Himalayan regions. But with introduction of modern education and social awareness both polygyny and polyandry are on decline. However, no stigma is attached to a man who has more than one wives. Polygyny is normally practised where population of females are greater than males. Y.S. Parmar writes 'Polygyny is usually practised where there are more females than males. But in a place where there are fewer females this custom cannot be widespread for the majority of the male population would have to remain unmarried. Thus, it is that polyandry is prevalent in Kullu and Saraj, Bashahr, Shimla hills, and Sirmur and so even those who cannot afford to have a wife separately manage to do so jointly. It is only the rich or well-to-do who have more than one wife. The rich sometimes keep as many as four wives and moneyed men with two wives are quite common.[2]

However, the fraternal form of polyandry is extensively practised in Bashahr, Kullu, Jubbal, Keonthal and the trans-Giri of Sirmur. We have to examine whether disparity in the proportion of the sexes is important reason for the origin and continuation of polyandry from anthropological point of view. According to some there is no correlation between the disparity of the sex. Whether disparity is brought about by female in infanticide or by other reason we have to examine also. The custom of polyandry is supported on the ground that it gives economic benefit as agriculture is confined to a limited area and it is not enough to support the larger population. Polyandry was encouraged by state in the past winch is evident from *Punjab States Gazetteer*, Vol. VII, Simla Hill States, 1910, Bashahr State, Part A, p. 16. As per this government order if the brothers divided movable property one half share of the whole was taken over by the state and the divisions of immovable property were refused official recognition.

Polyandry is not practised throughout the Kangra District, but it is confined to Kullu, Saraj and Lahaul. Dr. Parmar says while highlighting the importance of polyandry in containing the population. The density in other parts of the district, such as Nurpur, Dehra, and Hamirpupr, is only 666.9, 766.8, and 715.4 per square mile respectively as compared with 998.4 per square mile of Kullu and Saraj. These tracts have 75,124, and 102 square miles of land respectively still left uncultivated though they can be brought under cultivation. The inhabitants of Kullu and Saraj, therefore, having exhausted the land and not having the prospect of any more cultivable land, have had to devise means for providing for themselves and thus very probably had recourse to polyandry.[3]

The Kinnauris in Kinnaur like some other regions of Himalayan do praitice faternal form of polyandry. Along with the polyandry there is existence of polygamous marriages also. This north-eastern most district of Himachal Pradesh is situated bordering Tibet and it is very difficult mountainous terrain and people live in inhospitable climate. The bordering Tibbet is dominated by Buddhism whereas Nachar sub-division of Kinnaur is predominantly influenced by Hinduism. There is other part of Kinnaur where we find the co-existence of Hinduism and Buddhism. According to 1981 Census the population of Kinnaur is 59547 out of which 30598 are males and 27949 females. The Kanets (Rajput) is most dominant. Among all castes configuration the status group is known as *khels*. However, the *khel* system is not prevalent throughout Kinnaur.

Thornton has traced the existence of Polyandry in Himalayas.[4] Presently, this institution is very much in existence in Leh and in some parts of Kargil. Das Gupta states that the polyandry was in existence in Bushahr, Nahan, Mandi and Suket princely states of erstwhile Himachal Pradesh (1921: 147). Prince Peter in his monumental work "*A Study of Polyandry*" has stated that in Ladakh in early sixties 90 per cent people used to practice polyandry. He writes, "Asked what the proportion of polyandrous families was to the rest of the Buddhist population (the only one, naturally, among which polyandry is to be found) my informants told me that out of one hundred families, ninety of them lived in this form of matrimony."[5] As per the custom practised in Lahaul & Spiti eldest brother goes for formal marriage and the wife of the eldest brother becomes wife of all the brothers. D.D. Sharma writes, "From time immemorial polyandry is an honourable sacrosanct and socially approved custom of marriage among the Lahaulese. The practice of polyandry, prevalent among the Lahul is of the adelphic fraternal type, in which only the eldest brother weds a woman ceremoniously and she becomes a *de facto* joint wife of all brothers having a common parentage."[6] *The Gazetteer of Sirmur* 1969:14 concurs the practice of polyandry in trans-Giri tract in Rainuka Tehsil. *The Sirmur Settlement Report* 1881 states that it was found that women of all castes married more than one husband provided they were own brothers or sons of the same fathers and in special cases only could some other member of the family or an outsider hold a wife in common.

The anthropologists have failed to give a proper definition of marriage. The definition has given in the *Notes and Queries in Anthropology* (sixth edition) fails to give coverage to the different forms of marriages prevalent in Himalayas. There are prevalence of polyandry, polygyny and polygynandry marriage custom side by side with monogamy, Kinnaurese are basically endogamous. They follow fraternal or adelphic form of polyandry according to which the wife becomes after marriage common to all brothers.

With the waves of modernization as a result of education, communication system and high rate of mobility among the educated young Kinnaurese monogamy is becoming very much pronounced and polyandry is a dying institution. Mr. M.K. Raha writes, "besides; polygyny—both sororal and non-sororal types, is also prevalent but only in a few cases. Polygyny coupled with polyandry leading to polygyandry is found only in a few cases."[7] According to Raha, the polyandrous marriages count 23.38 per cent in Kinnaur. There is a gradual transformation among the marriage system of Kinnaurese. The polyandrous and the polygynandrous marriages are becoming unpopular and one husband one wife combination has also significant strength of 11.33 per cent. However, if we are to consider the ethnic groups then we find in comparison to the Koli, polyandry is higher in percentage among the Rajputs. The polygynandrous and polyandrous marriages among the Rajput is about 47.82 per cent. There is one important factor from anthropological point of view that polyandry is pronounced in villages near urban centres. The polygynandry in Kinnaur seems to be the outcome of the notional monogamy as practised by some Kinnaurese in the traditional polyandrous setup which they have failed to discard totally in spite of strong anti-forces prevalent in the present day Kinnaur particularly in the well communicated area like district Headquarters.[8] This practice is strongly imbedded in the mind of many Kinnaurese. But the idea that more wives will give better and more chances to fulfil carnal apetite and will also help in developing a feeling among one to have 'own' wife, brother started marrying more than once, resulting in the formation of polygynandry in polyandrous system. Polygynandry is bad omen for the existence of polyandry in Kinnaur. The polyandry in Kinnaur and some other parts of Himachal Pradesh was a revered social and cultural institution and it is in existence which has been confirmed by many sociologists and the antoropologists who have done a monumental research work in this field. As far as the Gazetteer of Shimla Hills States of 1910, it mentions about polyandry practised in Kinnaur. Andrew Wilson also confirms that polyandry was commonly practised in Taranda in the Sutlej valley, and this social custom was observed from Shimla up to Chinese border.[9]

The polyandry marriage in Kinnaur is known as *zanchang*. As per this system the eldest brother goes to the house of bride for marriage but after the solemnisation of *zanchang* marriage the newly bride becomes the wife of all the brothers through rituals which is known as 'turban tying ceremony'.

A unique socio-cultural custom of *Reet* gives a special status of woman in polyandrous marriage system of Himachal Pradesh. It is a very complex practice and to understand its impact in the socio-cultural life of society, it needs indepth study and research. In some parts of Sirmur a regular marriage sanctified through religious rites and rituals, is known as *Jhajrah*. The word *Jhajrah* stands for putting the nose-ring in the bride's nose. However, this custom of *Jhajrah* in Kullu, Kangra and Chamba stands for widow marriage. As there is no concept of divorce in traditional Hindu system as the marriage is considered a religious sacrament and not a contract, the relation between husband and wife is indissoluble tie and the custom of *Reet* emerged to solve the problem of strain and stress of marriage life. According to this custom woman has freedom to desert her husband and selects her new friends and spends free time with them. The sexual morality is very weak in Himalayas and the practice of *Reet* provides a wayout of the strain and stress of marriage life. When a woman takes a decision to part company with her hubsand she can get herself separated from her husband by arranging payment of *Reet* amount by her new husband which is called *ched karai*. By breaking the *dingi* (small sticks) by wife the divorce is formalised. *Reet* is a social custom according to which remarriage is solemnised. The woman of Himachal Pradesh has an identity and enjoys liberty. The status of woman of Himachal Pradesh is in some respects greater than any other parts of India. When woman finds it difficult to live with her husband she can get the marriage annulled by paying the *Reet* amount to husband and remarry with her lover. However, this custom of *Reet* marriage has been greatly misused and scandalised as it is not confined to a woman remarrying once or twice. Y.S. Parmar observes, "For an average peasant of the hills it is difficult enough to find money even for one marriage in his lifetime and that is why he has to pool his resources with others so that he may pay for a wife. But, if he has to pay for a bride more than once he is doomed. The women of the hills do not, however, content themselves with marrying once or twice according to *Reet* but as every subsequent *Reet* adds to her attraction, she must marry as many times as she can find new husbands willing to pay for her."

Massamat Shibi of Naini Dhar in trans-Giri tract of Sirmur had as many as 16 husbands in her life time.[10]

The institution of marriage is an enigmatic socio-cultural custom. Prince Peter has done a pioneering work in understanding the institution of polyandry from anthropological point of view. His book entitled *'A Study of Polyandry'* is a great work. He traces the practice of polyandry amongst the Sumerians of Mesopotamia in 2900 B.C.[11] The community of wives in Britain was of polyandric origin. He writes "According to Bruno Meissner in his Babylonian and Assyrian, 1,401, "relics of polyandry are apparent until the time of Uru-kaggina. The women of that period were owned by two men." This passage was communicated to me by Professor Sp. N. Marinatos, Rector of the University of Athens, in free translation from the original German. He adds that Uru-kaggina was one of the last Sumerian kings of the dynasty of Lagash, today Tello, in modern Iraq.

In Athens, in classical times, an heiress whose husband was incapable of performing his marital duty was legally entitled to ask for the embraces of a near relative of his. Polybius tells us that at Sparta, actual polyandry did exist, several of the brothers often having one wife whom they shared in common, as they did also the children which she bore them.

"*Uxoris habent deniduo denique inter se communes, et maxime fratres cum liberis*." This quotation from Julius Caesar's De Bello Gallico (lib. v, xiv) concerning the ancient Britons is, of course, very well known. "In their domestic life" runs the full text "they practise a form of community of wives, ten or twelve combining in a group, especially brothers with brothers and fathers with sons. The children born of such wedlock are then recknoned to belong to that member of the partnership who was the first to receive the mother as a bride in the household."[13]

E. Westermack has analysed and elucidated the concept of marriage is his celeberated book *The History of Human Marrriage*. His analysis of the concept of marriage is based on his wide reading and thorough understanding of this institution both from historical and socio-cultural perspective. He has contributed research paper in the *Encyclopaedia Britannica* in which he presents an authentic account of prevalence of polyandry throughout the world. He says that this socio-cultural custom is in practice throughout the four continents of America, Asia (which including the islands of the Pacific), and Australia and Africa.

In Chapter XXX of his book, *The History of Human Marriage*, Westermack while summarising the origin and prevalence of polyandry, he thinks that the disproportion of sexes, economic reason, long absence of male from home, motivation of offspring in men and women and the wishes of women are the main five causes of the continuation of polyandry in different parts of the world. However, Prince Peter does not agree wholly with the views of Westermack. He says, "Polyandry is initially due, I believe, to the fact that certain people find themselves living in a difficult and insecure natural environment which imposes upon them a strenuous economic and social organization. This necessarily takes the form of a very great interdependence between the men in society, who, in order to work either fields or herds of animals, have to put the good of the community before their own selfish and individual aims. Great solidarity between them is thus cultivated; they repress their natural aggression to a marked degree, and develop feelings of interdependence and of love for one another to a much greater extent than other people living in more clement environmental conditions. The balance of love and hate which exists normally in every individual is thus upset in favour of affection between these men, who come to look upon their unity as the supreme social ideal to be attained."[14]

All the reasons that have been enunciated for the origin and continuation of the institution of polyandry do not fully explain the phenomenon of this socio-cultural practice in different parts of world in general and in Himachal Pradesh in particular. Nancy E. Levine in her celebrated book, '*The Dyanamics of Polyandry*' have analysed and elucidated the concepts of kinship, cultural identity, ethnicity, traditional village structure, hardship of hilly agriculture, village economic and labour systems, concludes that polyandry cannot be explained by any of the above single factor. The economic and demographic factors are not sufficient to justify the existence and continuation of polyandry. She concludes that structurally autonomous domain of social life, symbolised in ideals of non-sexual love, of brotherhood, of equality in sharing, of giving without expectation of obligatory return, and above all, of involuntary, perpetual and inescapable bounds of complete mutuality are some of the main factors for the continuation of this cultural custom.[15]

This system of polyandrous marriage in Himachal Pradesh has exercised great impact on the socio-cultural life of the people. The division of labour where the male folks have specialised diverse subsistence activities such as long distance trade and commerce, while their wives take care of agricultures and other domestic activities, have given rise to autonomous domain of socio-cultural life.

This is a fact that polyandry is a dying institution. The process of modernization has created a schism and disintegration in this system. However, from sociological point of view we cannot ignore that it would create great demographic, economic and other social problems. For the people of Sirmur and Kinnaur where polyandry is still in existence, this is a sacradotal and sacramental institution. It is a source of their religious and ethical norms and practice. Toynbee has rightly stated that "Society is the total network of relations between human beings. The components of society are thus not human beings but relations between them."[16] Religion and ethics provide the contents of human relations in the absence of which no society can be formed. Polyandry in Himachal Pradesh derives its religious and ethical inspiration and *elan vita* from *Mahabharata*, and it has provided sound socio-cultural moorings.

In this modern age when the very existence of the institution of marriage is threatened, polyandry is not just exotic preoccupation. It has given meaning and purpose in the spheres of cultural and social life. I conclude with Aristotle's famous saying that "the union of man and woman has no name."

Notes

1. D.N. Majumdar, *Himalayan Polyandry*, Asia Publishing House, Bombay. 1962.
2. Y.S. Parmar, *Polyandry in the Himalayas*, p. 52. Vikas Publishing House Pvt. Ltd., Delhi, 1975.
3. *Ibid*., p. 131.
4. Thornton, E. *A Gazetteer of the Territories under the Government of the East India Company*. London, 1862.
5. *A Study of Polyandry*, p. 344, Mouton & Co. The Hague.
6. M.K. Raha (ed.) *Kinship Organisation of Polyandrous Lahaul. The Himalayan Heritage*. Gian Publishing House, Delhi, 1986.

7. *Polyandry in India*, p. 71. Gian Publishing House, Delhi, 1987.
8. *Ibid.,* p. 79.
9. Andrew Wilson. *Abode of Snow*, p. 255. Edinberg, 1876.
10. *Polyandry in Himalayas*, pp. 41-42.
11. Prince Peter. *A Study of Polyandry*, p. 59. Mouton & Co. 1963, The Hague.
12. *Ibid.*
13. *Ibid.*, p. 59.
14. *Ibid.*, p. 568.
15. Nancy E. Levine. *The Dynamics of Polyandry*, p. 279. The University of Chicago Press, Chicago and London. 1988.
16. Arnold Toynee. *A Study of History*, p. 43. Oxford University Press. London, 1972.

Remembrances

Bharatiya Vidya Bhavan,
Chaupatty Road,
Bombay 7.

SMUNSHIS

November 19, 1967.

Dear Shri Lalan,
Your letter of 14th November to hand.

I am not competent to write about Tantra.

People are mad with linguistic chauvnism, but I am trying to prevent balkanization, though unsuccessful so far.

Yours sincerely,

(K. M. Munshi)

from General Cariappa

THE ROSHANARA
MERCARA
COORG

Camp Patiala

23 Nov 67

Dear Shri [illegible]

I thank you for your letter of 14th Nov 67 which I received in Delhi only yesterday it having been redirected from my home in Mercara.

I do appreciate the spirit in which you have written the letter. I share your anxieties and concern about the falling off in our national discipline and national character - in some of them. It is very distressing to see in the papers everyday of gheraos, strikes, burning of buses, destroying important buildings and so on. There does not seem to be any respect for law and order in quite a few places in our country.

The tragedy of our country is that we have no public opinion worth the name. People are too frightened to speak out their minds frankly and fearlessly for the good of our country.

I am doing my humble best to remind our youth in particular of their duty to the nation to work as a disciplined body of young men of the day they are and the future leaders they would be and to ensure that the freedom we have won is kept permanently for all time in a truly democratic way.

I hope more and more people would go round about the country not only to tell the youth but say to our people in this respect.

PTO

I will bear in mind all the things you have said in your letter. If you meet our common friend Shri N.D.Majumdar, please convey to him my best wishes.

All the very best. Yours Sincerely

KMCariappa

Shri Acharya Lal@n
Department of Philosophy
Ranchi University
Ranchi (Bihar)

P.S

I have enclosed a copy of my call to the nation in regard to the Five Year Plan which might interest you.

Telephone : Mercara 52
Telegram : Mercara

UNIVERSITY GRANTS COMMISSION
BAHADUR SHAH ZAFAR MARG
NEW DELHI-1.
***

No.F. 11-88/67(F) Dated: 22-1-68

To

The Registrar,
Ranchi University,
Ranchi.

Sub: Award of Junior Research Fellowships in Science/ Humanities and Social Sciences; during 1967-68 (Second Award)

Sir:

I am directed to say that the University Grants Commission has selected Shri Lalan Prasad Singh

for the award of a Junior Research Fellowship of the value of Rs.300/- p.m. to work on "Tantra - Its Mystic and Scientific Basis".

in the Department of Philosophy with Shri R. S. Srivastava as his Supervisor. The award is subject to the rules and regulations as per Appendix I and will be effective from the actual date on which the fellow commences research work at your Institution or the date of issue of this letter, whichever is later.

2. The last date for joining the award is ~~29th February 1968~~ 31st March 1968. failing which the fellowship will be withdrawn.

3. Payment of fellowship amount and the normal contingent grant of Rs.1,000/- for meeting authorised expenditure as detailed in Appendix II during the first year of the award will be made to the fellow through the

(P.T.O

-2-

Institution on receipt of statement of particulars as in Appendix III and the joining report of the fellow duly countersigned by the Supervisor.

4. The six monthly reports of the work done by the fellow may please be sent in the prescribed proforma (Appendix IV). At the end of each financial year a utilization certificate from the Government Auditors/Chartered Accountants to the effect that the grant paid to the Institution has been spent for the purpose for which it was sanctioned may kindly be sent to this office.

5. The receipt of this letter may kindly be acknowledged.

Yours faithfully,

(A. B. Gupta)
For Secretary.

1. Copy forwarded to Shri Lalan Prasad Singh, Deptt., of Philosophy, Ranchi University, Ranchi with the request that he/she may kindly inform the Commission immediately whether the offer is acceptable to him/her.

2. ______________________

(A. B. Gupta)
For Secretary.

Sahani ***

19

VISVA-BHARATI

CENTRE OF ADVANCED STUDY IN PHILOSOPHY
ALL-INDIA SUMMER INSTITUTE IN PHILOSOPHY
(JUNE 1 TO 28, 1973)

This is to certify that

Sri/ Lalan Prasad Singh

of Magadh University has successfully completed the courses in Philosophy offered at All-India Summer Institute in Philosophy held at the Centre of Advanced Study in Philosophy, Visva-Bharati under the auspices of The University Grants Commission. His/Her subjects were :

Compulsory Subjects

1. Indian Theory of Knowledge
2. Western Theory of Knowledge
3. Symbolic Logic

Elective Subjects (Any Two)

1. Contemporary Indian Philosophy
2. Contemporary Western Philosophy
3. Analytic Ethics
4. ✓ Analytic Philosophy of Religion
5. ✓ Philosophy of Science

SANTINIKETAN

DATED 27. 6. 1973

DIRECTOR

भारतीय उच्च अध्ययन संस्थान

indian institute of advanced study

राष्ट्रपति निवास • समर हिल, शिमला 171005 • दूरभाष: 2235

RASHTRAPATI NIVAS • SUMMER HILL, SIMLA 171005 • PHONE 2235

श्यामाचरण दुबे
निदेशक

S. C. DUBE
DIRECTOR

No. 909

May 30, 1974

8 JUN 1974

Dear Dr. Singh:

The Indian Institute of Advanced Study proposes to organize a workshop on The Concept of Man from September 23-29, 1974. On behalf of the Institute I have great pleasure in inviting you to participate in the workshop. A background paper outlining the scope of the workshop is enclosed.

I very much hope that it will be possible for you to accept our invitation. Your acceptance may kindly be communicated to my colleague Professor Sibajiban Bhattacharyya, Visiting Fellow, Indian Institute of Advanced Study, Rashtrapati Nivas, Summer Hill, Simla 171005 (H.P.). In your reply to him kindly indicate the topic on which you propose to write a paper.

Rules regarding payment of TA and DA are explained in an enclosed sheet. If air travel is necessary, kindly write to me. While at Simla you will be a guest of the Institute.

To facilitate timely duplication and distribution the manuscripts of papers should reach us by August 31, 1974.

We shall look forward to your cooperation in this important venture undertaken by the Institute.

With warm personal regards,

Yours sincerely,

(S.C. Dube)

Encl: As above.

Dr. L.P. Singh
Guest Fellow
Indian Institute of Advanced Study
Rashtrapati Nivas: Summer Hill
Simla 171005 (H.P.)

कैम्प आफिस: डी-1, हौज खास, नई दिल्ली 110016 दूरभाष: 78307

CAMP OFFICE: D-1 HAUZ KHAS, NEW DELHI 110016 PHONE: 78307

तार का पता : 'गुरुकुल'

ओ३म्

टेलीफोन नम्बर : ५१

गुरुकुल कांगड़ी विश्वविद्यालय

डाकघर : गुरुकुल कांगड़ी (सहारनपुर), उत्तर-प्रदेश

रेलवे स्टेशन : हरिद्वार, उत्तर-रेलवे

पत्र संख्या

दिनांक ६-२-७७

आदरणीय महोदय,

सादर वन्दे।

आधुनिक भारत के निर्माता स्वामी श्रद्धानन्द की बलिदान अर्द्ध शताब्दी पर विश्वविद्यालय की ओर से एक सन्दर्भ ग्रंथ अप्रैल में प्रकाशित हो रहा है। इसमें भारतीय मनीषा को प्रतिबिम्बित करने वाले ज्ञान-विज्ञान सम्बन्धी लेख प्रकाशित होंगे। आप भारतीय चिन्तन के प्रमुख स्तंभ हैं। अत: आपका ज्ञान-आलोक साहित्य, दर्शन और संस्कृति के विविध आयामों को प्रकाशित करने में हमारा पथ प्रदर्शन करेगा, इसका हमें पूर्ण विश्वास है।

हमारा नम्र निवेदन है कि निम्नांकित विषय पर अपना मौलिक निबन्ध जो बीस पृष्ठ से अधिक न हो प्रकाशनार्थ २५ फरवरी,७७ [४ मार्च] तक भेजकर अनुगृहीत करें। हम इसके लिए ग्रंथ की २ प्रतियां और अनुमुद्रण सादर भेंट कर सकेंगे।

सादर सप्रीति।

विषय - शाक्त दर्शन।

भवदीय,

(रघुवीरसिंह शास्त्री)
उपकुलपति:

प्रति,

डा० ललन प्रसाद सिंह,
दर्शन विभाग,
मगध विश्वविद्यालय,
बोधगया, बिहार।

30
CONGRESO INTERNACIONAL DE CIENCIAS HUMANAS EN ASIA Y AFRICA DEL NORTE

30
INTERNATIONAL CONGRESS OF HUMAN SCIENCES IN ASIA AND NORTH AFRICA

MEXICO, D. F.
3-8, VIII, 1976

PRESIDENTE
GRACIELA DE LA LAMA
SECRETARIO GENERAL
JORGE ALBERTO LOZOYA
SECRETARIO ADJUNTO
MANUEL RUIZ

EL COLEGIO DE MEXICO
GUANAJUATO 125
MEXICO 7, D. F.
MEXICO

August 23, 1976

This is to certify that Dr. L. P. Singh of Magadh University, India, presented his paper entitled "The Phenomenology of the Sacred in Hinduism" under the panel 'Tradition and New Horizon' at the 30th International Congress of Human Sciences in Asia and North Africa held at Mexico City.

Graciela de la Lama
President

PRINCIPAL

Phone No. 605

GAYA COLLEGE, GAYA.

Dated the.......... 197

This is to certify that Dr.L.P.Singh, Lecturer in Philosophy, Department of Philosophy, Magadh University, Bodh Gaya joined Magadh University Service on 26th Feb. 1973 on the recommendation of Bihar Public Service Commission and was first posted at Gaya College, Gaya and subsequently transferred to P.G.Department of Philosophy, M.U. on 11th June 1979. During this period he engaged Hons. and Post-Graduate classes. Dr. Singh has presented his papers at World Philosophy Congress at Delhi 1975 and International Congress of Orientalist at Mexico 1976 and he has the honour of Co-chairing the Scriptural Literature in Cultural Context Session of 10th International Congress of Anthropological and Ethnological Sciences in 1978. He is a very successful teacher of his subject and if given higher responsibilities he is sure to prove himself worthy of the same.

B. Prasad 15.11.80

(Dr. B. Prasad)
Principal
&
Dean, Faculty of Arts
Magadh University, Bodh-Gaya.

Dr. Lalan Prasad Singh
M.A.D.LITT

Department of philosophy
Magadh University
Bodh-Gaya.

Dated 9th March 1981.

Dear Dr. Deppert,

Namaskar

This is to express my sincere thanks for your warm hospitali--ty. This was my first encounter with a German Scholar. My meeting with you confirmed my faith in wisdom and Scholarship of German people. Anyway, I was greatly impressed by your deep understanding of Vedic and Tantric traditions along with indepth knowledge of your own Ontological systems.

Well, I have not as yet finalised my visit to Amsterdam. However, I propose to visit your great University on 26th April 1981 and I would like to stay there for a week or so. I can deliver some talks on Indian Philosophy specially on Tantra if you so like. I shall feel greatly obliged if you kindly make arrangements of my stay in your University. I am interested in meeting some German thinkers specially Indologists. Will you kindly suggest some names? Do you have the address of French Scholar who has done some pioneering work in Tantra ?

Rest is O.K.

Hope this will find you in best of health and happiness.

With kind regards,

Yours Sincerely,

LPSingh

(L. P. Singh)

Dr. Joachim Deppert
Director,
South Asia Institute,
University of Heidelberg,
Max Muller Bhavan,
3½ Kasturba Gandhi Marg,
New Delhi

The International Association of Buddhist Studies

c/o Dept. of South Asian Studies University of Wisconsin
1258 Van Hise Hall Madison, Wisconsin 53706 USA (608) 262-3012
262-5881

July 1, 1981

GENERAL SECRETARY
A. K. Narain
TREASURER
Beatrice Miller

Dr. Lalan Prasad Singh
Dept. of Philosophy
Magadh University
Bodh Gaya
Bihar, INDIA

Dear Dr. Singh,

We are pleased to inform you that the 4th Conference of the International Association of Buddhist Studies will be held in Madison, Wisconsin, USA, from August 7-9, 1981. This letter is to officially invite you to attend this conference and present a paper on Buddhist Tantra.

Enclosed is our 2nd circular announcement for the conference. Please fill in the enclosed registration from and return it to the IABS office along with a brief abstract of your paper, so as to reach us as quickly as possible.

With best wishes,

Yours sincerely,
A.K. Narain
A.K. Narain
General Secretary, IABS

प्रथमम्
अन्ताराष्ट्रियसंस्कृतचर्चा

SIMPOSIO INTERNACIONAL DE LENGUA SANSCRITA
SIMPÓSIO INTERNACIONAL DE LÍNGUA SÂNSCRITA
SYMPOSIUM INTERNATIONAL DE LA LANGUE SANSKRITE
INTERNATIONAL SYMPOSIUM ON THE SANSKRIT LANGUAGE
II CONFERENCIA LATINO-AMERICANA DE SANSCRITISTAS

Mexico City, 21st February, 1982

TO WHOM IT MAY CONCERN:

This is to certify that Dr. Lalan Prasad Singh attended the First International Symposium on the Sanskrit Language held at the National Autonomous University of Mexico from the 15th through the 21st February, 1982, and has read a paper on:

"Tantra and Veda in Hindu Cultural Context"

The professor has not received any financial assistance from the Organizing Committee.

THE ORGANIZING COMMITTEE

President

Dr. Juan Miguel de Mora

Secretary

Marja Ludwika Jarocka, M.A.

Coordinación de Humanidades
Universidad Nacional Autónoma de México

Asociación / Associação } Latino-Americana de Sanscritistas

Torre de Humanidades II Piso 13 Ciudad Universitaria México D. F.

SEMINARS AT THE INDIAN INSTITUTE OF ADVANCED STUDY

HINTS FOR PARTICIPANTS

1. *Arrival* : Participants are requested to reach Simla a day before the inauguration of the Seminar.

2. *Hospitality* : Patricipants receive free accommodation and dining room hospitality, from the mid-day of the day previous to the Inauguratiou to 24 hours after the closing of the Seminar.

3. *Accommodation* : Accommodation at the Institute is limited. Participants are requested not to embarass the Institute by bringing members of their families or friends.

4. *Travel Costs* : First Class railway return fare (at hill concession rate when available) and Rs. 12.50 for every 24 hours or part thereof for the journey will be paid by the Institute. When the Railways' hill concession is available, the Institure reimburses costs only on this basis.

5. *Air Fare* : Air travel may be permitted, if the distance is more than 800 kilometres, at the discretion of the Director provided prior approval is obtained. For travel by ACC/rail car, however, normal Government of India rules will be applicable.

6. *Train from Kalka* : It is best to take the train leaving Kalka at about 7-30 a.m. and reaching the Summer Hill station at about 1-00 p. m. and Simla a few minutes later. Please alight at Summer Hill—representatives of the Institute will be available there for help and guidance.

7. *Arrival by Road* : Those coming from Kalka by car should proceed from the Motor Barrier Post along the road leading to Boileauganj Bazar and then to Rashtrapati Nivas.

8. *Clothing* : May-June and September-October are usually dry, sunny, and cool, but if it rains, it may become chilly. Kindly bring your warm clothes and bed-rolls which should include a blanket, a quilt, and other essentials. The Institute does not normally provide bedding.

9. *Publication of Papers* : The Institute publishes a Transactions volume based on the seminar proceedings. If it is decided to include your paper is this volume, we shall seek your formal permission to do so, and you will have an opportunity to revise it. When the paper is published, the Institute will pay a token honorarium of Rs. 200.

To enable us to plan the seminar and to take good care of you here, would you kindly mail the enclosed cards, pink and blue, right away ?

-: 5 :-

LIST OF INVITEES

1. Professor Daya Krishna
Philosophy Department
University of Rajasthan
Jaipur (Rajasthan)

2. Professor S.S. Barlingay
Philosophy Department
Poona University
Poona (Maharashtra)

3. Professor K. Satchidananda Murti
Philosophy Department
Andhra University
Waltair (Andhra Pradesh)

4. Professor K.J. Shah
Philosophy Department
Karnataka University
Dharwar (Mysore)

5. Professor Rajendra Prasad
Indian Institute of Technology
IIT P.O.
Kanpur-16 (U.P.)

6. Dr. S.N. Mahajan
Philosophy Department
Indian Institute of Technology
IIT Post Office
Kanpur-16 (U.P.)

7. Professor S. Vahiduddin
10-C, Maurice Nagar
Delhi-7

8. Professor Santosh Sengupta
Director, CAS in Philosophy
Visva-Bharati
P.O. Shantiniketan (W.B.)

9. Dr. Suresh Chandra
Philosophy Department
Visva-Bharati
P.O. Santiniketan (W.B.)

10. Professor N.S.S. Raman
Centre of Advanced Study in Philosophy
Banaras Hindu University
Varanasi-5

11. Dr. R.K. Sinari
S.I.E.S. College
Bombay

12. Dr. R.K. Gupta
St. Stephen's College
Delhi-7

-: 8 :-

13. Dr. Mrinal Miri
Visiting Fellow
Indian Institute of Advanced Study
Rashtrapati Nivas, Simla-5.

14. Dr. Ramchandra Gandhi
Philosophy Department
University of Rajasthan
Jaipur (Rajasthan)

15. Dr. Yogendra Chopra
C/o Mrs. Heda Dayal
Chakkar
Simla-5 (H.P.)

16. Mrs. Sujata Miri
Guest Fellow
Indian Institute of Advanced Study
Rashtrapati Nivas, Simla-5.

17. Dr. L.P. Singh
Guest Fellow
Indian Institute of Advanced Study
Rashtrapati Nivas, Simla-5 (H.P.)

Pol. Maj. Anant Senakant
Sec. 2 Klong Prem Central Prison
Bangken, Bangkok 10900

Jan. 3, 1984

Dearest Dr. Lalan,

Thank you very much for your kind letter of Dec. 1, 1983. I have also received the letter which you have sent to Mr. Upavong for me. When I saw him he mentioned that he is yet to receive my synopsis from you. I asked him to see you when a suitable opportunity presents itself. He also sent a gift to you and your family from me.

In my present situation my capacity to carry out my work is temporarily impaired, but my sacrifice in itself will not go unnoticed, as you have pointed out. Please bear in mind that my intention is not fame, but to see true democracy established in Thailand. This is the only aim of any sacrifice I have made, however meagre.

You are very kind to hope for my being released by a higher court of justice. But that is impossible. I cannot appeal my case to a higher court because I was sentenced by a military tribunal. The implications are obvious. I have been sentenced to another 3 years for my second charge of lese majeste. This brings my total sentence to 6 years imprisonment.

My only hope for reconsideration of my sentence or release lies with a royal pardon. I have made my application and am awaiting the outcome. It is a time consuming process but well worth the effort. Your offer to write the King's Privy Council and the Minister of Interior will be helpful in this regard.

My family's addresses are listed on the reverse. Please feel free to contact them. Warmest regards to all those who are dear to you. Thank you again for your continued correspondence.

Warm regards

Aman Senakant

my wife: Sunan Senakant
85 NGAM WONG WAN RD.
BANGKHEN, BANGKOK 10900
THAILAND

my son: Rom Senakant
P.O. BOX 1283
ST. JOSEPH COLLEGE
RENSSELEAR, INDIANA 47978
U.S.A.

my daughter: Joy Senakant
405 E. 17th St. I-7
BLOOMINGTON, INDIANA 47401
U.S.A.

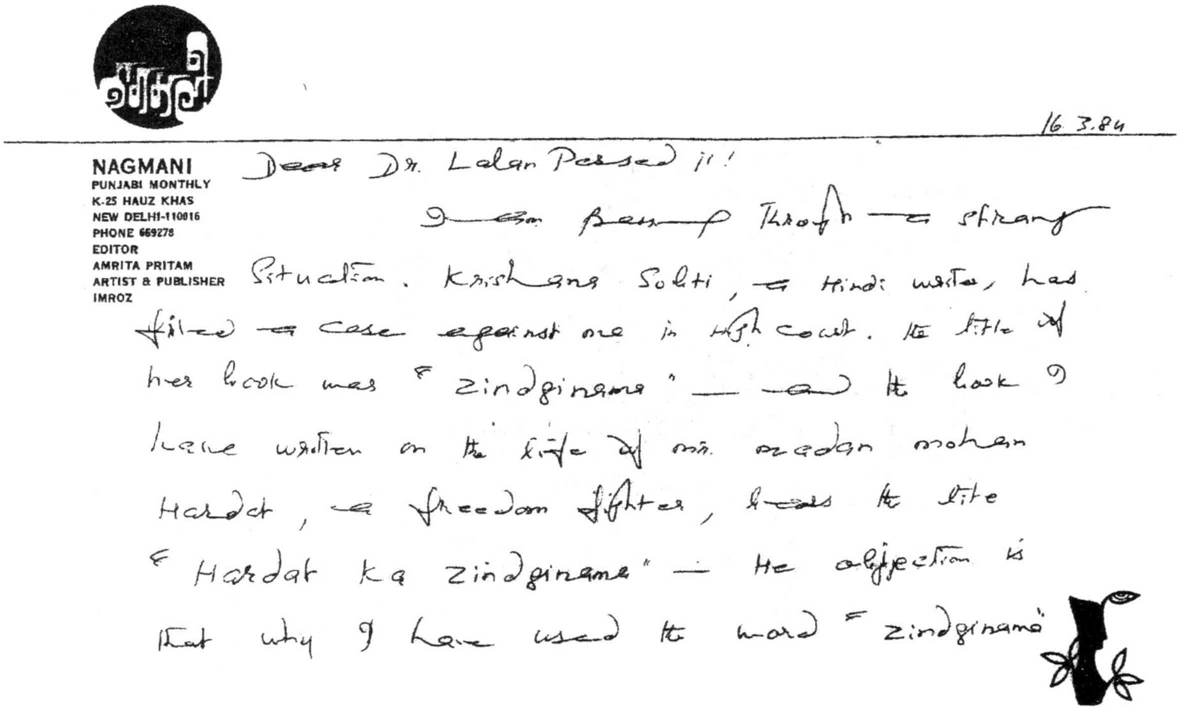

NAGMANI
PUNJABI MONTHLY
K-25 HAUZ KHAS
NEW DELHI-110016
PHONE 669278
EDITOR
AMRITA PRITAM
ARTIST & PUBLISHER
IMROZ

16.3.84

Dear Dr. Lalan Prasad ji!

I am passing through a strange situation. Krishna Sobti, a Hindi writer, has filed a case against me in High Court. The title of her book was "Zindginama" — and the book I have written on the life of Mr. Madan Mohan Hardat, a freedom fighter, has the title "Hardat ka Zindginama" — the objection is that why I have used the word "Zindginama" my book is published in three languages — Punjabi, Hindi, and Urdu. The title page of every book bears the photograph of Mr. Harder, and the full title "Harder Ka Zindginama" — I can not understand the complaint.

Nama is a persian word, which is used with an other noun — hundred times — as Zinda Nama, Furkat nama, Safar nama, Rosenama, Maha nama, Vasiat nama, Nikah nama, Talaq nama, Muhabat nama, Hadayat nama etc.

NAGMANI
PUNJABI MONTHLY
K-25 HAUZ KHAS
NEW DELHI-110016
PHONE 669278
EDITOR
AMRITA PRITAM
ARTIST & PUBLISHER
IMROZ

27.4.84

Dear friend Lalanji!

I have heard that the biggest library of Persian books is in Hyderabad there are more than eighteen thousand books. Please find out from the librarian — the list of Zindaginama's available in the library.

or you can ask from any library of Persian books and let me know.

Thank you

Amrita Pritam

3

NAGMANI
PUNJABI MONTHLY
K-25 HAUZ KHAS
NEW DELHI-110016
PHONE 669278
EDITOR
AMRITA PRITAM
ARTIST & PUBLISHER
IMROZ

she has claimed one lakh + fifty thousand ~~da~~mages to her reputation.

Please find an urdu + persian scholar to write a letter to me regarding the use of many nouns with nagma word.

One thing more — I can not understand that why all these things are happening to me, who does not harm any body.

6

you have the power to know about it.

I want to devote all my remaining years to work, not to these silly things.

Yours — Amrita Pritam

Perhaps you can contact some one of Aligarh University.

11.7.88 night

NAGMANI
PUNJABI MONTHLY
K-25 HAUZ KHAS
NEW DELHI-110016
PHONE 669278
EDITOR
AMRITA PRITAM
ARTIST & PUBLISHER
IMROZ

Dear Lalan ji

At 7. A.m. I met a Scholar-Saint Shri Mithran Namoodripad, and had a wonderful experience. I was full of it, when you rang me at 8.30. It was not just a chance, it has some deeper link. Imroz was with me, when I met Namoodripad ji, and I think you are the only person, I can share the experience with. That is the reason I asked you to come to Delhi. I think I know the power, who inspired you to ring me. With respect — Amrita

S. Nijalingappa

V. P. Extension,
CHITHRADURGA.

Ist April I984

Dear Dr. Prasad Singhji,

After I left Patna I was in Delhi for a weak and had to visit several places in Karnataka iteelf and could only see your kind letter of the 16th only a couple of days back. I am happy that I met you in Patna. Your letter to me is a correct analysis of the present unhappy situation brought about by the self-willed autocratic, power-mad policies of the Prime Minister Indira Gandhi who has not respect for any of the accepted principles and policies but is entirely devoted to her own interests in holding on to power at any cost. I am in entire agreement with you that Gandhian principles and policies alone can save this country politically, socially and economically.

I am sure Morarji Bhai will take necessary interest in strengthening the Janata Party which, as I can see, is the only alternative to Indira Congress. I am ready to serve it and doing so since its inception.

Regarding your kind enquiry about the 12th Century reformers, Sri Basaveshwar who as I know is the only person who wanted to build up a society based on euqlity, non-exploitation religious or social, removal of untouchability, equality of sexes, education of the masses through simple language, avoidance of irriational beliefs and observances, avoidence of concentration of wealth etc. I am enclosing a copy of my letter to Dr.Siddaiah Puranik retired IAS Officer who has been one of the respected literary figures in Karnataka, a scholar, a poet, a free thinker. He is well versed in the philosophies of Basaveshwar and is in charge of the institution "Basava Samithi" which is doing commendable work to propagate that philosophy. He will send you the necessar literature.

I hope this finds you in the best of health and spirits

With warm regards,

Yours sincerely,

(S. Nijalingappa)

Dr. Lalan Prasad Singh, M.A., D. Lit,
Department of Philosophy,
Bodh-gaya.

Ist April 1984

Dear Dr. Puranik,

On the 23rd evening when I met you in Ilkal T.B. I mentioned Dr Lalan Prasad Singh as Professor of phylosophy in Magadh University. I had mentioned to him at Patna during the Janata Party Session, the life and Philosophy of Sri Basaveshwar. He is interested in knowing everything about Sri Basaveshwar. I have written to his as per enclosed copy. Kindly write to him and let him have all the available literature in English about Basaveshwar. I think it is necessary and in the furtherence of the objectives of Basava Samithi. I would be grateful for an early repley.

With kind regards,

Yours sincerely,

(S.Nijalingappa)

Dr.Siddaiah Puranik,
Directer in charge of
Publication Division,
Basaveshwara Samithi.
Bangalore.

Bodh-gaya.

Klong Prem Central Prison
Bangkok

Dr. Lalan Prasad Singh
Department of Philosophy, Magadh University,
Bodh-Gaya, India.

7th June, 1984.

Dear Dr. Lalan Singh,

Thank you for your letter of 4th May 84. I sincerely appreciate your best wishes and offer of further assistance.

The policy of censorship practised in the prisons of Thailand enables limited access to reliable information and impedes communication with the world outside. This means that I receive little news of the real world and I am therefore unsure of developments in my case to gain freedom. I appreciate your communications to the King's Secretary on my behalf as most helpful.

It had now been five months since I have applied for a pardon from His Majesty the King and my progress towards an early release is being retarded; both intentionally by those who will employ any tactic to stifle the development of democracy in this country, and intentionally by the procrastination and inaptitude of the bureaucracy or red tape. Thus so far my application for a King's pardon has not been sent to His Majesty for consideration, but is being delayed at the Department of Corrections. I would be very grateful for your help in this regard if you would write to the Minister of Interior, General Sithi Jirooj and request his help in persuading the Department of Corrections to forward my application.

My wife expresses her happiness on receiving your letter. I feel certain that she and the children share my appreciation for your kind assistance and support. My children would also be very happy to meet you in person during your visit to the United States. I am pleased with my son for making good progress towards his degree at Indiana State where he still has one year to complete, but my daughter will be returning to Thailand this month having completed her B.A.

Once again, thanking you and with best Wishes from all of us

Yours Sincerely,

Anand Senakhant

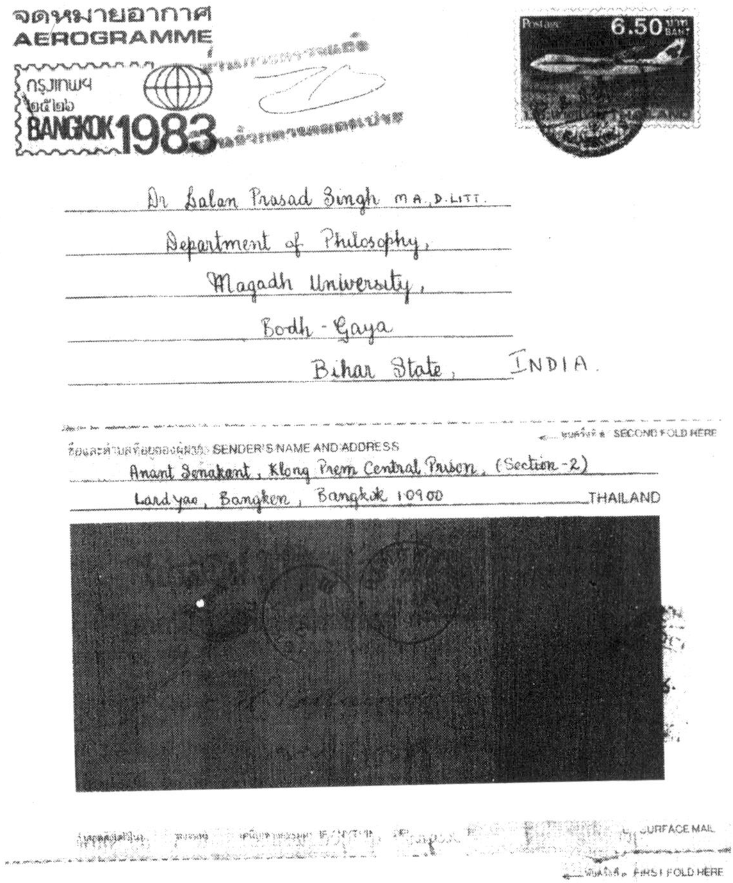

จดหมายอากาศ
AEROGRAMME

กรุงเทพฯ
๒๕๒๖
BANGKOK 1983

Postage 6.50 บาท BAHT

Dr Lalan Prasad Singh M.A., D.LITT.
Department of Philosophy,
Magadh University,
Bodh-Gaya
Bihar State, INDIA.

SECOND FOLD HERE

SENDER'S NAME AND ADDRESS
Anant Sonakant, Klong Prem Central Prison, (Section-2)
Lardyao, Bangken, Bangkok 10900 THAILAND

SURFACE MAIL

FIRST FOLD HERE

Telegram : UNIGUJARAT

Telephone : Office : 442562
Resi. : 446704

UNIVERSITY SCHOOL OF
PSYCHOLOGY, EDUCATION AND PHILOSOPHY
GUJARAT UNIVERSITY

Director
Dr. J. A. Yajnik
M.A., Ph.D.
Professor of Philosophy

AHMEDABAD-380 009
GUJARAT (INDIA)

PHIL/JAY/911 /84-85 October 9, 1984

Dear Dr. Singh :

This is to express our sincere thanks for your kind visit to the department of Philosophy on 26th September, 1984 and for your lecture on Philosophy of Wittgenstein. The students were enlightened by the lucid presentation of the theme and it was pleasant experience for all of us to hear you.

Thanking you once again and with regards,

Yours sincerely

(J. A. Yajnik)
Director

To
Dr. L. P. Singh
Reader
Department of Philosophy
Magadh University
Bodhgaya (Bihar)

rjm/9/10

XXXII International Congress for Asian and North African Studies

25-30 August 1986

Organizing Committee
c/o Seminar für Kultur und Geschichte Indiens
Grindelallee 53, D-2000 Hamburg 13
Federal Republic of Germany
Telefon: 4123 33 85

ICANAS Hamburg

Dr. L.P. Singh
Department of Philosophy
Magadh University
Bodh-Gaya - 824234

Indien

21 April 1986

Dear Dr. Singh,

I thank you very much for sending us the abstract of your paper on "The Esoteric Basis of Buddhism".

On behalf of the Organizing Committee I wish to extend to you a formal invitation to present your paper to the Congress.

We are sure that you will make a significant contribution in your field of specialization, and we would be glad if you would be able to read your paper to the section on "Buddhist Studies" in person.

Sincerely yours,

A. Wezler

(Prof. Dr. A. Wezler)

Secretary General
Organizing Committee
XXXIIICANAS

UNIVERSITY GRANTS COMMISSION
BAHADURSHAH ZAFAR MARG
NEW DELHI-110 002

D.O.No.F. 3-42/93(IC-I)

Dated: OCTOBER, 1993
27 OCT 1993

Dear Registrar,

Kindly refer to this office endorsement of even number dated 21.9.93 regarding the visit of Dr. L. P. Singh Magadh University, Bodh Gaya (Bihar) French to France under the Indo-French Cultural Exchange Programme.

The French authorities have accepted his/her/their visit to Paris for a period of 45 days. The University, is therefore requested to arrange his/her/their air tickets from nearest international airport in India to the capital of the country concerned and back (by excursion category for the whose sector or a part thereof if available, otherwise by economy class shortest route) directly from Air India and not through travel agent.

For his/her/their internal travel in India, the University may provide him/her/them funds for his/her/their travel from his/her/their place of duty to the nearest international airport in India and back by air if his/her/their basic pay is between Rs.5,100/- and above in the revised Scale. In case his/her/their basic pay is between Rs.4,100/- and Rs.5,100/- he/she/they may also travel by air provided the distance involved is more then 500 kms and the overnight journey cannot be performed by a direct train service/direct slip coach service; otherwise he/she/they may travel by train (first class).

The Commission will reimburse the expenses incurred by the University on his/her/their air/rail tickets journeys between residence to Airport/Railway station and back on mileage basis according to University rules plus airport tax on receipt of a pre-receipted bill duly revenue stamped. No other expenses will be reimbursed by the University Grants Commission.

A proforma for report by the scholar on his/her/their visit is enclosed. This may kindly be got completed from the scholar immediately after his/her/their return and sent to the University Grants Commission.

Contd...

:2:

~~Dr. Lalan Prasad Singh, Magadh University, Bodh Gaya~~ may be paid full salary and allowances for the period of his/her/their visit abroad and treated as 'on duty'. The nature of leave to be given to the teacher may be decided by the university according to its rules.

With regards,

Yours sincerely,

(M.M.Chawla)

The Registrar
Magadh University
Bodh Gaya (Bihar) 824 234

Copy to:-

~~Dr. Lalan Prasad Singh, Deptt. of Philosophy~~
~~Magadh University Bodh-Gaya (Bihar) 824 234.~~

He/she/they are requested to intimate the date and flight number by the which he/she/they would be arriving in the capital of the host country atleast two weeks in advance to the undersigned. He/she/they are also requested to (i) avoid reaching the host country on Saturdays and Sundays and (ii) change in arrival particulars at eleventh hours. After his/her/their arrival in the host country, he/she/they may get in touch with Indian Embassy and keep in touch with them during his/her/their stay there. In case of any difficulty during the stay in the host country he/she is advised to take up the matter through our Embassy in the country and not directly with the host authorities.

(M.M.Chawla)

UNIVERSITÉ EUROPÉENNE DE LA RECHERCHE

Montagne Sainte Geneviève

20 Mai 1994

Lalan Prasad Singh

Magadh University
Bodh Gaya, India

Dear Professor L.P. Singh,

You will find hier the French translation of your profound project of ***Inter Faith Dialogue.*** With the thoughts of Louiza Gallèze, and also mine.

We propose the creation of
a **Center of Knowledge,**
which would be the spiritual space of ***Inter Faith Dialogue***, in Bodh Gaya, and also in Paris : in the European University of Resarch, connected with the Mediterranean University of Rome. Whith the help of the Maison des Sciences de l'Homme.

This would be the beginning of a long way towards ***Inter Faith Dialogue***, as a spiritual prospective in your own terms.

Very sincerely yours,
with our deep hopes and conviction,

J P Faye

Jean-Pierre Faye

Université Européenne
de la Recherche

1 rue Descartes
Montagne Sainte Geneviève
75005 Paris

Fax 4634.3678

1, rue Descartes - 75005 Paris

चन्द्रशेखर

CHANDRA SHEKHAR

June 18, 2007

My dear Manmohan Singhji,

It gves me great pleasure in introducing to you one of my closest friend and follower Prof. L.P. Singh. He is a distinguished professor of Philosophy and a thinker. He is associated with me for last four decades. Keeping in view his qualifications and achievements he is most deserving person for the post of an Ambassador or to some equivalent position and thereby make him the member of your mission of making India as a great nation.

It will not be out of place to mention here that Pandit Jawahar Lal Nehru started a rich and glorious tradition by inducting eminent professors and social activists as Governor, Ambassador and other high Govt. officials. I hope and expect that you would revive that tradition by inducting eminent academicians and social workers in your team of good governance.

I shall be grateful if you kindly give an opportunity to my friend Prof. L.P. Singh to serve the country as an Ambassador or some highest Govt. official.

With personal regards,

Yours sincerely,

Chandra Shekhar

(CHANDRA SHEKHAR)

Dr. Manmohan Singh,
Prime Minister,
Government of India,
New Delhi-110011

3, साउथ एवेन्यू लेन, नई दिल्ली-110 011 टेलीफोन 2301-2587, 2301-2163
3, South Avenue Lane, New Delhi-110 011 Tele : 2301-2587, 2301-2163

Bibliography

A.J. Ayer. *Language, Truth and Logic,* London, Victor Gallanez Ltd. 1936.

A.S. Altekar, *The Position of Women in Hindu Civilization,* 3rd edition, Delhi: Motilial Banarsidass.

Abhinavagupta, *Tantrāloka*, 12 vols. Kashmir Sanskrit Texts and Studies, vols. 27-39, Kashmir Government Publications, Srinagar, 1921-38.

Albert Schweitzer. *Philosophy and Ethics, The Philosophy of Civilization,* A & C Black Ltd., 4, 526 Soho Square, London, W. 1, 1929.

Arnold Toynee. *A Study of History*, Oxford University Press. London, 1972.

Avalon, Arthur (Sir John Woodroffe), *Mahānirvāṇa Tantra* (The Great Liberation), 3rd ed., Ganesh & Co., Madras, 1953.

Bagchi, P.C., *Studies in the Tantras*, University Press, Calcutta, 1939.

Besant, Annie, *Brahma Vidyā*, Theosophical Publishing House, Adyar, Madras, 1927.

Bhaskara, *Shiva Sūtra Vārtika*, Kashmir Sanskrit Texts and Studies, Srinagar, 1916.

Bhattacharya, Benoytosh (ed.), *Guhyasamāja Tantra,* Gaekwad Oriental Series, Baroda, 1931.

Brown, W. Norman (ed.), *Saundaryalaharī*, Harvard Oriental Series, vol. 43, Cambridge, Massachusetts, 1958.

D.N. Majumdar, *Himalayan Polyandry*, Asia Publishing House, Bombay. 1962.

Davids Rhys, *The Psalm of the Sisters.* London: Pali Text Society, 1930,

Deendayal Upadhyaya, *Integral Humanism: An Analysis of Some Basic Elements*, Prabhat Paperbacks, New Delhi.

Diana Y. Paul, *Women in Buddhism,* Berkeley: University of California Press, 1979.

Erich Fromm (Ed.) *Socialist Humanism*, Allen Lane, The Penguin Press London 1967.

Erwin Schrodinger, *Nature and the Greeks and Science and Humanism*, Cambridge University Press.

Farquhar, J.N., *Religious Literature of India*, Motilal Banarsidass, Delhi, 1966.

Friedrich Nietzsche. *Thus Spoke Zarathustra*, Translated by Walter Kaufmann. The Viking Press, New York, 1954.

Galileo, 1632. *Science and Religion: Opposing Viewpoints,* ed. Janelle Rohr, Greenhaven Press, 1988.

George Buhler (trans.), *Laws of Manu, Sacred Books of the East,* Vol. 25, Oxford, 1986.

Greertz, C. *Religion* as a *Cultural System,* New York: Basic Books Inc., 1973.

H.R.H. Prince Peter, *A Study of Polyandry*, Mouton & Co. The Hague, 1963.

Henri Maspero, *Taoism and Chinese Religion,* tr. by Frank A. Kierman Jr., University of Massachusetts Press, 1981.

I.B. Homer, *Women Under Primitive Buddhism*, Delhi; Motilal Banarsidass, 1975.

J.C. Chatterjee, *Kashmir Shavism*, Srinagar, Research and Publication Department, 1962.

James, William, *The Varieties of Religious Experience*, The Fontana Library, London, 1960.

Justus Hartnack, *Wittgenstein and Modern Philosophy*.

K. Marx and F. Engels, *Works,* Vol. III.

Katha Upanisad I. Hi. 15, Verse 14.

Kaviraj, Dr. Gopinath (ed.), *Tripurā Rahasyam*, Saraswati Granthamala, vol. 15, Varanasi, 1965.

Kaviraj, Dr. Gopinath, *Bhāratiya Saṁskṛti Aur Sādhanā*, Bihar Rastrabhasa Parisad, Patna.

Ken Wilber (ed.), *Cosmic Religious Feeling*, *Quantum Questions*.

Lakhmanadesikendra, *Sāradā Tilakam*, Chowkhamba Sanskrit Series Office, Varanasi, 1963.

M.N. Roy, *Radical Humanism*, Eastern Economist Pamphlets. Eastern Economist Pamphlets 14, General Editor E.P.W. da COSTA.

M.S. Venakataramaiah *Tripura Rahasya: The Mystery Beyond the Trinity,* Sri Ramanasramam, Tiruvannamalai, 2011.

Marquis De Laplace. *A Philosophical Essay on Probabilities,* Dover Publications, Inc. New York, 1951.

Marshall, Sir John, *Mohenjo-daro and the Indus Valley Civilization*, 41, Great Russell Street, London, 1931.

Max Muller (Ed.), *Atharva Veda, Sacred Books of the East*, Vol. XXIX, Motilal Banarsidass, Delhi.

Mircea Eliade, *Yoga Immortality and Freedom*, Bollingen Series/Princeton, New York, 1952.

Mircea Eliade, *The Quest: History and Meaning in Religion,* University of Chicago Press, 1984.

Nancy E. Levine. *The Dynamics of Polyandry*, The University of Chicago Press, Chicago and London, 1988.

Oldenberg, Hermann, *Vedic Hymns*, Part II, *Sacred Books of the East*, Clarenson Press, Oxford, 1897.

Pratyagatmananda, Swami *Japasūtram*, Bharatiya Vidya Prakashan, Varanasi, 1966.

Radhakrishnan S., *Indian Philosophy*, Volume I, Oxford University Press, 1999.

—, *Indian Philosophy*, Vol. II, George Allen & Unwin, London, 1931.

—, *The Idealist view of Life*, Goerge Allen & Unwin, London, 1932.

—, *The Philosophy of Rabindranath Tagore*, MacMillan & Co., London, 1918.

Rene Descartes. *Meditation and Other Metaphysical Writings*, The Complete Essays, Penguin Books. London, 1998.

Rene Descartes. *Replies to the penultimate counter-objections. Meditations and other Metaphysical Writings* Penguin Books. London, 1998.

Rene Grousset, *In the Footsteps of the Buddha*. J.A. Underwood (trans.), Orion Press. New York. 1971.

Russell, Bertrand, *Religion and Science*, Oxford University Press, London, 1960.

Satkari Mookherjee. *The Buddhist Philosophy of Universal Flux*, Motilal Banarsidass Publishers, 2006.

Schilpp P.A. (ed.), Philosophy of Sarvepalli Radhakriṣhnan, Motilal Banarsidass Publishers, Delhi, 1992.

Singh, Lalan Prasad, *Buddhist Tantra: A Philosophical Reflection and Religious Investigation*, Concept, 2010.

—, *Science, Spirituality and Ontological Mysticism: The Philosophical Enquiry and Reflection*, Concept, 2016.

—, *Tantra: Its Mystic and Scientific Basis*, Concept, 2010.

—, *Zen Buddhism*, Concept, 2018.

Snellgrove, D.L. *The Hevajra Tantra*, 2 vols., London Oriental Series, Oxford University Press, London, 1959.

Soumyendranath Tagore, *Rabindranath Tagore and Universal Humanism*, Rabindranath Tagore Centenary Year.

Sri Aurobindo, *Foundations of Indian Culture,* The Sri Aurobindo Library, New York, 1953.

Stephen Hawking & Leonard Mlodinow. *A Briefer History of Time,* Bantam Press, London. 2010.

Stephen Hawking & Leonard Mlodinow, *The Grand Design,* Bantam Press, London, 2010.

T.R.V. Murti. *The Central Philosophy of Buddhism*, George Allen and Unwin Ltd. London. 1960.

The Fundamental Wisdom of the Middle Way. Nagarjuna's Mulamadhyamakakarika, Translation and Commentary by Jay L. Garfield. New York, Oxford University Press, 1995.

Thomas Cleary, *The Essential Tao*, Translated and Presented, Harperone San Francisco. 1993.

Thornton, E. *A Gazetteer of the Territories under the Government of the East India Company*. London, 1862.

Tractatus, 5.634.

Tucci, Giuseppe, *Theory and Practice of Naṇḍala*, Rider & Co., London, 1961.

V.G. Childe, *Social Worlds of Knowledge,* In Hobhouse Memorial Lectures 1941-1950 p. 18, London: Oxford University Press, 1952.

Werner Heisenberg. *Physics and Philosophy, The Revolution in Modern Science,* Harper Perennial Modernthought Publishers, New York. 2002.

Werner Heisenberg, *Physics and Philosophy*, Harper Perennial Modern Thought, 2007.

Y.S. Parmar, *Polyandry in the Himalayas*, Vikas Publishing House Pvt. Ltd., Delhi, 1975.

—, *Tantrik Vāṅmaya men Śāktadṛṣṭi*, Bihar Rastrabhasa Parisad, Patna, 1963.

Index